AT HOME WITH JAPANESE COOKING

ALFRED A. KNOPF NEW YORK 1986

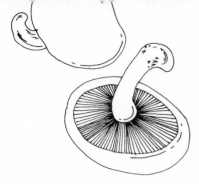

AT HOME
WITH
JAPANESE
COOKING

by Elizabeth Andoh

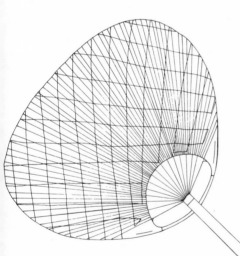

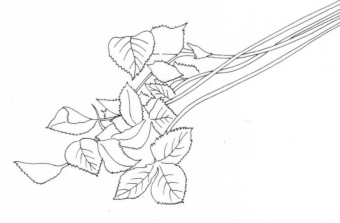

This is a Borzoi Book Published by Alfred A. Knopf, Inc.

Copyright © 1974, 1975, 1980 by Elizabeth Andoh
All rights reserved under International and Pan-American Copyright Conventions.
Published in the United States by Alfred A. Knopf, Inc., New York,
and simultaneously in Canada by Random House of Canada Limited, Toronto.
Distributed by Random House, Inc., New York.

Many of the recipes which appear here were originally printed in slightly
different form in Gourmet magazine, 1975, as part of a 6-part series entitled
"The Seasonal Japanese Kitchen" by Elizabeth Andoh.

Information concerning the nutritional and caloric value of Japanese
foodstuffs was provided by the Dai-Ichi Chori Kenkyu Kai
of Japan.

Library of Congress Cataloging in Publication Data
Andoh, Elizabeth.
At home with Japanese cooking.
Includes index.
1. Cookery, Japanese.   I. Title.
TX724.5.J3A52   1980   641.5952   79-3501
ISBN 0-394-74634-1 (pbk.)

Manufactured in the United States of America
First Paperback Edition, May 1986

TO MY DAUGHTER, RENA

Contents

Acknowledgments

Many people helped me in many ways: I first learned about the Japanese kitchen from my dear friend Eiko Ohta. She patiently showed me how to make rice one evening while her daughter Masumi (tired, hungry and only three years old at the time) scolded, "What's the matter with you? Married, and you don't even know how to make rice! Ridiculous!!" My husband, Atsunori, comes from a large family, and his mother and sisters have shared many of their culinary secrets with me. I owe my formal training to the Master of the *Kinsa Ryu* School of Classical Japanese Cuisine, Toshio Yanagihara. He and his son, Kazunari, were understanding of my early doubts and frustrations and encouraged me to teach and write in the English language about the food of Japan.

But knowing the cuisine and putting that knowledge into writing are very different things. My editor, Judith Jones, showed me how to bring the two together. In the United States, Julie Lovins and Cecile Lemons, friends and former students of mine, read the manuscript and tested the recipes with care and enthusiasm. In Tokyo, two more friends-and-students Berta Davis and Pamela N. Phillips, listened to me, talked with me and read the manuscript at many stages. Also in Tokyo, Akémi Shimizu, friend and assistant, helped in an infinite number of ways. Michiko Fujiwara, whose sensitive drawings illustrate this book, was a pleasure to work with, and Sonoé Enmei typed my work with patience and devotion.

Iro iro to oséwa ni narimashité, arigatō gozaimashita. I am indebted to you all—many thanks.

Introduction

Each time I come home to America, I am struck at how increasingly popular Japanese cooking has become in this country. Americans seem to savor the subtle yet spicy flavors of the cuisine, and they are intrigued by the attractiveness of the presentation. Yet for all the enthusiasm, few people I know in the United States feel that Japanese food is something they can prepare themselves. They seem reluctant to try to recreate in their own kitchens the dishes they have enjoyed while eating out. I think they're afraid that they haven't the skill or temperament required—they seem to think that the deft slicing of raw fish they see performed at restaurant counters or the artistic carving of a radish twirl are essential skills that must be mastered before they can enjoy Japanese food at home.

I probably would have felt the same way, too, had I not lived with a Japanese family and later married into a large, rather traditional one. I remember my first trip to Japan fourteen years ago. I had traveled a long way to visit the Andoh family on the island of Shikoku (who would have thought then that I would marry their son two years later?), and I was tired and very hungry when I arrived. I was served a steaming bowl of thick white noodles in a hearty broth that was topped with a poached egg and a sprinkling of finely chopped scallions. Absolutely delicious . . . such simple things combined in such a unique and satisfying way! Seeing how hungry I was, they quickly brought me a side dish of squash that had been simmered in a sweetened soy broth and napped with a marvelous dark chicken sauce. The aromas that wafted from the Andoh kitchen were very inviting. I wanted to learn more about this wonderful cooking, but I had no book available that really helped me to understand the basic techniques or that offered good everyday authentic recipes, and my knowledge of Japanese then was very limited. I had to rely mostly on instinct and pantomime during that first year.

Shortly after I married, I signed up for a first course at the Yanagihara School of Classical Japanese Cooking. I got my husband to join the evening class with me since he loved good food and I needed his help in explaining the nuances of the language and the cuisine. After the basic course there, I was so intrigued that I continued on my own, and finally the master of the school took me under his wing and gently prodded and guided me through a five-year apprenticeship.

Meanwhile, I realized that many Westerners living in Tokyo were in the same dilemma I had been in, so I started teaching Japanese cooking. I would take my students to market, introducing them to unfamiliar ingredients and seasonings, and we would cook together the kinds of dishes that the Japanese themselves enjoy so much from one season to the next.

It is precisely this kind of home cooking that I would like to share with you. And because I don't have you in my own kitchen to show you some simple but ingenious equipment that the Japanese use, or to demonstrate techniques that may be just a little different from what you're used to in Western-style cooking, I have tried to describe in detail, at the beginning of this book, all the methods that are peculiarly Japanese. At the end, I take you to market, describing the look and characteristics of the ingredients you are likely to encounter in cooking Japanese food. These ingredients are readily available now in most major cities in the United States, or by mail order from the larger stores.

In between are the recipes—the things I learned and the dishes I've made over the years in the Andoh household and picked up from other Japanese friends and relatives. Everything from those steaming noodles and simmered squash to enticing aromatic grills, crispy fried fish, piquant pickled vegetables, and very much more. I think you'll find a whole new world of Japanese cooking that you'll want to do at home, whether you are making a complete Japanese meal or incorporating Japanese dishes into your own kinds of menus.

I hope this book will make you feel entirely at home with a cuisine that may seem formidable to you before you start, but is in reality as relaxed as it is exciting. What I've tried to write here is the very book I wish I'd had with me when I started out fourteen years ago.

Elizabeth Andoh
Tokyo, August 1980

A Note about the Romanization
of the Japanese Language

For those who have discovered the delights of Japanese food but cannot read the language, it is particularly frustrating to find that the spelling and word division on menus and food labels can vary so much. Unfortunately, there is a great deal of controversy in both governmental and academic circles over the best means of transcribing Japanese to the Roman alphabet.

For spelling, I feel that the well-known and respected Hepburn System of Romanization is most helpful, since it closely follows the speech patterns of standard American English. It also makes use of the macron, or "long mark," over certain vowels that are meant to be extended in sound. In Japanese, this difference in sound length can be crucial in conveying meaning: *ōjisan* is a prince, but *ojisan* is an uncle.

However, no system to date has provided a visual clue to the reader for the correct pronunciation of the letter "e" (which really is "ay"). So I have borrowed a familiar symbol from the French to show that *saké* is indeed "sa-kay" and not sake as in "for heaven's sake," and that *agé* is not age—an indication of life span—but "ah-gay." Incidentally, in Japanese all "g's" are hard (as in *g*ood or *g*reat): soft "g" sounds are written with a "j."

Written Japanese is a steady flow of symbols rarely broken by spaces between words, or even by punctuation. This is very different from English, in which written words are grouped into units of meaning. Since no system of romanization provides guidelines for word division, confusion abounds. After giving the matter a great deal of thought, I opted for a system that would reflect the English language—that is, would divide words by units of meaning—in the hope that this will be the simplest to follow. Thus, *yaki tori* is two units (*yaki* = "grilled"; tori = "chicken") and *ingen no goma miso aé* is five units (*ingen* = stringbeans, *no* = possessive article, *goma* = sesame, *miso* = bean paste, *aé* = tossed). Whenever a close association of words causes a phonetic change (like *tamago-dōfu,* where the "t" of *tōfu* changes to a "d"; or *miso-zuké,* where the "tsu" of *tsuké* becomes a "z"), I have hyphenated the compound.

Above all, the romanized Japanese in this book is meant to serve as a pronunciation guide to the original Japanese for those without reading knowledge of the language. I hope you find it helpful.

AT HOME WITH JAPANESE COOKING

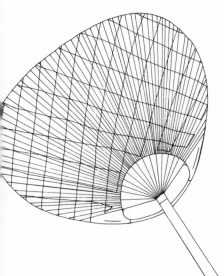

IN THE JAPANESE KITCHEN: TECHNIQUES AND EQUIPMENT

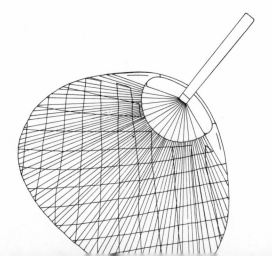

There is a lot that goes on in any kitchen before a meal can be served, and many things about the Japanese kitchen are sure to surprise you. First, a peek inside a home kitchen will reveal a small, cluttered, not very gaily colored room. Typically, Japanese families prepare their meals in a 9-by-12-foot space with only a single gas burner, a small sink (with perhaps a separate water-heating unit) and a tiny refrigerator, the top of which doubles as counter space. You are sure to find at least two very sharp knives (the blades may be a bit discolored, but the edges are razorlike), a sturdy cutting board or two, odd-shaped pots and pans and gadgets galore hanging from hooks on the wall or piled high on shelves. I know that the first time I saw my mother-in-law's kitchen I was flabbergasted. Having just eaten a truly elegant, almost austerely beautiful meal, I could not believe that it had been prepared in such surroundings. The art of Japanese cooking—order created from chaos.

Japanese home kitchens are rarely on display (even if invited into a home, you would never be shown the kitchen), and chances are you would puzzle over most of the objects found there. So what I've done here is to catalogue it all, explaining what the techniques and equipment are and how you can cook Japanese food in your own kitchen. But this doesn't mean you have to rush out and buy a lot of new things— I've given suggestions on how to use American utensils, too.

First come the details on cooking methods: grilling and skillet grilling, steaming, braising and simmering, deep frying and dry roasting. By the way, the Japanese do not bake foods in the Western sense of dry heat in an oven. In fact, what few ovens there are in Japan are used for making Western-style dishes.

Other important procedures you'll want to know about are grinding, crushing and mixing; slicing and chopping; cleaning and dressing fish; skewering, straining, mashing and grating. Then there are miscellaneous pieces of equipment you may not be familiar with: chopsticks, rice paddles and rice tubs, flat fans, assorted pots and pans, bamboo mats, trays and bark, metal molds. I also thought you might want to know about special linen cloth, aprons and kitchen curtains, too.

5

Despite the novelty of many of the items and procedures, you'll find that the more Japanese cooking you do the more its seasonings, textures and rhythms will influence the way you handle other cuisines. It would be hard to remain totally unaffected by one of the most fascinating and delicious cuisines in the world.

❖

Grilling

Grilling in Japan is done over a source of very intense heat. It is quick, high heat that makes for moist, flavorful fish, meat and vegetables. In the old days this meant home hearths *(robata yaki)* or outdoor pits; now most people have taken to grilling directly over kitchen gas ranges. Not surprisingly, this creates a great deal of smoke and smell, especially when grilling a nice oily fish. But the Japanese have a rather convenient laissez-faire attitude about this. I can remember my own astonishment, when I first lived in Tokyo, as I woke up one morning to find thick smoke filling my small rented room. My first thought was to call the fire department. Then I realized that no one else in my neighborhood was showing any signs of alarm, and usually everyone in Japan lives in dread of fire. I took another whiff, and on second thought decided the aroma was rather good. Following my nose, I arrived at the kitchen of my *ōya-san* (landlord). My curiosity (I spoke hardly any Japanese at the time) was apparent and I was invited to breakfast. In addition to pickles, hot rice and soup, I was offered grilled dried fish. It had an appealingly smoky flavor and aroma, albeit a chewy texture that took me quite a while to appreciate.

I doubt if in the West most cooks—and their neighbors—would put up with the smoke and the smells that grilling directly over gas produces. However, there are now on the market smokeless electric grills that eliminate these problems and make indoor grilling a pleasure. If you don't have one, you may have to confine your barbecuing to the outdoors. But also bear in mind that broiling (cooking under rather than over the source of heat) will give you flavorful results, similar in taste and texture to something that has been grilled.

Outdoor Grilling

Many Americans have barbecue sets and most of these are fine for grilling foods in the Japanese manner. The Japanese have their own cast-iron barbecues called *hibachi* (literally "fire boxes") which are nice to own, though not essential. In either case use charcoal for your fuel, since it imparts a subtle flavor accent to the final dish. In addition, you will need:

1. Several very sharp, thin, round skewers (preferably metal, but if bamboo, soak them in cold water for 15 minutes before using). Flat skewers, such as ones used for shish kebab, are difficult to insert in most cases and the foods tend to stick to them, making removal difficult, but if that's all you have, oil them lightly before using.
2. Most barbecue units have detachable grill tops and these can be removed to allow skewers to rest on the frame. If this is not possible with your unit, you will need several bricks or large rocks to elevate and support the skewers above the grill.
3. An *uchiwa* (flat circular fan) or a piece of stiff cardboard to help control occasional flare-ups and provide better ventilation for the fuel box.

Ideally, you should be grilling above very hot, glowing coals with a fair amount of ash already formed, and you will probably have to start your fire at least 20–30 minutes ahead to achieve this.

Indoor Grilling

Unfortunately most American kitchens are not set up for this type of cooking and you may find cleaning up afterward a bit discouraging. If you don't have a smokeless electric grill and if, like me, you've decided that the flavor of grilled fish and poultry must be savored more often than at an occasional summer barbecue, here is what you'll need:

1. Excellent ventilation—this is as much for your sake as it is for your neighbors'. A powerful hood fan and/or an open window are a must.
2. Several very sharp, thin, round skewers (preferably metal, but if bamboo, soak them in cold water for 15 minutes before using). See note about flat skewers above.
3. A stand (called a *tekkyū;* two types are pictured here) or several bricks or large stones on which your skewers can rest.

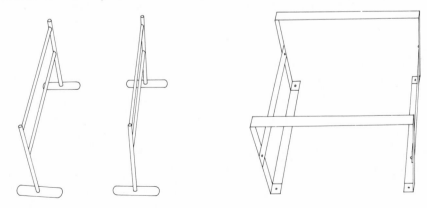

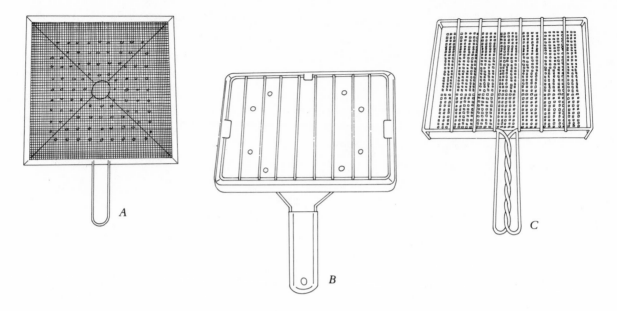

4. A net to lay over your source of heat—either type A or B will help to disseminate the heat and protect the gas or electric range from drippings. If you plan to use a net to grill fish or poultry in lieu of skewering, use either type B or C.
5. An *uchiwa* (flat circular fan) or stiff piece of cardboard to help control occasional flare-ups.

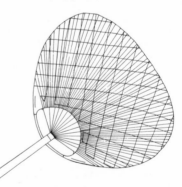

Broiling as an Alternative to Grilling

Most American kitchens have broiling units and these can be used to produce flavor and appearance similar to those of net-grilled foods. There should be a pan or tray beneath your broiling rack, and ideally there should be a few inches both between the rack and pan and between the pan and the source of heat. You may have to prop one or the other up with bricks, large stones or empty cans to achieve this. Lightly oil your rack to prevent sticking. Preheat the entire broiling unit before placing food on the rack to ensure quick exposure to high heat.

The Japanese are concerned with appearance as well as taste and they distinguish between "right" and "wrong" sides of their food. With whole fish the "right" side presented on the platter is with the head to your left, belly toward you, and tail to the right. With fish steaks or chicken breasts, skin side up is the "right" side. Broil the "wrong" side first for one third of the total cooking time. Then turn and finish broiling on the "right" side. This will make for more attractive and flavorful broiled foods.

Skillet Grilling

Although grilling is most often done with skewers or nets, the Japanese also "skillet grill," a technique many Westerners may think of as "pan-frying." Heavy, flat, cast-iron skillets, called *teppan,* are lightly oiled and pre-heated so that the food sizzles upon contact.

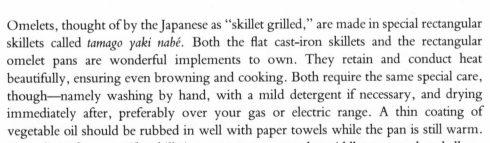

Omelets, thought of by the Japanese as "skillet grilled," are made in special rectangular skillets called *tamago yaki nabé.* Both the flat cast-iron skillets and the rectangular omelet pans are wonderful implements to own. They retain and conduct heat beautifully, ensuring even browning and cooking. Both require the same special care, though—namely washing by hand, with a mild detergent if necessary, and drying immediately after, preferably over your gas or electric range. A thin coating of vegetable oil should be rubbed in well with paper towels while the pan is still warm.

In lieu of a *teppan* (flat skillet), you can use a pancake griddle or any other shallow, heavy-duty frying pan. For thin omelets, any crêpe pan will do, though for thick omelets forming a square block will be troublesome. If you like the recipe on page 152 and you're an omelet lover in general, you'll surely want to own a Japanese rectangular pan. The very best are made of lined copper and are expensive. Medium-priced aluminum ones are usually quite good, especially after being seasoned. I would avoid the Teflon-coated pans, though, as they don't stand up to high heat well.

Steaming

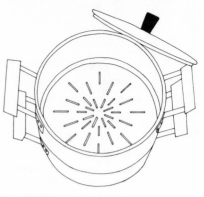

Steaming is a very simple method of food preparation that produces moist, tender, delicately seasoned dishes. The Japanese steam fish, poultry, vegetables, egg custards and some rice-flour cakes. Little skill is required of the cook in steaming, but choice of equipment is important.

Steaming requires moist heat that circulates throughout the cooking vessel, and the food should never touch the liquid. So you'll need to either purchase or improvise a steamer. The Japanese make both round and square steamers. Nearly all are made of aluminum, though some are golden-toned in appearance. They generally come in only one size (9½-inch diameter), though occasionally you will see a smaller one. Japanese steamers are a good investment and can be used for all kinds of steaming, but if you want to improvise, here are a few suggestions.

The simplest improvisation requires a very deep pot such as a stock pot, and one or more fairly wide, tall empty cans. Remove both tops and bottoms of the cans and wash the insides well. Fill your pot with sufficient water (the chart on page 12 will help you to calculate your needs), stand the can (or cans) in the center of it and place your plate or mold directly on top of these, then cover.

Since steaming Japanese style requires a flat surface upon which dishes or molds can be placed, the popular size-adjustable aluminum baskets are not suitable. Their sloping sides and tall vertical "handle" in the center make it impossible to balance a plate on top.

If you already own woven bamboo Chinese steamers, these are excellent. Make sure that they fit securely over or into whatever pot you have chosen to use them with. Check, too, that there is sufficient space for water in your pot. (Refer to the chart at the end of this section to calculate your needs).

No matter what type of steamer you have or have improvised, the principle of heat control remains the same. Namely, use very high heat until you have brought the water in the bottom of your steamer to a boil. Reduce the heat then, but maintain a simmer. Steaming is traditionally an economical method of cooking since little fuel is needed to generate a great deal of moist heat. And it is this moist heat that makes steamed foods incredibly tender and flavorful.

Even with the best of equipment and careful heat control there are two major problems you will face when steaming. The first of these is dripping condensation from the underside of the lid, causing water spots (which can be a problem, particularly with custards) and/or diluting the flavor of the food.

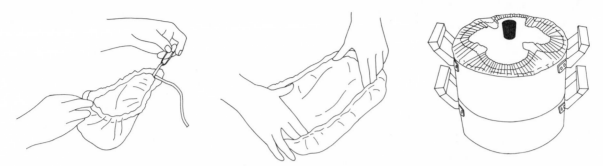

To solve this, make a cloth "cap" for your lid to absorb the excess moisture that collects on the underside. Use a towel or piece of cloth several inches larger than your lid. Sew a hem on all four sides of the cloth, leaving the corners open. Insert elastic or ribbon through this track and tie the ends together. Place this cap over the underside of your lid. The cloth should be taut—the elastic or ribbon will prevent the edges of the cloth from slipping and/or drooping down.

The second problem is the difficulty in fishing out a very hot dish, particularly when it fits quite snugly into your steamer. The solution is to make a sling from one or two narrow strips of cloth, long enough to extend well beyond the rim of your pot. Place the cloth sling beneath your plate or mold before steaming. Place your lid (with or without a cap) on the pot and fold the end pieces of your sling over the top of your lid. You could secure these with a clothespin, if necessary. When ready, remove the lid and lift out your hot mold or plate with the aid of the sling, steadying it with a pot-holdered hand.

Always be sure to use a heat-proof plate, mold or other container when steaming. (Glass will shatter, and most unglazed pottery will crack.) It should be at least ½ inch smaller in diameter than the pot you are using for steaming, to ensure sufficient circulation of steam throughout the vessel.

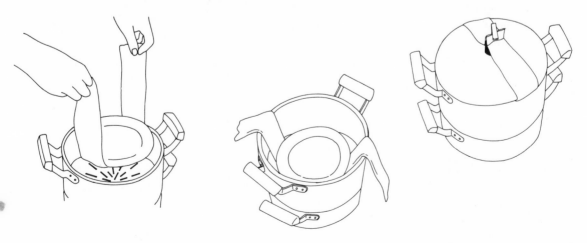

Below is a table to help you calculate the amount of water necessary for steaming:

Diameter of pot	Depth of water	Number of minutes can steam
6½–7 inches	1–1½ inches	8–10 minutes
	2 inches	15–20 minutes
7½–8 inches	1½ inches	15–20 minutes
	2 inches	25–35 minutes
9½ inches	1–1¼ inches	40–45 minutes
	1½–1¾ inches	60–80 minutes
12-inch wok	1½ inches	10–15 minutes

(If you've miscalculated your needs and have to add water to the bottom of your steaming pot while cooking, use boiling water to ensure a continuous flow of steam.)

Braising and Simmering

Braised and simmered foods are the mainstay of Japanese cuisine, and although there are no special skills required of the cook, choice of utensils is important. Any good heat-retaining and conducting metal is fine but I would avoid glass and ceramic pots since the final exposure to high temperatures required in many recipes may cause these to crack.

Size is determined by the quantity of food to be cooked at one time. Your pot should be wide enough to hold the pieces of food in one layer, but not so wide that the food floats about. Your pot should be deep enough to hold the food and braising and simmering liquid comfortably with 1–2 inches to spare.

You'll have to have a straight-sided pot to accommodate the Japanese "dropped" lids or *otoshi-buta,* which are flat, circular slabs of wood, usually made of fragrant

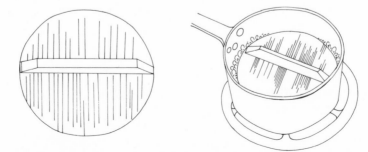

spruce or cedar with a standing handle in the center. They come in a variety of sizes and ideally yours should be ½ inch to 1 inch smaller in diameter than your pot so that it drops down into your pot comfortably and rests upon the food itself. The difference in size between lid and pot allows vapor from the cooking liquid to evaporate gradually. Moisture retained by ordinary lids, even partially askew, is undesirable since it condenses and dilutes the braising liquid. Direct contact of the dropped lid with the food prevents exposed surfaces from drying out. As the bubbling liquid touches the *otoshi-buta* it is forced back into the pot in a recycling that intensifies the flavor of the final dish.

Once you have sampled foods simmered or braised in this manner you will be wanting to use this simple technique quite often. You may want to purchase *otoshi-buta* in several sizes to suit your needs. With constant use, the wood of an *otoshi-buta* mellows and self-seasons. Avoid harsh soaps or detergents, though, and do not expose the wooden lid to the extreme temperatures of a dishwasher. Allow it to dry naturally, yet thoroughly, before putting it away. Properly cared for, *otoshi-buta* will last many, many years.

If *otoshi-buta* are unavailable, you may improvise, using a flat lid from a slightly smaller pot. If the lid is metal, though, the heat it retains is often so great that foods may stick. Too, a slightly metallic taste occasionally mars the flavor of the final dish.

If you are handy with simple tools, *otoshi-buta* are quite easy to make. In addition to cedar and spruce, cherry or a close-grained pine are good woods to use. Cut a flat, circular cross-grained piece about ½–¾ inch thick. Carefully sand any rough edges. Do not varnish the wood. A handle can be fashioned from a variety of objects: a small hook that screws into (but not through) the wooden lid, a small knob from a dresser drawer that screws into the wooden lid, or an extra piece of wood nailed onto the lid. If you are very skilled with tools you could carve a groove to hold your wooden handle (this is the way in which *otoshi-buta* are really made, by the way). Do not use glue or paste to attach your handle, as it will fall off with exposure to moist heat.

Should you not be able to purchase, improvise or make an *otoshi-buta*, you can approximate the flavor results by simmering with no lid at all, at a slightly lower temperature than suggested in each recipe. Be sure to ladle the braising liquid over the food many times (much as you would baste a roast) during cooking.

Frying

Foods that are fried properly are crisp, golden and not in the least greasy. Fine fried foods depend on proper preparation (batter-coating, breading, flour-dusting, etc.) and the quality and composition of the oil, as well as careful heat control.

The Japanese use vegetable oils almost exclusively. American corn oil or combinations of cottonseed, soybean and corn oils are fine. The Japanese market a combination of processed vegetable oils known as *tempura abura,* and although it is rather expensive it doesn't turn cloudy the way some oils do at high temperatures. Dark sesame seed oil or *goma abura* is a flavoring and seasoning agent. Though it should not be used alone for deep frying because it is too overpowering, a small amount added to vegetable oil can impart a pleasant accent. Olive oil is too heavy and distinctively European in flavor to be acceptable, and though peanut oil is not much used by the Japanese, it is fine in combination with other vegetable oils.

For reasons of economy, most Japanese clean and save oil for future frying. If you wish to do so, use a fine-meshed strainer to filter the used oil. Allow it to cool naturally to room temperature (much of the flour, batter or bread crumbs that litter the used oil will have sunk to the bottom, making the job of straining easier). Place your strainer over a thoroughly dry glass, plastic or ceramic container (metal cans often give a metallic taste to the oil) and let the oil filter through it. Refrigerate the clean used oil until you are ready to use it again. I have found that such oil stays fresh for several weeks. I would not, however use filtered oil more than 3 or 4 times. Used oil becomes darker in color, particularly after eggplant, burdock root or lotus root has been fried in it, but don't let that worry you.

Maintaining proper heat control for deep frying does not require expensive or complicated equipment. The size of the pot or pan you use for frying will depend upon what you are making and how much. It should be deep enough to allow the foods at least 2 inches of oil to fry in and wide enough to provide a surface area that can accommodate one-third to one-quarter of the total number of pieces being fried. Most fried foods should be eaten hot, and the time lapse from start to finish can be crucial. As for the shape of the pan, I (and most Japanese) prefer a flat-bottomed, straight or slightly flared pan. I have used small Chinese woks with success, though I found maintaining lower oil temperature a bit difficult. Pots which curve slightly inward at the top, such as a fondue pot, should be avoided, as steam from the frying foods will condense along the sides and cause unnecessary and unwanted splattering. Otherwise any pot made of good heat-conducting material is fine. Teflon-coating is unnecessary (nothing should stick to the pan if foods are fried properly). There are special *tempura nabé* (pots for cooking *tempura*) which have a detachable rack for draining already fried foods. These are nice to have, but certainly not essential.

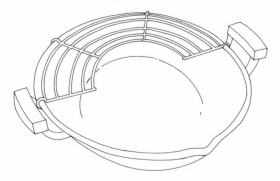

It is always important to know the temperature of the oil and how it will react to the foods you wish to fry in it. The Japanese do not use a thermometer. Instead, they determine the temperature by observation and testing. Begin to heat your oil over medium heat. The first indication that the temperature of your oil is rising is change in its viscosity: cold oil is thick and flows poorly while warm oil is thin and flows easily. Let the oil heat undisturbed until streaks appear on the bottom of your pot. The oil is now approximately 275 degrees Fahrenheit. Stir the oil and continue to heat it for a minute more. Place the tips of wooden chopsticks (or the hand of an unvarnished wooden spoon) in the oil. Small bubbles should begin to rise from the chopsticks' tips. The oil is now approximately 375 degrees.

If you are frying batter-coated foods (such as *tempura*), now is a good time to begin testing the batter in your oil. Drop a very small amount (less than ¼ teaspoon) of the batter into the oil. Ideally, the batter should sink (but not stick) to the bottom of your pot before rising to the surface of the oil, where it will dry and puff out quickly. If the temperature is too low, the batter will sink (and occasionally stick) to the bottom and stay there for several seconds. Frying in such oil produces greasy, doughy foods. If the temperature of the oil is too high, the batter will sizzle and brown quickly on the surface, so that the outside will burn before being cooked through.

For breaded foods such as pork cutlets *(tonkatsu)*, test the oil with a few crumbs, preferably those with a bit of egg wash and flour clinging to them. Ideally, the crumbs will drop into the oil, surface immediately and begin to sizzle and foam slightly. If the oil is not hot enough, the crumbs will become oil-logged and sink slightly with no sizzle at all. If the oil is too hot, the crumbs will sizzle and burn within a few seconds.

For foods which have been dusted in flour and/or cornstarch such as *Kara Agé* (Gingery Fried Chicken), test the oil's temperature with a pinch of the dusting agent. If the oil is too cool, the flour will travel with the current of the oil (moving toward the center on the surface and toward the edges on the bottom) and barely sizzle. Ideally, the flour sizzles in place but does not burn. If the oil is too hot, it will begin to smoke; flour used for testing will foam and sizzle, burning around the edges of the pot.

No matter what dish you make, batter, crumbs and flour will litter the oil as you are frying. Use a fine-meshed wire skimmer or strainer to clean the surface of the oil after frying each batch of food. Not only will this make the final clean-up job easier, but your fried foods will taste better.

Dry Roasting

Dry roasting enhances and releases the flavor of many ingredients, most notably sesame seeds and laver (sheets of dried seaweed), which are used in many dishes. Ideally, ingredients requiring dry roasting should be prepared just prior to use. This is not as great a chore as you might imagine, since it is a quick and simple procedure.

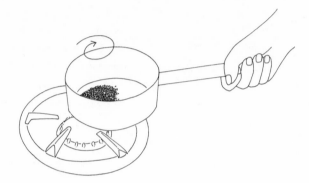

For seeds and nut meats, you will need a heavy, ungreased, thoroughly dry skillet. Place what you are dry roasting in the skillet over medium-high heat. Shake the skillet gently in a circular pattern to keep the food in motion. This will ensure even roasting and coloration and prevent unwanted scorching. Most foods are dry roasted in less than a minute and should be removed from the skillet while still hot.

To dry roast sheets of laver, hold the corner of a single sheet with your finger tips. Or, if your hands are as sensitive to heat as mine are, hold the sheet with tongs. Wave the laver back and forth slowly over direct, medium-low heat. It should take about a minute for the laver to crispen and turn a slightly greener hue.

Grinding, Crushing and Mixing

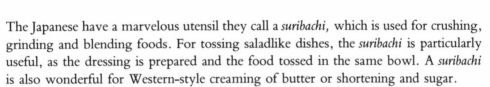

The Japanese have a marvelous utensil they call a *suribachi,* which is used for crushing, grinding and blending foods. For tossing saladlike dishes, the *suribachi* is particularly useful, as the dressing is prepared and the food tossed in the same bowl. A *suribachi* is also wonderful for Western-style creaming of butter or shortening and sugar.

The bowls of most *suribachi* are ceramic, though some modern versions are made of tough plastic. The stick (called *bō* or *surikogi* in Japanese) is usually made of fragrant cedar wood. Often *suribachi* come with plastic or rubber grips on the base to prevent the bowl from sliding about. A damp towel or cloth placed between the *suribachi* and counter will do quite well, too. The friendliest arrangement is to have someone else hold the bowl while you grind with the stick.

With a bit of practice it's a simple matter to grind a tasty sauce or dressing in a few minutes. Here's how: Hold the stick with one hand cupped over the top, the other hand gripping the bottom. Press down firmly with the top hand while rotating the bottom of the stick in a circular motion. It's a bit tiring at first, but you can alleviate fatigue by alternating left and right hands on top and bottom, and by alternating clockwise and counterclockwise strokes. To collect the contents of the *suribachi* at the bottom of the bowl, scrape the food down with a wooden spoon or spatula.

When all finished, fill the empty *suribachi* with warm sudsy water and let it soak for 5–10 minutes before washing out with a soft sponge. Rinse it well under fresh running water. Do not put a ceramic *suribachi* in a dishwasher. Turn the clean *suribachi* upside down, then towel it dry.

Although a blender or other food processor can crush and grind most foods, these machines are not very effective when it comes to the scant quantities called for in most Japanese recipes. You may have to double or even triple quantities to have sufficient volume to engage the blades of your machine. For a small amount an ordinary mortar and pestle will do the job.

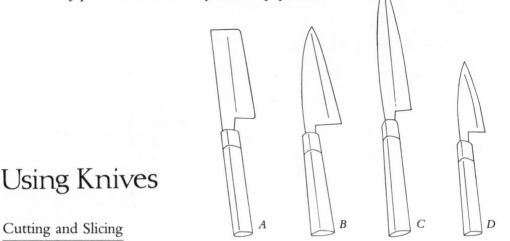

Using Knives

Cutting and Slicing

Japanese cuisine is often admired for its visual effect, and artful cutting and slicing play a major role in creating this. Of course cutting affects flavor, too, and it becomes an important part of food preparation.

Essential to any and all types of cutting are good, sharp knives. You will need at least two different kinds: a broad-bladed vegetable knife (called a *na-giri-bōchō*)— A—and a heavy-duty tapered knife (called a *déba-bōchō*)—B. If you already own a Chinese cleaver, this may be used in lieu of the vegetable knife, though you may find the weight of the Chinese implement cumbersome in preparing Japanese food. In addition to these two basic knives, a professional set includes a swordlike *sashimi-bōchō*—C—for slicing fillets of raw fish and a small dagger *(kodéba-bōchō)*—D—for preparing shellfish. Fancy cutting often requires small straight-bladed knives, but most fruit knives are fine for this. Traditionally, Japanese knives are made of tempered iron and have single-surface cutting edges (fashioned for use by right-handed persons). Today stainless steel and many other metal combinations are available, though for precision cutting finely honed iron still cannot be matched. Of course iron knives rust easily and must be kept absolutely dry when not in use. A light scrub with a non-chlorinated cleansing powder will usually remove stains and rust from iron knives.

Knives should always be kept sharp. A fine way to test sharpness is to hold a sheet of typing paper with an extended hand. Slash it with the knife. A sharp knife will cut a clean line; a dull blade will make a ragged tear. Most Japanese use a medium-coarse stone for sharpening their knives. Always wet your stone and knife with water before starting. Secure your stone by placing a towel beneath it.

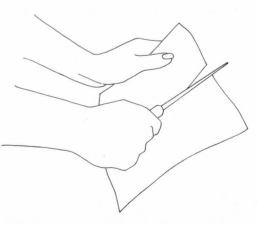

Hold the handle of your knife in your right hand with the cutting edge facing left. (Note: Left-handed persons will have to reverse all procedures. Also, if ordering professional knives be sure to state that they are for use by a left-handed person.) Place the edge of the blade on the stone and secure it by pressing down with the thumb and two or three fingers of your left hand. Exert pressure on the cutting edge as you push the knife away from you, sweeping the entire cutting edge over the stone. Retain your hold on the knife but relax the pressure and lift it as you pull the knife back over the stone to the starting position. Repeat 20–30 times in an even rhythm. Wet the stone and knife several times while sharpening.

Now turn the knife over and "clean" the edge with 5–6 scraping strokes flat across the stone.

Make sure you are applying even pressure to the cutting edge throughout the sharpening procedure. Professional knives have an established angle to the cutting edge that must be followed when they are sharpened. You will need to tilt the blade slightly in order to achieve this. Household knives are flatter and you create your own angle as you sharpen them.

Polish your knives after sharpening them. You will need a sponge and non-chlorinated, fairly abrasive, cleansing powder—if you can't find one, baking powder works quite well. Sprinkle the powder liberally over one side of the blade and scrub with a damp sponge. Repeat on the other side. Rinse the knife under running cold water. Dry with a soft absorbent towel. Hold the knife with the blade pointing down, drying the handle first. Then slowly work down and out over the entire blade.

Basic Holds for Cutting and Slicing

You should always hold your knife firmly to maintain control over the blade, but there is no need to tense up. Aim for a light, steady, even rhythm in cutting—speed will come with practice. When cutting on a board with your knife held perpendicular to it, use Basic Hold 1.

Basic Hold 1 (a): Most Japanese place the thumb on top of the blade and the first finger extended along the side. The remaining three fingers then grip the handle from the bottom.

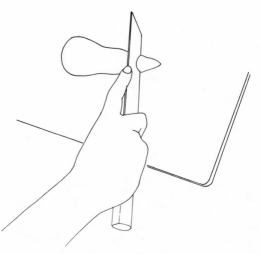

Basic Hold 1 (b): Or you can place your thumb on the inside of the handle and extend your first finger along the top of the blade, wrapping the remaining three fingers around the handle from the outside.

When using Basic Hold 1, hold your ingredient firmly with fingers tucked under. The blade of the knife will then lie parallel to the knuckles, preventing fingers from being cut. Move your fingers back a bit with each slice.

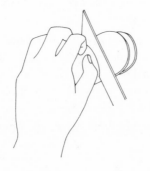

Basic Hold 2: Use this hold for peeling. The cutting edge of the knife should be facing in. Place your thumb flat on the broad base of the blade with your first finger slightly rounded on the underside of it. Curl your other fingers around the handle.

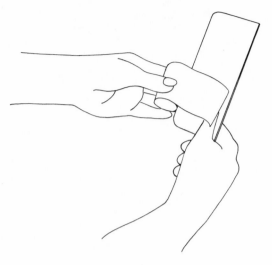

Basic Hold 3: Here cutting is done at an angle to the board. Place the tip of your thumb on the inner side of the handle with the cutting edge pointing inward. Extend your first finger along the top, gripping the handle with your remaining fingers. Start your cut with the base of the blade, pulling the knife toward you, and finish with the tip of the knife. Hold ingredients on the board with your other hand, fingers extended flat.

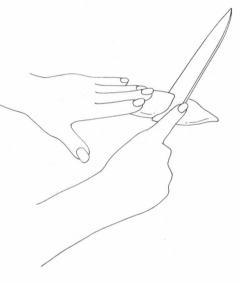

Ground Fresh Fish, Seafood and Poultry

Japanese cooking calls for a good deal of ground fish, seafood and poultry—all of which are easily obtainable in Japanese markets. But if you have a meat grinder or a food processor there's no problem. You can also hand chop to a fine mince.

Whatever equipment you plan to use, it should be clean, dry and well honed. Be sure your raw ingredients are thoroughly cleaned and trimmed. Carefully shell and devein shrimp; skin and bone chicken or fish, removing as much fat as possible. Towel-dry your ingredients and cut them into small pieces before feeding them into whatever machine you use.

For hand chopping, use either a Japanese heavy–duty knife (known as a *déba-bōchō*) or a Chinese cleaver. If you are using a *déba-bōchō*, cut and slice with the narrow, pointed tip, but chop with the thicker base blade. If you are using a Chinese cleaver, use the entire blade for chopping.

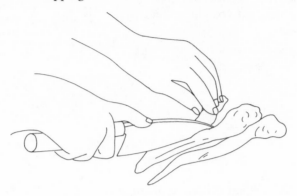

Before starting, make sure your board or chopping block is secure. One way to prevent a small board from slipping on a chrome or Formica surface is to place a dampened, though well wrung-out, terry or other textured cloth between board and counter. The Japanese chop with only one hand, keeping the other out of the way. Speed of hand movements is irrelevant. A steady rhythm of fairly light strokes is far more effective than occasional heavy blows. Turn your food, not the board or knife, several times at quarter turns to ensure even chopping. Traditionally, the Japanese finish off the hand-chopping process by grinding in a *suribachi* (see page 17). This reduces the ground seafood, poultry or fish to a pastelike consistency.

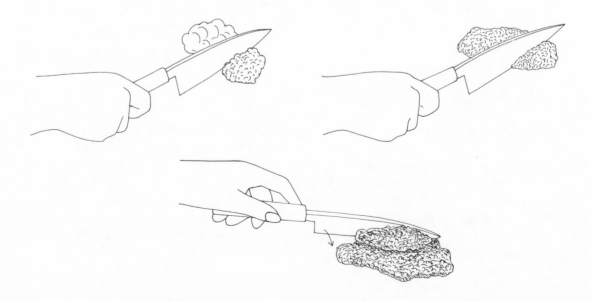

Some Basic and Decorative Cuts

1. **EXTRA FINE JULIENNE** *(sen-giri):* This is a basic cut for vegetables, meat and fish. Sometimes it is referred to as "shredding." Lay several thin slices, one on the other. Hold the knife as in Basic Hold 1. Cut across the slices to make thin strips, pushing forward and away with the whole of your arm. Lift the blade and repeat.

2. **HALF MOON** *(han gétsu-giri):* Use Basic Hold 1. Cut your vegetable in half lengthwise, then into thick half-circle slabs. This cut is commonly used for pickles.

3. **WIDE PEEL** *(katsura muki):* Use Basic Hold 2 on a 1½–2-inch-long cylinder of carrot, *daikon* (Japanese white radish) or cucumber. Rotate the vegetable into the blade. You can use a short up-and-down sawlike motion with the knife if that seems more effective. It's a bit like learning to pat your head and rub your belly at the same time—eventually you coordinate it all. Be prepared to practice quite a bit before you can peel a continuous piece several inches long.

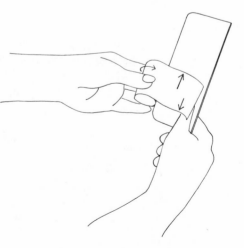

4. CORKSCREW *(yori udo):* Make your wide peel of carrot, cucumber or *daikon,* described above, at least 1 ½ inches wide and 6 inches long. Lay this flat on your cutting board. Cut it on the diagonal into 5 or 6 thin strips. The strips will curl like corkscrews. Place them in a bowl of cold water for a few minutes, then drain them. Corkscrews add a nice decorative touch to salads or soups.

5. CURLICUE CUT *(kaminari):* Cut several pieces of cucumber into wide peels (see no. 3). Roll the peels as tightly as possible without splitting them. Slice the peels crosswise as thin as possible, using Basic Hold 1. Place the curly shreds in a bowl of ice water and let them soak for 10 minutes before draining them well.

6. BRAID CUT *(tazuna):* This is a decorative cut used for *konnyaku* (pearly-toned gelatinous cake) or *kamaboko* (fish sausage). Make a slit in the center of a block and pull one end through it.

7. PINE NEEDLE CUT *(matsuba):* This cut is most often used for fruit peels, though it's possible with red pickled ginger, too. Make two slits in the peels to form a Z shape, then twist the ends to make a standing triangle.

8. SHAVINGS *(sasagaki):* This cut is used with burdock root *(gobō)* and carrot. Make several vertical slashes at the narrow end of the vegetables. Then point your blade away and whittle, much as you sharpen a pencil.

9. FLOWER CUT *(hana-gata):* A common decorative cut used for carrots. Flower-shaped cutters are available at many Oriental stores. They usually come as part of a set: plum blossom, cherry blossom, pine cluster (cloudlike in appearance) and maple leaf. Cut ¼-inch-thick slices of carrot, then stamp out a flower from each with the cutter.

You'll need a small sharp knife (a paring knife is fine) if you want to sculpt these flower shapes further. Make 5 shallow slits, each beginning from between the "petals" and working toward the center (the dotted lines in illustration). Now slice at an angle a thin wedge from the middle of each petal to the slit between petals (the shaded area in the illustration).

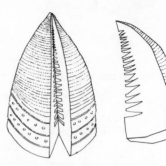

10. COMB CUT *(kushi-gata):* Vertical wedges of
bamboo shoot look like hair combs and this is
the origin of the name. Other vegetables, such
as onions, turnips and potatoes, are cut into
vertical wedges, too. Use Basic Hold 1.

11. MOUNTAIN CUT *(yama-gata):* Cucumbers are cut to look like mountains and help
to "landscape" many a platter of fish. Use two small straight, sharp knives. Insert
one into a 1½-inch cucumber cylinder. Use the second knife to make a horizontal
slash to the depth of the blade of the first knife. Pull out the second knife and flip
the cucumber over. Now slash horizontally again in the same way. Remove both
knives and pull the two "mountains" apart.

12. DIAGONAL SLICE *(sogi-giri):* Use Basic Hold 3 and
place the knife at a 45-degree angle to the board.
Make sure that each slice is a clean one; don't
saw back and forth.

13. OBLIQUE CUT *(ran-giri):* A cut used for vegetables such as carrot, *daikon* (Japanese white radish) and *gobō* (burdock root), it is particularly suited for use in braised dishes. The bulky multi-surfaced shape offers two advantages: it allows for greater absorption of braising liquids yet it retains its original shape, even with prolonged simmering.

Slice your peeled vegetable slightly on the diagonal, using Basic Hold 1. Without changing the direction of your blade, roll the vegetable toward you (about one-quarter turn) and make another slice. Continue rolling and cutting to form multi-surfaced, triangular-like shapes.

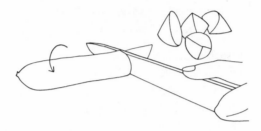

14. FAN CUT *(suéhiro):* This is a nice decorative cut for unpeeled cucumbers and small eggplants. Make sure your slits are evenly spaced. Salt cucumbers lightly before fanning them out.

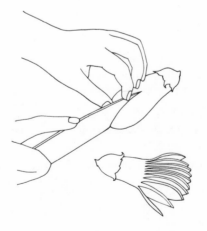

Cleaning and Dressing Fish

This is work that not all cooks enjoy. Although most fishmongers will dress and prepare fish for their regular customers, for some dishes, such as Mackerel Loaves, page 88, you might prefer to do the work yourself. And you might have your own fresh catch to eat one day. So here are the basics of fish preparation.

Generally, the order of events is as follows: scaling if necessary, decapitation, evisceration, filleting. When smaller fish are to be grilled or fried whole, they are scaled if necessary, then eviscerated. Before starting, have all your tools at hand:

1. A sturdy, easily washable cutting surface.
2. Several sponges and/or cloths for wiping and patting dry.
3. A sturdy knife (preferably a *déba-bōchō*).
4. Tweezers (preferably those meant for removing small bones; called *honé nuki* in Japanese).
5. For some fish, a scale remover (called *uroko tori* in Japanese). This last item is not essential though nice to have; you can use the back of your knife instead. In addition, you'll need plenty of fresh cold running water.

Scaling: Porgy, snapper and other similar fish need to have scales removed before being eviscerated. Using either an *uroko tori* (implement for scale removing) or the back of your knife, scrape from the tail to the head in short, jerky motions. Rinse under cold water several times during the scaling.

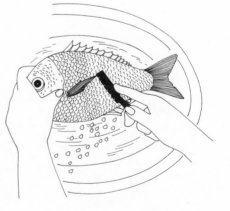

Decapitation and Evisceration: Rinse the fish and pat dry. Lay it on your board, belly toward you, tail to the right. Lift up the fin behind the head and insert your knife at an angle and cut halfway through *(1)*. Turn the fish over (back toward you, with tail still to the right) and insert knife again, cutting through to remove the head *(2)*. Rinse off your board and the fish and lay it belly toward you, tail to the left. Slit open the belly *(3)* and rinse out the cavity thoroughly, discarding the innards. Wash board, hands and fish with cold water and pat everything dry.

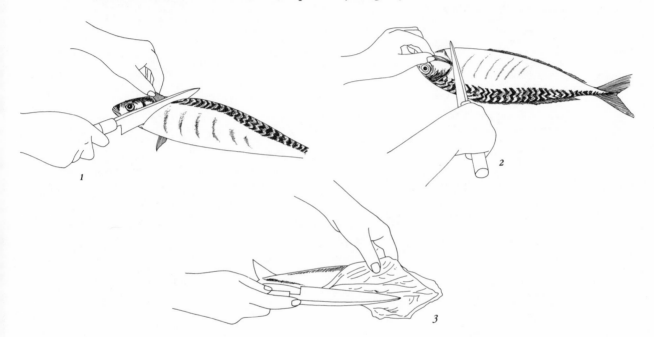

Eviscerating Small Whole Fish: Wash your fish and pat dry, laying it on your board with head to the right, belly toward you. Make a slit from just behind and under the gills to the anus. This will expose the entire intestinal cavity. Remove the innards carefully, lightly rinse, then pat the cavity dry.

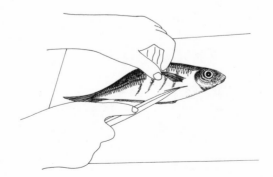

Filleting: Depending upon the skeletal structure and size of the fish, there are two ways of filleting. *Sanmai oroshi* or "three-pieced" cutting is most common and yields two large fillets and the backbone. *Gomai oroshi* or "five-pieced" cutting is used with large flat fish such as flounder and halibut and yields four smaller fillets and the backbone.

Sanmai oroshi (three-pieced filleting) is explained and illustrated here with mackerel: Lay the decapitated fish with its back toward you, tail to the left. With the tip of your knife, trace a line along and just above the backbone. Repeat this drawing motion several times, inserting more of the blade with each stroke until the flesh is cut through *(1)*. Turn the fish around and cut into the tail piece to the bone *(2)*. Bring the knife across the length of the whole fish *(3)*. Do not saw back and forth. If necessary, repeat smooth sweeps several times until the top half of the flesh is removed. Put aside this first fillet, turn the fish over (tail still to right, but belly toward you now) and repeat. If you are using mackerel fillets to make *sushi*, trim off the belly bones at an angle.

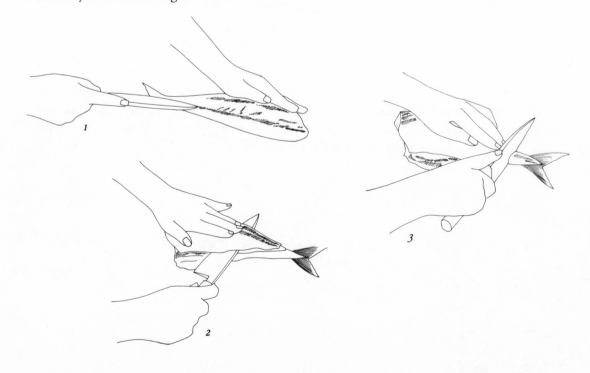

Gomai oroshi (five-pieced filleting) is explained and illustrated here with flounder: Remove any scales, decapitate and eviscerate the fish. With flounder and most flat fish, the intestinal cavity is small and located just beneath and behind the gills. A small slash should expose enough of the cavity to remove all the innards. Lay the fish with its dark skin side up. Draw a line with the tip of your knife down the middle of the fish *(1)*. Reinsert the knife, cutting through to the backbone. Now make a slash across the tail *(2)*.

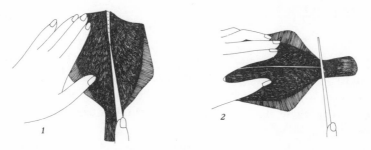

Now place the fish flesh side up with the tail toward you, and use light, sweeping strokes to lift up one of the fillets. Try to keep the blade of your knife flat against the bone structure as you cut *(3)*. If the fillet does not come loose from the fins at this point, lay it flat again and trace a line with the top of your knife along the outside *(4)*. Lay the fish so that the tail points away from you and remove the other half of the flesh in the same manner *(5)*. Turn the fish over and repeat the same procedures. This will yield four fillets and one backbone with tail and fins attached *(6)*.

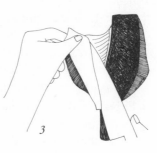

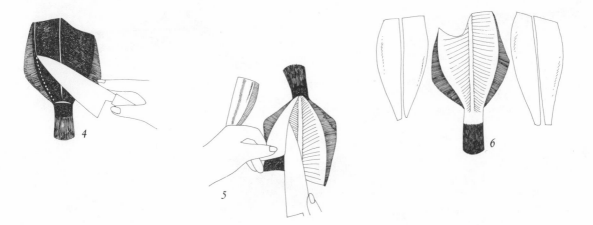

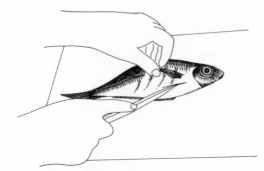

Skewering

Whole Fish: Place the fish on your board with the belly toward you and the head to the right, tail to the left. This is the "wrong" side, on which all cutting and skewering are done to insure a pretty presentation on the "right" side after cooking. Make a 1½–2-inch incision along the belly, starting from under and just behind the gills. Eviscerate the fish and rinse out the cavity with cold water. Pat the fish dry and place it wrong side up on a clean, dry board. Slightly above the evisceration cut and just behind the eye, insert the first skewer *(1)*. Twist and push it into the flesh but not through to the right side. Now bring the tip of the skewer out on the wrong side about ½ inch from the original insertion *(2)*. Bend the fish slightly and reinsert the skewer ¾ inch further along the side toward the tail. Again, twisting the skewer, push into the flesh, but not through to the other side, bringing the point of the skewer out just below the tail *(3)*. If grilling two or more whole fish at one time, insert a balancing skewer horizontally between every two or three fish. If grilling a single large fish, thread a balancing skewer parallel to the first but a bit more shallow.

    Shallow decorative slashes are often made on the right side of the fish. These should be done after skewering and just before grilling.

Fish Steaks and Chicken Breasts: If there is skin covering part of one side, this is considered the right side, to be presented face up on the final dish. If the skin merely borders the thickness of the steak, you may choose either side for final presentation. Lay the fish or chicken wrong side up on a clean dry board. You will need two skewers for each steak or chicken breast. These skewers can be inserted either parallel to each other or slightly fanned apart. Twirl and push the skewer into the flesh but not through to the other side.

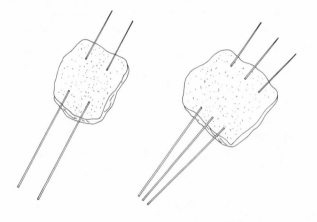

Straining and Mashing

The Japanese use an *uragoshi* for straining and mashing. An *uragoshi* consists of a flat, fine-meshed net stretched drumlike over a hollow wooden frame. A bowl is placed beneath it to collect food that has been forced through the netting by a *shamoji* (wooden paddlelike spoon).

The *uragoshi* serves a variety of purposes in the Japanese kitchen. Primarily it is used to mash or rice cooked vegetables such as squash, sweet potatoes, dried beans or *tōfu* (bean curd). The resulting purée is velvety smooth, and unwanted stringy vegetable fibers or skins from dried beans are left clinging to the net. The *uragoshi* is also used to strain uncooked custards and other egg preparations.

Although nothing else really performs these tasks so well, you can mash with a potato masher or a food processor, and then if your vegetables are a bit stringy after mashing, force them through a fine-meshed wire colander or strainer. If you need to purée cooked dried beans, try to remove the skins before mashing them or force the mashed beans through a fine-meshed strainer to isolate their skins. For straining liquids, use a cheesecloth-lined colander in lieu of an *uragoshi*.

If you like the Chestnuts in Yam Paste (*Kuri Kinton,* page 204) recipe enough to make it frequently, though, and are a mashed-potato-eating family in general, I think it's well worth the trouble and expense of buying an *uragoshi*. They may not be regularly stocked, but almost any Oriental store or dealer will order one for you. Good ones are handmade of real horsehair netting to give just the right amount of resiliency. Before using, soak the net surface in warm water for a moment or two. Using a towel, lightly pat off any excess water. Place a small amount of the food to be puréed on top of the net. Using a fair amount of strength, press down on the food with the flat part of a wooden spoon *(shamoji)*. Continuing to apply pressure, drag the spoon diagonally across the surface of the net. Alternate between right and left for these dragging strokes, as though you were drawing an upside-down figure V. Repeat, as necessary, until all the food has been forced through the net. Turn the *uragoshi* by quarter turns, occasionally, to utilize the entire surface. Should the netting seem clogged at any time, gently scrape the purée from the underside and add it to purée in the bowl.

After using, soak the net to loosen any fibers, skins or other food particles that may be clinging to it. Gently rub with a soft sponge and mild detergent before rinsing the *uragoshi* thoroughly in warm or cold water. Pat dry with an absorbent towel. Do not put your *uragoshi* in a dishwasher; the wooden frame will warp and the net will split. Properly cared for, an *uragoshi* will last a lifetime.

Grating

The Japanese grate fresh ginger and *daikon* (Japanese white radish) frequently. Occasionally other roots, vegetables and fruits are grated, too. The Japanese use an *oroshi-gané,* which is a grater with very fine, sharp "thorns" and a cupped well at the bottom to collect the gratings and juice. Most modern *oroshi-gané* are made of aluminum and require no special care. A four-sided metal grater set over a plate will do well, too.

To extract juice from freshly grated ginger, gently gather the gratings collected in the cupped well, tilt the *oroshi-gané* slightly, and squeeze. Pour the juice directly into a measuring spoon if you're not sure of the quantity.

Pots and Pans

The Japanese use an assortment of shapes, sizes and materials for their cooking vessels. Three interesting and useful ones are described here:

Do Nabé (earthenware pots) are particularly nice to use at the table either for serving or for cooking one-pot dishes that require simmering in a fair amount of liquid. These ceramic pots are glazed only on the inside; avoid placing a pot that is damp on the outside directly over high heat—it may crack. Wash *do nabé* by hand with a mild detergent and soft sponge. Rinse in warm water and turn upside down to let dry naturally. Allow at least an hour for it to "drip dry." With proper care, *do nabé* can last a lifetime. I recommend buying one that has at least a 2-quart capacity. They are available at many Oriental grocery stores.

Oyako Nabé are small skillets with upright handles. They are used primarily for making a special chicken omelet in broth that is served on rice (page 75). The handle is placed to allow for ease in swirling the contents of the pan. *Oyako nabé* can be ordered from most Oriental suppliers. They should be hand washed and dried.

Sukiyaki Nabé are black, heavy skillets made of cast iron— perfect for making the braised beef and vegetable dish *sukiyaki* for which they are named. Hand wash, dry over high heat immediately, and very lightly oil the inner surface, before letting the skillet cool down. They are available at most Oriental grocery stores.

Miscellaneous Equipment

Chopsticks: Called *hashi* in Japanese, they are used for eating and food preparation. Once you become accustomed to the necessary finger movements, I think you'll agree that they are the two most useful sticks of wood you have ever handled. Here is the basic hold. The top stick is the one to be manipulated up and down with thumb and forefinger; the other stays put.

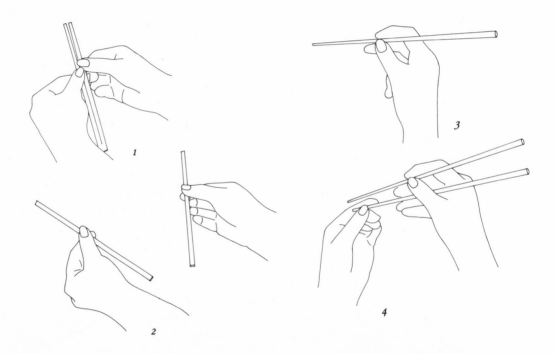

For eating, there are plain tapered wood and lacquered-wood chopsticks and disposable wooden ones in paper sheaths called *wari-bashi* (most of these need to be pulled apart). There are small ones for children, but most adult chopsticks measure nearly 9 inches. The long (14–16-inch) plain wooden chopsticks are meant for cooking, and for deep frying you should use the longest you can comfortably handle. Most of these cooking chopsticks are tied together at the base (thicker end) to facilitate handling, but if you find it more difficult this way just cut the string.

To stir, mix or whip foods, hold the chopsticks as illustrated. To lift foods, first insert the bottom chopstick under the food, then bring down the top chopstick to secure it in place. To cut or break apart foods, follow the illustrations. Insert the tips of both chopsticks together. Now steady the food by holding the bottom stick still and push away with the top chopstick.

All groceries and suppliers dealing in Oriental goods will have a variety of chopsticks in stock. They will last longer if hand washed.

Rice Paddle: Used for scooping and stirring, *shamoji* are paddle-shaped wooden spoons. Available at most Oriental groceries that carry basic equipment in addition to foodstuffs, they should be hand washed and dried to avoid splitting and cracking.

Rice Tub: Called a *handai* or *sushi oké* in Japanese, it is made of fragrant cedar wood. Some come with lids, others do not. Cooked rice intended for *sushi* is placed in a *handai* to facilitate seasoning. *Handai* may be ordered from most Oriental groceries if not in stock. They make attractive serving dishes in addition to being very useful in preparing many rice dishes. After using, wash *handai* by hand with a mild detergent and warm water. Rinse thoroughly and towel dry.

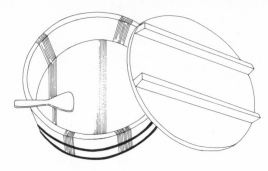

Flat Fan: Called an *uchiwa* in Japanese, it is waved back and forth to cool down rice in preparing *sushi* or to help control occasional flare-ups in grilling. A stiff piece of cardboard, though not as attractive, is excellent as a substitute.

Bamboo Mats: Called *sudaré,* these are used for rolling foods such as *sushi*. Made of thin bamboo slats (some modern versions are made of plastic) that have been lashed together, *sudaré* should be hand washed and dried to avoid splitting and cracking. Available at most Oriental groceries that carry basic equipment, you could improvise with a pliable placemat.

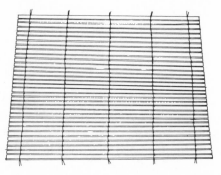

Bamboo Trays: Called *zaru,* they are of two types. The first is a round, slightly concave tray which is used in lieu of a colander in the traditional Japanese kitchen. The second is a square slatted mat which fits inside a wooden box used for serving cold buckwheat noodles. Both are sold at most stores stocking simple equipment. They should be hand washed and allowed to drip dry naturally.

If round *zaru* are not available, substitute a strainer for straining and draining. If noodle boxes are unavailable, make sure your noodles are very well drained before serving on ordinary plates.

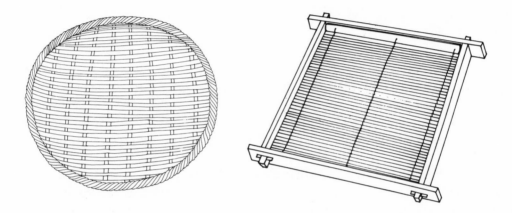

Bamboo Bark: Called *také no kawa* in Japanese, it is used for wrapping some rice and fish dishes. Five sheets come packaged in a cellophane bag. The bark should be soaked in water for about 20 minutes. Just before using, pat dry with a towel.

Metal Mold: Called *nagashi-bako* in Japanese, it has a removable inner tray, making it a most convenient mold for any use. Fit the tray flat in the box and pour in your liquid gelatin or custard. Unmold when firm by lifting up and removing the inner tray. Spread the flanged sides of the inner tray slightly to help loosen the contents,

and if necessary, trace the inner surface
with a dull knife, too. Your jellied loaf or
custard will slide out easily in one block.

Nagashi-bako are available at most Oriental
stores stocking simple equipment. They usually
come in one size only (6½ by 4½ by 1¾
inches) and have a maximum capacity of 2½
cups liquid. No special care is required in
washing or storing.

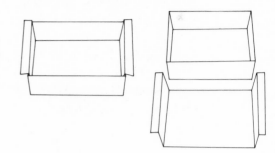

Linen Cloth: Called *sarashi* in Japanese, it has many kitchen uses. It is perfect for
straining stocks, wrapping fish to be marinated in bean paste, wrapping grated
vegetables that need to be drained of excess liquid, or forcing lumpy sauces through.
If unavailable, substitute a plain napkin or several layers of surgical gauze. *Sarashi* is
usually sold in a long roll of 5 meters—split your purchase with several friends.

Aprons: Although ordinary aprons are quite appropriate for any cuisine, the Japanese
kappōgi are particularly nice. Literally "the thing worn for cooking," a *kappōgi* has full
sleeves with elasticized wrists designed to keep a *kimono* from getting soiled. Perfect
over Western clothes, too—especially when using flour. Available at many Oriental
novelty shops and groceries, they are traditionally white with a pleated and lace-
trimmed square neck.

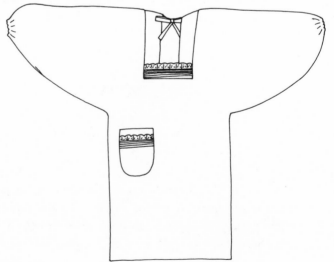

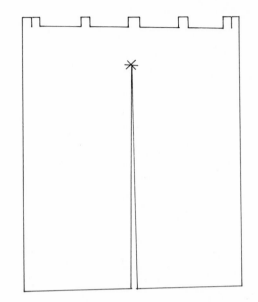

Curtains: Called *noren,* they are hung at the entrance of restaurants and home kitchens. The custom of hanging such curtains is several centuries old and originally served two different purposes. The floor-length curtains hanging outside commercial establishments were a means of advertising (the restaurant's name and specialty were decoratively woven into the fabric) and protection from the strong summer sun or blasts of cold winter wind. In the home, *noren* were used to hide the kitchen from general view. Today, *noren* are much shorter and usually made of cotton cloth printed with a variety of designs. Some *noren* have two panels, others three. They can add a nice decorative touch to your kitchen, too. They are sold at many Oriental novelty shops and occasionally at groceries.

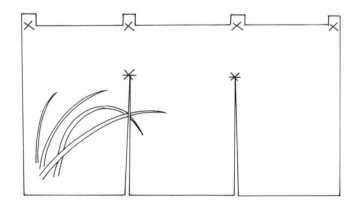

MEALS
AND
MENU
PLANNING

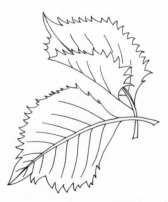

Whether you decide to add a few Japanese touches to your everyday menus or prepare full-course Japanese dinners, you'll find the cuisine lends itself to many different interpretations. Browse through the recipes and see what interests you. If you're looking for something a little different to serve with a roast turkey or chicken, try the Red and White Salad on page 173 or the Chestnuts in Yam Paste on page 204. Spinach with Sesame Seed Dressing (page 182) makes a nice vegetable accompaniment to meat loaf, pot roast or baked ham. Ribs of celery stuffed with Walnut Paste (page 183), pink shrimp served with Tart Yellow Sauce (page 176), Spicy Braised Livers (page 127) and Grilled Oysters (page 141) make delicious appetizers for any meal. Or if Fried Stuffed Eggplant (page 161), Mackerel in Bean Sauce (page 121) or Stewed Turnips and Chicken Balls (page 118) tempts you, serve any of these with a clear consommé and tossed green salad plus hot white rice or rolls.

Don't be apprehensive about trying full meals. The basic principle behind Japanese meal planning is really rather simple: meals are thought of as a combination of several dishes, each prepared by a different method and served with rice, or occasionally noodles.

A formal meal (called *kaiseki ryōri*), served in two or three stages (see page 51), would include at least one dish from each of the following categories: *aé mono* (a sauced and tossed dish), *su no mono* (a tartly dressed dish), *yaki mono* (a grilled dish), *agé mono* (a deep-fried dish), *mushi mono* (a steamed dish), *ni mono* (a simmered or braised dish), *sui mono* (a soup) and *tsuké mono* (pickles). An informal meal (referred to as "home cooking" or *katei ryōri*) would have fewer courses—maybe only two or three in addition to rice and pickles—that are served all at once; they would not be elaborately garnished.

In the strictly Western sense there are no main courses in formal or family eating but that doesn't mean that all the various dishes are of equal importance. More emphasis is placed on some foods and less on others, not only through a larger serving, but also because the dish is more intense in flavor and more complex to prepare. Most featured dishes are braised, fried or grilled. Seasonal foods in Japan naturally get important billing, too. If eggplants are particularly tasty, it would not be unusual to find them slivered and floating in a soup, deep fried and sauced in a featured dish, and served pickled at the same meal.

Here are some menu suggestions. The balance of flavors and textures they represent is typical of Japanese cuisine, though the emphasis on meat, fish and poultry isn't. I've also added dessert, which would not be served with the meal in Japan. Tea can be enjoyed throughout the meal, or at the end—whichever you prefer. Beer and chilled plum wine are popular summertime beverages in Japan; warmed *saké* is favored in the cold months.

MENU 1
Egg Drop Soup
Deep-Fried Pork Cutlet
String Beans in Thick Bean and Sesame Sauce
White Rice
Pickles
Jellied Apricot Loaf
Rice Tea

MENU 2
White Turnips in Dark Bean Soup
Cold Steamed Chicken
Braised Sea Vegetable
Rice with Peas or Chestnuts
Sweet Sticks
Green Tea

MENU 3
Salt-Grilled Salmon Steaks, Garnished
with Sweet and Sour Lotus Root
Braised Eggplant in Sesame and Bean Sauce
White Rice
Assorted Pickles
Candied Sweet Potatoes
Chilled Barley Tea

MENU 4

Gingery Fried Chicken
Steamed Egg Pudding
Spinach with Sesame Seed Dressing
Vegetables and Seasoned Rice
Kumquats in Syrup
Green Tea

❖

The following are more typical of formal-style dining:

MENU 5

Seaport-Style Grilled Oysters
(grilled; an appetizer)

Red and White Salad
(tartly dressed; an appetizer)

Crispy Fish
(fried; featured on this menu)

Bamboo Shoots Simmered in Amber Broth
(simmered; a vegetable accompaniment)

Cold Egg Custard
(steamed; a side dish)

Red Tuna with Creamy Potato Sauce
(sauced and tossed; a side dish)

Pink Pickled Radish and Pickled Greens
(pickles)

Sparkling Bowl
(soup)

Red Rice and Beans
(rice)

MENU 6

Cuttlefish in Pink Dressing
(sauced and tossed; an appetizer)

Braised Chicken Cubes and Vegetables
(an appetizer)

Salt-Grilled Whole Trout
(grilled; featured on this menu)

Tempura Vegetables
(fried; a side dish)

Silver Boats
(steamed; a side dish)

Green Sea Salad
(tartly dressed; a side dish)

Cucumber Rice Bran Pickles and Yellow Pickled Radish
(pickles)

Snake's Eyes
(soup)

Chestnuts and Rice
(rice)

These are breakfast menu ideas:

MENU 7

Thick Sweet Omelet or
Fine-Crumb Chicken Tossed into Scrambled Eggs
Sea Greens and Bean Curd in Light Bean Paste Soup
Rice
Assorted Pickles

MENU 8

Golden Braised Icicle Radish or
Bamboo Shoots Simmered in Amber Broth
Pork and Bean Curd in Light Bean Soup
Crisp Dry-Roasted Laver
Rice
Pickles

In planning a Japanese breakfast menu always include *miso* soup, rice and pickles. Then fill in with some protein (eggs, fish, chicken or bean curd) and sea vegetation (crisp *nori,* or soft and slippery *wakamé,* or maybe braised leftover *hijiki*).

Japanese food lends itself well to buffet-style eating, since most dishes are served at room temperature and meant to be nibbled a bit at a time in various combinations. Thinly sliced Oriental Pork Pot Roast (page 120) garnished with red pickled ginger, braised soybeans and assorted vegetables (page 136), Fried Chicken Balls Simmered in Dark Sauce and sprinkled with poppy seeds (page 162), and Clams in Mustard and Bean Sauce (page 185) are all delicious. Fish dumplings stuffed with shrimp or burdock root (page 116) and Treasure Bags filled with ground chicken and vegetables (page 124) can be kept warm for many hours without becoming "overcooked," making them perfect chafing-dish choices.

Entertaining even a large crowd can be simple with Scattered Crab *Sushi* (page 86) or Assorted Vegetarian *Sushi* (page 87). Either of these seasoned rice dishes looks impressive and tastes fabulous. Most of the work can be done well in advance of the party. At more informal gatherings, it's fun to have your guests bring some of the ingredients with them. It won't seem like such a formidable task either, if one friend brings the braised mushrooms (page 129), another the sweet and sour lotus root (page 175), still another the ribbons of thin omelet (page 151). As host or hostess, you cook the rice and organize the assemblage, letting everyone toss in their contribution and help in the final decoration. The *sushi* is a meal in itself and needs only a clear soup (Egg Drop, page 58, is the simplest) and a large bowl of fresh fruit to complete the menu. Both of these *sushi* dishes, by the way, are very popular with the Japanese for entertaining at home on birthdays, festivals and other happy occasions.

One-pot cook-at-the-table dinners, called *nabé mono,* are fun when entertaining a small group. The Braised Beef and Vegetable dish known as *Sukiyaki* (page 110) is probably the best known in the West. I've included recipes here for pork (page 113), chicken (page 115) and shellfish (page 112), *nabé mono* also, and each has its own distinctive seasonings. For any of these you'll need a tabletop cooking unit (gas or electric) and a large platter or tray on which to arrange your ingredients attractively— hours before your guests arrive, if you wish. You get to join everyone at the table without any last-minute fuss, especially since you need only rice and pickles to round out the meal. In Japan, these one-pot dinners are very congenial affairs, particularly in the cold months, as everyone gathers around the steaming pot to help themselves.

No matter what the occasion, one of the joys of Japanese cooking is the leisure with which it may be done. There is none of the split-second timing of Chinese stir-fried dishes, none of the tedious and time-consuming stock or sauce making of the European cuisines. Since most Japanese dishes are seasoned to taste best when served at room temperature (soup and plain rice being the major must-be-served-hot exceptions), you don't have to juggle several dishes in order to finish them at the same time. Presentation is important, too, and you'll find there's plenty of time to lavish attention on garnishing or table settings if you're so inclined.

Just as Western convention tells us where to place our knives, forks and spoons, so Japanese place settings have their own set of rules. The basic setting is illustrated here: with Menu 1.

Rice is placed to the left, soup to the right and the featured dish (fried pork cutlet, in this example) is in the center behind these. To the right and left of the featured dish, and slightly behind it, come the side dishes (the string beans and pickles here). Any sauces or condiments are usually placed to the immediate right of the food they are intended for.

Clockwise from top left: string beans with sesame and bean sauce, pickles, sauce, soup, rice, pork cutlet (with cabbage).

The most common informal variation on this theme is with the featured dish forward in lieu of a missing bowl of soup or rice (as in Menus 3 and 4). Tea and sweets should be served separately. Chopsticks always point to the left; often they rest against a "pillow" or the serving tray to keep the tips from touching the table.

Clockwise from top left: spinach in sesame dressing, steamed pudding, fried chicken, rice.

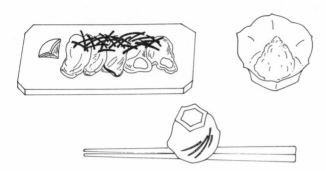

Clockwise from top left: grilled oysters, red and white salad, saké cup.

Full-course meals are often served on trays in two or three parts. In Menu 5 the grilled oysters and tartly dressed vegetable and fruit peel would act as appetizers and be served with a small cup to be filled and refilled with warm *saké*. When those have been finished and cleared away, the fried fish would be brought out as the featured course, flanked by simmered, sauced and steamed side dishes. Typically, the final tray holds soup, pickles and rice.

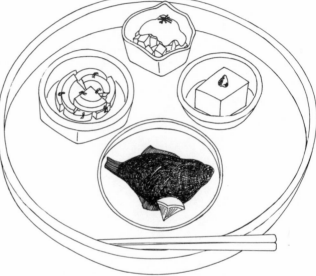

Clockwise from top: tuna with creamy potato sauce, cold egg custard, crispy fish, bamboo shoots.

Clockwise from top: pickles, soup, rice.

If your place setting has a soup, that's where you begin to eat—if not with a taste of rice. After that, it's a matter of personal choice; you nibble and bite from any or all of the dishes spread before you. One last point of etiquette: before eating we say, *"Itadakimasu,"* which is a polite way of announcing your intentions to dig in. Upon completing the meal, we say, *"Gochisō sama deshita,"* or "I've been royally feasted."

Next come the recipes. Let's eat!

Itadakimasu!!!

THE RECIPES

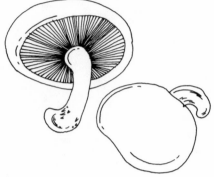

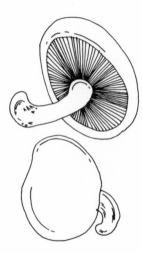

Soups

(S U I M O N O)

The Japanese love soups and serve them for breakfast, lunch and dinner. Most soups are based on an amber-colored, sea-flavored stock called *dashi,* but a gingery chicken broth, and occasionally a clam or pork stock, are also enjoyed.

Clear soups are thought to be the most elegant and are likely to be served as part of a full-course dinner or with a delicate *sushi* (vinegared rice) entrée. Typically, a few bits of vegetable carved in a seasonal motif and fish or shellfish will rest in a delicately seasoned sea broth.

Soups that are thickened with fermented bean paste are called *miso shiru,* and they are the mainstay of Japanese soup cookery. They are commonly served for breakfast as well as for lunch or at an informal dinner. Nearly every household in Japan has its own "house special" in addition to a variety of nationally enjoyed favorites. I've included one of my own "house soups" and a wide selection of basic vegetable and shellfish combinations.

The Japanese pound steamed glutinous rice into something that resembles taffy, which is shaped into small rounds or rolled into sheets and then cut into squares. These cakes are called *omochi* and, grilled or boiled, they find their way into soups, especially around the New Year. Lavishly garnished with chicken, shrimp or vegetables, one of these soups makes a light meal in itself.

Finally, a thick rice porridge aromatic with ginger completes my selection of soups here.

❖

BASIC SOUP STOCK *(Dashi)*

Good stock is crystal clear, without a trace of oil or fat. It is a subtle blend of flavor, smoky yet sweet, with a hint of the salty sea. It is made from *konbu* (dried cultivated kelp) and *katsuo bushi* (dried bonito), both of which may appear unappealing to the uninitiated. *Konbu* is a sturdy sea plant which, when dried, resembles strips of dark,

55

dusty leather. It imparts a mellow sweetness to the stock that no other ingredient could. *Katsuo bushi* looks like sawdust or wood shavings and smells a bit fishy too. Yet these flakes of dried bonito lend a subtle smoked flavor and aroma to the final stock.

The essence of good stock making is timing. If the *konbu* is allowed to boil, the broth will be bitter and cloudy. If the *katsuo bushi* is not strained out within a few minutes, the stock will indeed taste fishy. *Dashi* making, though, is not the time-consuming process that stock making often is in the West. From start to finish, it should take no more than ten minutes. Leftover *dashi* may be refrigerated for up to 4 days, but its delicate flavor does not hold up to freezing. *Yields approximately 1 ½ quarts of stock.*

10–12 inches *dashi konbu* (dried kelp for stock making)
6½ cups fresh cold water

¾ cup loosely packed large shavings of *katsuo bushi* (dried bonito flakes) OR 2 packages (5 grams each) fine shavings of *katsuo bushi*

Place the kelp in a large saucepan, measure in the cold water and bring it to a boil over high heat. Remove the kelp immediately. (Note: several recipes make use of softened kelp and it can be stored in the refrigerator for several days.) Take the saucepan from the heat. Add the bonito flakes and let them settle to the bottom of the broth naturally.

Then line a colander with a finely woven white cloth and strain the stock through it. Gather up the edges of the cloth to make a bag, twisting and gently squeezing it. Discard the water-logged bonito flakes.

鳥がらの出し ORIENTAL CHICKEN BROTH *(Tori-Gara No Dashi)*

Many Japanese soups are made from a clear chicken broth that may be more appealing to you than the traditional sea-flavored basic stock. This chicken broth is not difficult to make, though it does take more time than basic *dashi*. It may be frozen successfully for up to 1 month. *Makes a generous quart of broth.*

6 cups fresh cold water
1–1½ pounds uncooked chicken bones with meat (necks, wings, backs, etc.)
5–6 slices fresh ginger (each slice approximately 1 × 2 × ¼ inch)

2–3 leeks OR 5–6 scallions (white and green parts)
1–1½ teaspoons salt
3 whole black OR green peppercorns
3–4 raw eggshells OR 1 raw egg white

Put the water in a very large pot, and add the chicken bones and meat. Peel the ginger and cut the leeks or scallions into 1- or 2-inch lengths and add them to the pot. Bring the water to a boil rapidly over high heat and skim off any large clouds of froth. Add the salt and pepper and adjust the heat so that the broth is kept at a steady simmer. Partially cover the pot and cook the broth for at least 30 minutes and up to 1 hour.

Line a colander with several layers of cheesecloth or a single layer of linen and strain the hot broth through it. Discard the bones, vegetables and peppercorns. Place the strained broth in a clean, deep pot and bring it to a boil. Crush the eggshells slightly and toss them into the pot, or pour in the egg white, swirling it with a chopstick or spoon. Let the broth return to a foaming, rapid boil, then quickly remove the pot from the heat. Strain the broth again through a cloth-lined colander. Blot away any fat from the surface of the broth by dragging strips of paper towel over it. Or chill the broth and remove the solid fat with a spoon.

さわ煮椀 SPARKLING BOWL *(Sawani Wan)*

Here thin threads of colorful vegetables float in a clear sea broth that has been enriched by the addition of finely shredded pork. Fragrant pepper provides a glittering and aromatic final accent. This is an elegant soup—and particularly lovely when served in black lacquerware lidded bowls. *Serves 4.*

3 cups *dashi* (Basic Soup Stock, page 55)
½ teaspoon *usu kuchi shōyu* (light soy sauce)
¼ teaspoon salt
2 ounces lean pork loin
½ small carrot

½ small boiled bamboo shoot (use bottom only; save comblike top for another use)
5–6 fresh snow peas
⅛ teaspoon *sansho* (Japanese fragrant pepper)

In a saucepan, heat the basic soup stock and season it with the light soy sauce and salt.

In order to slice the pork thin, partially freeze the meat first and use a very sharp knife. Slice as thin as possible, then cut across the grain of these slices to make very fine shreds. Pour some boiling water into a small bowl and add the pork, stirring to separate the shreds. Drain the pork and add it to the seasoned soup stock. Keep the stock barely simmering as you cut the vegetables.

Scrape the carrot and cut it lengthwise into very thin slices. Use the vivid orange outer slices only and cut them into 1½–2-inch-long threads. Slice the bottom of the bamboo shoot into very thin rounds. Trim these into squares and pile several of them on top of each other. Cut the slices into threads. Add the carrot and bamboo threads to the soup and bring it to a boil over high heat. Skim off any froth that rises, reduce the heat to maintain a steady simmer, and cook the soup for 3–4 minutes.

Break off the stem of each snow pea and pull it back, removing the string. Blanch the snow peas in boiling salted water for 30 seconds. Drain immediately and plunge them into a bowl of cold water. Remove the snow peas, pat them dry and slice on the diagonal into very fine threads.

Add the snow peas to the soup, remove the saucepan from the heat and serve immediately in individual bowls. Sprinkle a pinch of fragrant pepper over each bowl.

卵 と じ EGG DROP SOUP *(Tamago Toji)*

This is a simple and wonderfully light, clear soup that goes well with any meal. It also makes fine use of any beaten egg left over from other recipes, such as breaded cutlets. *Serves 4.*

3 cups *dashi* (Basic Soup Stock, page 55) OR 3 cups Oriental Chicken Broth (page 56)
¼ teaspoon salt
½ teaspoon soy sauce
2–3 fresh button mushrooms, optional

At least 1 tablespoon beaten egg and up to 1 whole beaten egg
2–3 stalks chopped *mitsuba* (trefoil) OR coriander OR ½ tablespoon chopped chives, optional
Pinch *sansho* (Japanese fragrant pepper)

Heat the basic stock or chicken broth in a saucepan and season it with the salt and soy sauce. For greater volume and depth of flavor include mushrooms. Trim, wash, and pat the mushrooms dry, then slice thin before adding to the seasoned soup. Simmer for 3–4 minutes.

Bring the soup to a boil and with either a ladle or chopsticks, stir the soup clockwise. Pour in the beaten egg, remove the soup from the heat, and stir counterclockwise. Chopped trefoil, coriander or chives add a colorful and interesting flavor accent. Add some to the soup, cover for 30–40 seconds, then uncover and season with a pinch of fragrant pepper. Serve the soup immediately.

じ ゃ の め 汁 "SNAKE'S EYES" SOUP *(Janomé-jiru)*

The name of this soup derives from the curled, striped shrimp that lie at the bottom of each bowl. Typical of Japanese clear dinner soups, a few artistically designed morsels rest in a subtly flavored broth. *Serves 4.*

8 jumbo shrimp

1 teaspoon *saké* (rice wine)

8–12 stalks *mitsuba* (trefoil) OR coriander

Peel from ½ lemon or lime

3 cups *dashi* (Basic Soup Stock, page 55)

½ teaspoon *usu kuchi shōyu* (light soy sauce)

¼ teaspoon salt

Shell and devein the shrimp and sprinkle the rice wine over them. Blanch the shrimp in rapidly boiling water for 1 minute and drain them. Place two curled shrimp in the bottom of each of four individual bowls.

Plunge the trefoil or coriander into fresh boiling salted water until it barely wilts. Remove the greens immediately to a bowl of cold water. Knot together 2 or 3 stalks to make a single bunch and lift it out of the water. Repeat with remaining stalks. Pat the bunches of greens dry and lay one over the shrimp in each bowl.

Carefully remove as much pith from the underside of the fruit peel as you can. With scissors, cut out 4 small flower shapes, rinse them under cold water, then pat them dry. Place a lemon flower in each bowl.

In a saucepan, heat the basic soup stock and season it with the light soy sauce and salt. Bring the broth to a boil, then carefully ladle it over the arrangements of food in the individual bowls. Serve immediately.

小
か
ぶ
の
味
噌
汁

WHITE TURNIPS IN DARK BEAN SOUP
(Kokabu No Miso Shiru)

Pearly white turnips are in season in the cold months in Tokyo and I make this Andoh "house special" often. A simple, nutritious and delicious soup. *Serves 4.*

3 cups *dashi* (Basic Soup Stock, page 55)

1 scant teaspoon soy sauce

¼ teaspoon salt

4–6 small white turnips, with their leaves

1½ tablespoons *Sendai miso* (dark bean paste)

Heat the soup stock in a saucepan and season it with the soy sauce and salt. Peel the turnips and quarter them, and save 5–6 of the prettiest green leaves. (If there are none, substitute a few leaves of fresh spinach, collard greens or chrysanthemum leaves.) Add the turnip pieces to the seasoned stock and simmer them for 4–5 minutes, or until translucent but still firm.

In a separate bowl, dissolve the bean paste in a bit of the hot seasoned stock. Pour the dissolved paste into the saucepan and stir to distribute. Continue to cook the soup for 2–3 minutes over low heat.

Blanch the green leaves in boiling salted water for less than a minute; they should be barely wilted and bright green. Drain the leaves and squeeze out any excess moisture before chopping them coarsely. Add the leaves to the soup, heat through and serve immediately.

蛤
の
味
噌
椀

CLAMS AND SCALLIONS IN BEAN SOUP *(Hamaguri No Miso Wan)*

A flavorful clam broth, thickened with mellow bean paste and garnished with scallions, is good with almost any meal. *Serves 4.*

20–30 small hard-shelled clams	½ teaspoon soy sauce
Salted water	¼ teaspoon *saké* (rice wine)
1 quart water	2 tablespoons *Shinshū Ichi miso*
5–6-inch piece of *konbu* (kelp)	(medium bean paste)
¼ teaspoon salt	1–2 scallions, finely minced

Scrub the shells of the clams with a stiff brush. Then soak the clams in a large bowl of lightly salted cold water (¼ teaspoon salt for every cup) for 30–40 minutes, or until the shells have opened slightly (the clams "breathe" this way). With your hand, stir up the clams and water; the shells will close promptly. Pour off the sandy water and repeat this cleaning procedure two or three more times. Rinse the clams very well after the final soak.

In a large pot, place the clams, in their shells, in 1 quart of cold water. Add the piece of kelp and bring the water to a boil, uncovered, over high heat. The clams will open and the kelp expand. Reduce the heat, discard the kelp, and simmer for 3–4 minutes. Strain the broth through a cloth-lined colander.

Carefully rinse off any froth or sand that may be clinging to the clams and their shells. Divide the clams among 4 individual soup bowls.

Season the strained clam broth with the salt, soy sauce and rice wine. Use a small amount of warm broth to dissolve the bean paste in a separate bowl, then combine with the seasoned clam broth in a saucepan and heat. Pour it over the clams in individual soup bowls and garnish with the minced scallions. Serve immediately.

わかめと豆腐の味噌汁 SEA GREENS AND BEAN CURD IN LIGHT BEAN SOUP (Wakamé To Tōfu No Miso Shiru)

This is a very popular soup in Japan, particularly in the early spring when tender sea greens are their sweetest. A good soup to serve with fish, chicken or eggs. *Serves 4.*

1 ounce tangle of dried *wakamé* (lobe-
    leaf; a kind of sea green)
4 cups *dashi* (Basic Soup Stock,
    page 55)
1 teaspoon soy sauce

¼ teaspoon salt
2½ tablespoons *Saikyō miso* (light bean
    paste)
½ block *tōfu* (bean curd), about 4
    ounces

Soak the lobe-leaf tangle in a bowl of warm water for 20–25 minutes. It will soften and expand to many times its original volume. Rinse the softened, slightly slippery strands under cold water, then pat them dry. Cut away any tough stems before chopping the lobe-leaf coarsely.

In a pot, bring the basic soup stock to a simmer and season it with the soy sauce and salt. Add the chopped lobe-leaf, and cook for 2–3 minutes over low heat.

In a separate bowl, dissolve the bean paste in a bit of hot stock, then return it to the pot. Stir to distribute well.

Cut the bean curd into ½-inch cubes and add them to the soup. Continue to cook the soup, over low heat, for another minute, but do not boil it. Serve piping hot.

なめこ入りの味噌汁 JAPANESE VEGETABLES IN DARK BEAN SOUP (Naméko Iri No Miso Shiru)

Slippery, full-bodied golden mushrooms are paired with cubes of silky white bean curd in a pungent, dark soup. Garnished with crisp and aromatic trefoil, this soup is an interesting assortment of textures and flavors. *Serves 4.*

¾ cup *naméko* (slippery mushrooms)
3½ cups *dashi* (Basic Soup Stock,
    page 55)
1 scant teaspoon soy sauce
¼ teaspoon salt

2–2½ tablespoons *Sendai miso* (dark
    bean paste)
½ block *tōfu* (bean curd), about 4
    ounces
10–12 stalks *mitsuba* (trefoil) OR
    coriander

Blanch the slippery mushrooms in rapidly boiling water for 1 minute and drain them well (they will still be slippery). In a saucepan, heat the basic soup stock, season it with the soy sauce and salt, and add the blanched mushrooms. Simmer the soup for 2–3 minutes.

In a separate bowl, dissolve the bean paste in a bit of hot soup, then return this paste to the saucepan and stir to distribute it well.

Cut the block of bean curd into small cubes (about 50 or 60 of them) and add these to the soup. Continue to simmer for another minute.

Wash and pat dry the trefoil, and chop it, stalks and leaves, into ½-inch lengths. Toss these into the hot soup, cover the saucepan for 30 seconds, then remove it from the heat and serve immediately.

豚 PORK AND BEAN CURD IN
汁 LIGHT BEAN SOUP *(Ton-jiru)*

Foreign (pork) and native (bean curd and bean paste) elements combine to make a flavorful, uniquely Japanese soup. It's very good with vegetable and egg dishes. *Serves 4.*

¼ pound lean pork butt
5–6 inches dried *konbu* (kelp)
4½ cups water
1 generous teaspoon soy sauce
¼ teaspoon salt
¼ teaspoon *saké* (rice wine)

2–2½ tablespoons *Saikyō miso* (light bean paste)
½ block of *tōfu* (bean curd), about 4 ounces
1 scallion, finely chopped

Cut the pork into ¼-inch cubes and place them in a pot with the kelp and water. Bring it to a boil over high heat, discard the kelp and skim the froth from the surface. Lower the heat, season with the soy sauce, salt and rice wine and simmer uncovered for 20–30 minutes, or until the pork is very tender.

In a separate bowl, dissolve the bean paste in a bit of hot broth before pouring it back into the pot. Stir well to distribute.

Cut the bean curd into ¼-inch cubes and add them to the soup. Continue to simmer for 1–2 more minutes. Garnish with the chopped scallions and serve immediately.

さつま汁 CHICKEN AND POTATO SOUP *(Satsuma-jiru)*

A rich, hearty soup thickened with dark bean paste, *Satsuma-jiru* was born out of an acquaintanceship with European stews dating from sometime around the seventeenth century. Both chicken and pork versions appear on menus in Japan today, though the former is more common, and I think tastier.

Served piping hot with rice and pickles or dark bread and a green salad, it's wonderful on a cold and blustery day. *Serves 4.*

2 small chicken breasts, with skin and
    bone
1 tablespoon *saké* (rice wine)
2–3 small *sato imo* (Japanese country
    potatoes)*
2–3 inches *daikon* (Japanese white
    radish), about 4 ounces, OR 2 small
    white turnips

1 small carrot
½ cake *konnyaku* (gelatinous cake made
    from a tuber vegetable)
3½–4 cups water
1½ tablespoons *Sendai miso* (dark bean
    paste)
½ teaspoon *mirin* (syrupy rice wine)

Cut each chicken breast into 4 pieces and blanch them in boiling water for 30 seconds. Drain and pour the rice wine over the chicken and let it stand while preparing the vegetables.

Peel the potatoes and cut them obliquely into bite-size pieces. Soak in very salty cold water for at least 5 minutes, then rinse them under fresh cold water and drain.

Peel the radish and cut it into ½-inch-thick half moons, or peel the turnips and cut each into quarters. Peel the carrot and cut it obliquely into bite-size pieces.

Dice the *konnyaku* cake into 12–16 cubes and blanch them for 1 minute in boiling water. Drain well.

In a large pot, combine the chicken, potatoes, radish or turnips, carrot, *konnyaku* and enough water to cover all generously. Bring the water to a boil and skim the surface frequently for the first 5 minutes. Reduce the heat to maintain a steady simmer

*If you can't find Japanese country potatoes, use new potatoes scraped but left whole.

and cook the soup for 15 minutes. Measure out the bean paste into a separate bowl or pot and ladle some hot soup over it, stirring to dissolve. Add the dissolved bean paste to the big pot and continue to cook for 7–8 more minutes, but do not let it boil. Just before serving, stir in the syrupy rice wine.

鳥
雑
煮
CHICKEN IN GRILLED RICE CAKE SOUP *(Tori Zōni)*

Grilled cakes of glutinous rice taffy in a rich chicken broth make a very satisfying soup. It's really a small colorful meal in a bowl, with its generous garnishes of chicken shreds, snow peas, carrots and mushrooms. *Serves 4.*

1 chicken breast, skinned and boned
1 teaspoon *saké* (rice wine)
Pinch of salt
4 *omochi* (glutinous rice cakes)

3–3½ cups Oriental Chicken Broth
  (page 56)
8 large fresh button mushrooms
3–4 inches carrot
12 fresh snow peas

Season the chicken breast with the rice wine and salt, and grill or broil it over moderate heat for 8–10 minutes. It will char and dry slightly on the outside, but be moist inside. Shred the chicken with your fingers (the irregular strips will absorb the soup and thus be more flavorful here than if evenly sliced), and put it aside.

Keep the grill or broiler going and place the rice cakes about 2 inches from the source of heat. Grill them until slightly golden and well puffed. Turn the cakes once or twice during the grilling. Depending upon their freshness, it will take from 5–10 minutes for them to puff out and begin to split, exposing a soft, sticky, taffylike interior. While grilling them prepare the rest of the soup.

Heat the chicken stock through and add the shredded grilled chicken. Wash and pat dry the button mushrooms, then cut them in half before adding them to the soup. Peel the carrot and cut it into 12 rounds. Then cut each to resemble flowers (*hana-gata* cutting, page 25) for a special effect. Add the carrot flowers to the soup and continue to simmer for 3 more minutes.

Wash and trim the snow peas, removing the string down the back of each. Blanch in boiling salted water for 1 minute, then drain them well.

When the rice cakes are done, place a single cake in each of the 4 individual bowls. Pour hot soup over and garnish each bowl with strips of chicken, 2 mushrooms, halved, 3 carrot flowers and 3 snow peas. Serve immediately.

海老雑煮 SHRIMP IN RICE CAKE SOUP *(Ebi Zōni)*

Another colorful, flavorful combination of rice taffy and soup—here plump, pink shrimp, black mushrooms and bright green spinach garnish each bowl of amber broth. A final decorative slice of lemon peel lightens and brightens each serving. *Serves 4.*

4 dried *shiitaké* (black Oriental
   mushrooms)
1½ cups warm water
Pinch of sugar
1 cup liquid from soaking the
   mushrooms
2½ cups *dashi* (Basic Soup Stock,
   page 55)

1 teaspoon *usu kuchi shōyu* (light soy
   sauce)
½ teaspoon salt
4 jumbo shrimp
12–16 leaves of fresh spinach
Peel from ½ large lemon
4 *omochi* (glutinous rice cakes)

Soak the dried mushrooms for at least 20 minutes in 1½ cups warm water to which a pinch of sugar has been added. Remove and discard the stems, and rinse the softened mushrooms under cold water. Squeeze them dry, cut each in half, and place them in a saucepan. Strain the soaking liquid and pour 1 cup of it over the mushrooms. Add the basic soup stock to the saucepan, season it with the light soy sauce and salt, and bring it to a simmer. Cover and cook mushrooms in the soup for 12–15 minutes, while preparing the other ingredients.

Shell and devein the shrimp, leaving the tail pieces intact. Blanch the shrimp for 2–3 minutes in boiling salted water, then drain and reserve.

In another small saucepan, blanch the spinach leaves in fresh boiling salted water for 30–40 seconds until barely wilted. Drain, rinse under cold water to stop the cooking process, and drain again. Squeeze out all excess liquid from the greens and set them aside.

Cut the lemon peel into 4 decorative pine needle shapes (see page 25 for *matsuba* cutting), and set them aside.

Soak the rice cakes in a saucepan of warm water for 5 minutes, then bring the water to a boil. Cook for 1 minute if necessary to make them soft and stretchy. Drain off the water and transfer 1 cake to each of 4 individual bowls. (If using freshly pounded rice, just place 1 cake directly in each of 4 deep bowls without soaking and cooking.) Place a single shrimp on each of the cakes, then a few spinach leaves. Add 2 mushroom halves to each bowl and a single decorative pine needle lemon twist. Pour hot soup over all and serve immediately.

味
噌
雑
煮
VEGETABLES IN RICE CAKE SOUP *(Miso Zōni)*

A regional variation on the theme, vegetables and soft rice taffy float in a light-bean-paste-thickened soup. *Serves 4.*

3–3½ cups *dashi* (Basic Soup Stock,
    page 55)
1 scant teaspoon soy sauce
¼ teaspoon salt
5–6 inches *daikon* (Japanese white
    radish)
3–4 inches carrot

1 small wedge of boiled bamboo shoot
2–2½ tablespoons *Saikyō miso* (light
    bean paste)
1 small bunch chrysanthemum leaves
    OR dandelion greens (about 10
    stalks)
4 *omochi* (glutinous rice cakes)

Heat the basic soup stock and season it with the soy sauce and salt. Peel the radish and slice it into ½-inch-thick half moons (*han gétsu-giri* cutting, page 23). Peel the carrot and slice it into ¼-inch-thick rounds. Rinse away any white gritty material that may cling to the wedge of bamboo shoot. Slice the shoot lengthwise into ½-inch-thick "combs." Put the radish, carrot and bamboo-shoot slices into the seasoned stock and cook them, over moderate heat, for 10–12 minutes. Measure the bean paste into a small bowl and pour some of the hot soup over it. Stir to dissolve the paste, then return it to the soup. Remove the soup from the heat while finishing other preparations.

Blanch the chrysanthemum or dandelion leaves in rapidly boiling salted water for 15 seconds, then drain and rinse them under cold water to stop the cooking process. Squeeze out all excess liquid and set aside the green leaves.

Soak the rice cakes in a saucepan of warm water for 5 minutes, then bring the water to a boil. Cook for a minute if necessary to soften further. Pour off the water and transfer a cake to each of 4 deep bowls. (If using freshly pounded rice cakes, do not soak; just place 1 cake directly into each bowl.)

Over each rice cake place a few slices of radish, carrot and bamboo shoot and a few stalks of blanched greens. Stir and heat the soup to barely boiling before pouring some into each bowl. Serve immediately.

お
雑
炊

GINGERY RICE PORRIDGE *(Ozosui)*

I can't think of a tastier way of using leftover rice than to add it to this thick soup. Many Japanese enjoy *ozosui* when they're down with a cold or upset stomach from overeating; it's that final touch of ginger that both opens up nasal passages and aids in digestion. But there's no need to wait until you've caught a chill before trying this marvelous soup-that's-a-meal. *Serves 4.*

3 cups *dashi* (Basic Soup Stock, page 55) OR 3 cups Oriental Chicken Broth (page 56)
¼ teaspoon salt
½ teaspoon soy sauce
1½–2 cups cooked rice (leftovers are perfect)
1 chicken breast (leftovers from Cold Steamed Chicken, page 170, OR Salt-Grilled Chicken Breasts, page 140, are fine)

1–2 small *shiitaké* (black Oriental mushrooms), softened in warm water for 20 minutes
4–5 green leaves (spinach, collard greens, or chrysanthemum leaves)
1 egg, beaten
1–1½ teaspoons ginger juice, extracted from peeled and grated fresh ginger

In a saucepan, heat through the basic stock or chicken broth and season it with the salt and soy sauce. In a fine-meshed strainer or colander, rinse the cooked rice in cold water so that each grain is separate. Drain the rice well.

If you've got some steamed or grilled chicken left over, just shred it by hand into thin strips and toss them into the soup. If you're starting with uncooked chicken, skin and bone it and cut it into extra fine julienne (for a more delicate flavor sprinkle a few drops of rice wine over the chicken). In a separate small saucepan, blanch the chicken for 30–40 seconds, until barely white. Drain the chicken and add it to the soup. Slice the softened black mushrooms into thin julienne strips and add them to the soup. Continue to simmer, stirring occasionally, for 8–10 minutes. Add the rice, stirring.

Wash and pat dry the green leaves and quickly blanch them in boiling salted water until barely wilted. Drain and squeeze out all excess liquid before chopping the leaves coarsely. Toss them into the soup.

Bring the soup to a boil rapidly, then stir it clockwise with a ladle or chopstick. Pour in the beaten egg, remove the soup from the heat and stir counterclockwise. Cover the pot for 30–40 seconds, then add the ginger juice. Stir and serve immediately.

Rice

(GOHAN RUI)

Rice is so important to the Japanese that their word *gohan* means both "cooked rice" and "meal." You literally have not eaten until you've had your rice.

Although a bowl of pearly white rice is the epitome of elegance and simplicity, seasoned and mixed rice dishes play a significant role in Japanese cuisine, too. Often vegetables are cooked together with rice in a seasoned broth, or added at the last minute to plain rice while it is cooking. Such dishes are commonly garnished with a mixture of roasted black sesame seeds and coarse salt, and served in lieu of white rice at dinnertime. Or plain rice can be topped with different foods such as omelets, seafood or poultry. These dishes are usually served at lunchtime and make good use of many leftovers from other recipes in the book.

But the unique contribution the Japanese have made to seasoned rice cookery is their national dish *osushi* (the *o* is honorific; the *sushi* refers to vinegared rice preparations). Its origins go back well over a thousand years when, without refrigeration, fresh fish was cleaned, salted and sun-dried to preserve it. A few wealthy homes probably experimented with stuffing the salted fish with cooked rice. The fish were stacked one upon the other and in a few weeks' time must have fermented, producing an appealing tangy fish and rice dish. From the Nara Period on (A.D. 710–784) this natural tartness was cultivated by those who could afford to pay for the time-consuming service. It wasn't until several hundred years later that seasoned vinegar was tossed into freshly cooked rice, which was then garnished with a variety of fish, shellfish and vegetables.

The word *sushi* was originally written as a pun on the words "tart" and "fish," but today it is written with the characters for "happiness" and "purpose." *Osushi* is featured in menus on happy occasions—holidays, birthdays, anniversaries—and you'll find many of the *sushi* recipes here perfect for your parties, too. By the way, *sushi* is not synonymous with raw fish, as many Westerners have come to believe because that is the way it is almost always done in Japanese restaurants. Slices of fresh uncooked fish are called *sashimi;* fresh marinated but uncooked seafood goes by many names. Details on both are to be found in "Mixed, Sauced and Tossed Foods."

Since rice is such an important food, here is some basic information about its selection, preparation and cooking. The Japanese prefer a short-grain fairly glutinous white rice. California Rose or Blue Rose are two types of "Japanese rice" readily available in the United States. Long-grain American rice is fine for most recipes, too.

There are many theories and myths concerning the washing of rice. Most health-conscious Westerners don't like to wash their rice at all since they fear loss of vitamins and minerals. Most Japanese, on the other hand, wash their rice until the water runs clear, since the starchy powder that clings to unwashed rice results in a gummy texture and unattractive filmy surface, which affects the flavor adversely. It is in seasoned dishes, such as *sushi* (vinegared rice), that the washing of rice becomes an important issue, since the starchy film prevents proper absorption of later seasoning. I personally opt for the Japanese method of thorough washing when preparing seasoned rice dishes, but plain rice I wash only lightly. To wash rice, place the measured amount in a bowl and pour fresh cold water to cover. With your hand, stir, swish and swirl the rice and water. Drain in a fine-meshed strainer. Repeat several times for more thorough washing.

Greater quantities of rice are easier to cook than scant ones; 1¾ cups or more raw rice is really best and I suggest that 1 cup be the minimum.

The water used in cooking rice, whether short or long grain, in the Japanese fashion, should measure a generous 15 percent more than the raw rice. Here is a table for reference:

For 1 cup raw rice, use 1 cup plus 2 tablespoons water
For 1¼ cups raw rice, use a scant 1½ cups water
For 1½ cups raw rice, use 1¾ cups water
For 1¾ cups raw rice, use 2 cups and 2 tablespoons water
For 2 cups raw rice, use 2⅓ cups water

To the uninitiated, the timing of rice cooking may seem tricky at first. But be assured that with several attempts you most certainly can produce lovely pearly grains of cooked rice. There is an old Japanese nursery rhyme that tells how. It goes like this:

Hajimé choro choro   At first it bubbles
Naka pa ppa   And then it hisses.
Akago naité mo   Even if the baby is crying [from hunger]
Futa toru na.   Don't remove the lid.

This chant melodically describes the basic rule: never remove the lid to see what is happening. You should know from the sound the pot makes (bubbling or hissing) just how the rice is doing. Peeking inside allows precious moisture to escape and it also reduces the valuable cooking pressure within the pot.

The ideal pot for rice cooking is sturdy, flat-bottomed and straight-sided. It should have a lid that fits well. For cooking the amounts in the reference table above, a diameter of 6–8 inches and a depth of 4–6 inches would be best. Any good metal material (aluminum, copper, stainless steel) is fine.

More than half the households in Japan now have either an electric or gas powered automatic rice cooker. Thermostatically controlled, these cookers eliminate all the timing problems involved in cooking rice and give you more room on the stove. Use the same proportions of water to rice.

Rice cookers are just beginning to be sold on the American market, but unfortunately both the variety and quality are less than what's to be found in Japan. If you are a serious rice eater, though, a cooker is a good investment to make. Be sure never to immerse the entire cooker in water; only the inner, removable bowl can be thoroughly washed. Other parts must be wiped clean with a damp sponge. Unless your rice cooker specifically states that it is a warmer too, the cooked rice will stay warm in it only slightly longer than rice cooked in an ordinary pot. There are fancy (and more expensive) cooker-warmers called *jidō denshi hon-gama,* which will cook the rice and keep it warm for up to 24 hours thereafter.

Whatever pot or cooker you use, cleaning will be much easier if you remember to soak the pot right after using it for at least 10 minutes in warm sudsy water.

❖

御飯 MASTER RECIPE FOR COOKING RICE *(Gohan)*

Serves 3–4.

1 cup short-grain raw rice
1 cup and 2 tablespoons cold water

Wash the rice several times, draining it well after the final rinsing. Place the washed rice in a sturdy medium-size metal pot and measure in the water. Ideally, the rice should soak for 15–20 minutes before cooking. If you are pressed for time, though, add an extra teaspoon of water and cook the rice immediately.

Place the pot, tightly lidded, over high heat and cook for 4–5 minutes or until the rice water bubbles and foams. You can hear this and you'll also see the lid dancing up and down; there's no need to peek inside. Lower the heat to medium at this point and continue to cook for about 8–10 minutes or until nearly all the water has been absorbed. Again, you can hear this: it will be a low hissing sound. The lid, too, will be less active. Turn the heat up to high again for just 20–30 seconds to help "dry off" the rice. Remove the pot from the heat and let the cooked rice steam itself, tightly lidded, for about 10–15 minutes. Cooked rice will stay hot for about 20 minutes after steaming, and quite warm for yet another 15 minutes.

To serve, dampen a wooden spoon (the Japanese use a paddlelike one called a *shamoji*) in cold water and lightly toss the rice before scooping out individual portions.

NOTE: Since quick heat control is a major factor in good rice cooking, those of you with electric ranges will need to work with two burners, one at high and one at low.

Preparing Rice for *Sushi*

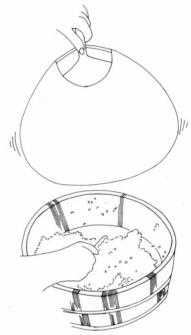

Sushi dishes require freshly cooked rice. Wash the raw rice until the water runs clear, then drain it well. Measure and add your cooking water to the pot and cook the rice according to the master recipe above. Transfer the cooked rice while it is still warm to a wooden bowl. The Japanese use a *handai* or *sushi oké,* which looks like a small tub. Some come with lids, others do not. Made of fragrant cedar wood, a *handai* is just porous enough to absorb excess moisture from the rice and its seasonings. You could improvise with a large unvarnished wooden salad bowl. Pour the seasoned vinegar called for in each recipe over the rice, a little at a time. Toss gently with a wooden paddle (*shamoji*) while fanning the rice with a stiff fan (*uchiwa*) or piece of cardboard. This helps to cool the rice to room temperature while avoiding unwanted condensation from the steam. The rice will take on a lustrous glow.

Leftover Rice

I highly recommend that any leftovers be used in Gingery Rice Porridge (page 67) or Sweet Rice Porridge with Red Beans (page 78). Of course such non-Japanese dishes as fried rice or rice pudding make fine use of leftovers, too. You can reheat cooked rice for 2–3 minutes in a steamer or double boiler, but texture and flavor will suffer somewhat. If you do reheat rice use it in dishes such as Parent and Child Bowl (page 75), Pork Cutlet Omelet on Rice (page 76), Batter-Fried Shrimp and Vegetables on Rice (page 77) or Garnished Rice with Tea (page 78).

豆
御
飯

PEAS AND RICE *(Mamé Gohan)*

Many cuisines throughout the world combine peas with rice and so do the Japanese. This dish is meant to replace plain white rice at the dinner table and is really not any more difficult to make. Use fresh peas, if available, since their flavor, color and texture are far superior to those of frozen or canned. A very nice alternative would be to use fresh lima beans or soybeans, though these require 2-3 minutes more blanching time than peas. *Serves 4–6.*

1 cup fresh shelled peas	1½ tablespoons *mirin* (syrupy rice wine)
1½ cups raw rice	1–2 tablespoons *goma shio* (mixture
1¾ cups water	of black sesame seeds and coarse salt)

Blanch the peas for 1 minute in boiling salted water to cover and drain them immediately. Rinse quickly under cold water to stop the cooking process and drain them again.

Wash the rice several times, draining it after each rinsing. Place the washed rice in a sturdy medium-sized pot and measure in the water. Allow the rice to sit in the water for 10 minutes or so; then add the *mirin*. Stir to distribute evenly and cook the rice according to the master recipe on page 70. Just before drying off the rice with a final exposure to high heat, remove the lid and quickly add the blanched peas. Replace the lid, cook over high heat for 10–15 seconds and remove the pot from the heat. Let the rice and peas self-steam, tightly lidded, for about 10–15 minutes.

Before serving, dampen a wooden paddle in cold water and gently toss the rice and peas. Scoop out individual portions and sprinkle some of the sesame-and-salt mixture over them.

栗
御
飯

CHESTNUTS AND RICE *(Kuri Gohan)*

In Japan, this is an elegant dish, in season during October and November when chestnuts are large and flavorful. The traditional manner of preparation requires shelling raw nuts, which is a difficult and time-consuming task. The nutmeats are soaked in an alum solution to prevent discoloration, then rinsed and drained before being cooked with sweetened rice.

The version I've given here makes use of cooked chestnuts in syrup, which simplifies the preparation tremendously yet results in a dish very similar to the original.

Chestnuts and Rice is meant to replace plain white rice on a predominantly fish or seafood menu. It is lovely, too, served with roasted poultry in a Western meal, in lieu of stuffing. *Serves 4–6.*

2 seven-ounce bottles of yellow chestnuts in heavy syrup (sold as *kuri no kanro ni* at Oriental groceries)	1¾ cups water
	1 teaspoon *mirin* (syrupy rice wine)
1½ cups raw rice	1–2 tablespoons *goma shio* (mixture of black sesame seeds and coarse salt)

Drain the chestnuts, reserving 2 teaspoons of the syrup. Cut the nuts in half, blanch them for 30–40 seconds in boiling salted water, then drain them thoroughly.

Wash the rice several times, draining very well after the final rinse. Combine the rice, water, reserved chestnut syrup and syrupy rice wine in a sturdy medium-sized pot, and stir lightly for even distribution. Cook the rice according to the master recipe on page 70, and just before drying off the rice, add the chestnut pieces, quickly replacing the lid. Cook over high heat for 20–30 seconds, remove the pot from the heat and let the chestnuts and rice self-steam for about 15 minutes.

Before serving, dampen a wooden paddle in cold water and gently toss the chestnuts and rice. Scoop out individual portions and sprinkle some of the sesame-and-salt mixture over them.

か や く 御 飯 VEGETABLES AND SEASONED RICE *(Kayaku Gohan)*

This is a subtly flavored rice dish that goes particularly well with grilled meat, fish or poultry. It will be welcomed by the many Westerners who find "plain white rice" uninteresting. It is also a fine way to use up bits of Oriental vegetables left over from other recipes. *Serves 4–6.*

2 slices *abura agé* (fried bean curd)	½ small carrot
½ cake *konnyaku* (gelatinous cake made from a tuber vegetable)	1½ cups raw rice
	1¾ cups water
5–6 inches *gobō* (burdock root) OR 1 small boiled bamboo shoot	1½ tablespoons soy sauce
	1 tablespoon *mirin* (syrupy rice wine)

Blanch the fried bean curd slices in boiling water to remove excess oil. Drain the slices before cutting them into thin strips about ⅛ inch wide and 1 inch long. Slice the *konnyaku* cake in julienne strips of approximately the same size. Blanch the *konnyaku* strips for 1–2 minutes and drain them thoroughly.

Wash and peel fresh burdock root and cut into julienne strips of approximately the same size as the *konnyaku* and fried bean curd. Soak the burdock strips in a bowl of cold water, to cover, for 5 minutes before draining them (this is known as *aku-nuki*, a technique the Japanese frequently employ to rid certain root vegetables of a bitter aftertaste). If using canned burdock root or bamboo shoot, drain it before plunging it into boiling water, which helps remove the canned taste. Drain again before slicing it.

Peel the carrot and cut into strips of the same size and shape as the other vegetables.

Wash the raw rice (see page 70 for master recipe), place in your cooking pot, add the measured water, and stir in the vegetables. Season with soy sauce and *mirin*, stir again for even distribution, and cook as you would plain white rice.

赤
飯
RED RICE AND BEANS (Sekihan)

Since red is the color of felicity in Japan, this dish is found on the menus of most formal, happy occasions. Here small red beans are pre-cooked to release a deep red liquid which is then used to tint the steaming rice and beans. It is not difficult to make, although it requires a great deal of time, mostly unattended. Unlike other recipes this particular dish uses glutinous rice, which is steamed and requires none of the tricky temperature changes of regular rice. Serve it with sweet simmered black mushrooms (page 129), Salt-Grilled Fish or Chicken (pages 138 and 140), and a green vegetable (such as Spinach with Sesame Seed Dressing, page 182) or a salad. *Serves 6–8.*

½ cup *sasagé mamé* (small dried red beans)	3 cups *mochi-gomé* (glutinous rice)
3 cups water	1–2 tablespoons *goma shio* (mixture of black sesame seeds and coarse salt)

Rinse and drain the beans, then simmer them in the water, uncovered, for about 10 minutes, until they give just a little when pinched. Drain the beans, reserving the deep red-colored cooking liquid.

Wash the glutinous rice several times, draining it very well after the final rinse. In a bowl, pour half of the reserved red bean liquid over the rice, adding water, if necessary, to barely cover it. Soak the rice in the deep red liquid for at least 4 hours at room temperature or overnight if refrigerated. Reserve, too, the parboiled beans and remaining red liquid, each in its own covered container in the refrigerator.

Just before steaming, drain the rice and mix it with the beans. Spread this mixture evenly on the rack of a Japanese steamer or on a plate in an improvised steamer.

Cover, and steam the rice and beans for about 15 minutes before sprinkling them with one-third of the reserved red liquid. Cover again and repeat the steaming-sprinkling procedure 2 more times, for a total of 40–45 minutes' steaming. Remove your steamer from the heat and allow the beans and rice to cool slightly before removing the lid. Lightly toss the tinted rice and beans with a dampened wooden paddle. Spinkle some of the sesame-and-salt mixture over it. Serve warm or at room temperature. Any leftovers may be refrigerated and resteamed for 3–5 minutes the following day.

親子丼 PARENT AND CHILD BOWL (Oyako Domburi)

The fanciful name given to this chicken omelet served on rice is typical of Japanese culinary humor. *Oya* means "parent" and *ko* means "child" and the age-old question of which came first (the chicken or the egg?) is given a tasty Oriental solution. You might find it surprising to use so much soup stock and sugar in an omelet. The resulting dish, though, is neither sweet nor soupy. The sugar is nicely balanced by the saltiness of the soy sauce, and the omelet is really poached in the seasoned broth. *Serves 4.*

1 boned chicken breast, about ½ pound	4 eggs
1 small onion	⅓ cup chopped *mitsuba* (trefoil) OR coriander OR watercress
2 cups *dashi* (Basic Soup Stock, page 55)	2½–3 cups hot rice, cooked according
4 tablespoons soy sauce	to the master recipe on page 70
3½ tablespoons sugar	with 1¼–1½ cups raw rice (OR
1 tablespoon *saké* (rice wine)	leftover cooked rice, briefly heated)

Remove all skin and fat from the chicken breast, slice it in half lengthwise and then slice into thin pieces slightly on the diagonal across the width (*sogi-giri* cutting, page 26). Peel and slice the onion thin on a vertical plane (*kushi-gata* cutting, page 26).

Heat the stock in a small saucepan and season it with soy sauce, sugar and rice wine, stirring until the sugar has dissolved. Then add the sliced chicken and onion to the seasoned broth. Cook it, uncovered, over medium heat for 3–4 minutes or until the onions have wilted and the chicken is cooked through.

The Japanese have a special skillet (*oyako nabé*) they use for making individual round omelets, described on page 35. If you have one of these or another very small round skillet, make 4 separate omelets using 1 egg for each and one-quarter of the chicken, onions and broth. You can keep the first ones warm by transferring them to a deep dish and covering with aluminum foil. If you have only a 6–8-inch or larger skillet, make 1 omelet and cut it in 4 pieces.

Beat the egg or eggs very well, trying not to incorporate air while doing so. Pour the chicken, onions and broth into a skillet and heat to simmering. Pour the well-beaten egg or eggs into the center of the skillet and cook over medium heat until the edges begin to set. Though skilled Japanese cooks use only a gentle swirling wrist motion to prevent the omelet from sticking to the bottom of the skillet, there's no reason why you couldn't use a spatula carefully to loosen the omelet. Simmer for 3–4 minutes and garnish the top with chopped trefoil, coriander or watercress. Cook for another minute.

Divide the hot cooked rice among 4 deep bowls. Place a small round omelet or a quarter of a larger one into each bowl. Pour any seasoned broth that may remain in the skillet over the omelets. Serve immediately.

かつ丼 PORK CUTLET OMELET ON RICE *(Katsudon)*

This makes a very filling lunch, especially if served with a hearty *miso* soup and several kinds of sharp, crisp pickles. *Serves 4.*

1½ cups *dashi* (Basic Soup Stock, page 55)	4 eggs
3 tablespoons soy sauce	¼ cup chopped coriander OR chives
2 tablespoons sugar	2½–3 cups hot rice, cooked according
1 tablespoon *saké* (rice wine)	to the master recipe on page 70
4 cooked boneless pork cutlets about ¼ pound each (page 159); leftovers are fine	with 1¼–1½ cups raw rice (OR leftover cooked rice, briefly heated)

Combine the stock, soy sauce, sugar and rice wine in a small saucepan and heat it, stirring, until the sugar dissolves.

The Japanese have a special skillet *(oyako nabé,* described on page 35) they use for making individual round omelets. If you have one of these or another very small skillet, make 4 separate omelets, using 1 egg and 1 cutlet for each, with one-quarter of the seasoned broth. If you are using a 6–8-inch skillet, make 2 omelets with 2 eggs at a time, or if using a larger skillet use all 4 eggs at once.

Slice each cutlet into long, narrow strips and line them up again to re-form the original cutlet shape. Pour the seasoned broth (⅓ cup per egg) into your skillet and bring it to a simmer before carefully placing the cutlet (or cutlets) in it. Beat the egg (or eggs if making multiple omelets) and pour it over the cutlet (or cutlets). Cook over medium heat until the egg is nearly set and sprinkle the coriander or chives over all. The Japanese like their omelets fairly loose, but if you prefer firm ones, cover and cook for another minute or so.

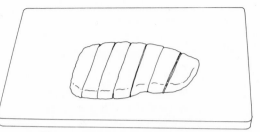

Divide the hot cooked rice among 4 deep bowls. Carefully remove the cutlet omelets from your skillet and place 1 on each bowl of rice. Pour any seasoned broth that may remain in the skillet over the omelets and rice. Serve immediately.

天丼　BATTER-FRIED SHRIMP AND VEGETABLES ON RICE *(Tendon)*

A simple and tasty way of using leftover *tempura* (batter-fried shrimp and vegetables) and rice. Serve this dish with hot soup and a colorful assortment of pickles. *Serves 4.*

Scant 1 cup *dashi* (Basic Soup Stock, page 55)
1½ tablespoons sugar
4 tablespoons soy sauce
2 tablespoons *mirin* (syrupy rice wine)
2½–3 cups hot rice, cooked according to the master recipe on page 70 with 1¼–1½ cups raw rice (OR leftover cooked rice, briefly reheated)

4 batter-fried shrimp (page 157); leftovers are fine
4 pieces of batter-fried green pepper OR other green vegetable (page 157); leftovers are fine
4 pieces of batter-fried eggplant OR mushroom (page 157); leftovers are fine

Combine the stock, sugar, soy sauce and syrupy rice wine in a small saucepan and simmer, stirring, for 2–3 minutes.

Divide the rice among 4 deep bowls. If using leftover batter-fried foods, heat them first for a few minutes in a warm oven before placing a shrimp and 2 vegetable pieces over each mound of rice. If using freshly fried foods, place them directly over the rice. Pour some of the piping-hot seasoned broth over each bowl and serve immediately.

お
茶
漬

GARNISHED RICE WITH TEA *(Ocha-zuké)*

This is a classic light meal or snack throughout Japan and a lovely way to make use of leftovers. There are many variations on the basic theme, most notably *tori cha-zuké* made with shreds of steamed chicken and *shaké cha-zuké* made with chunks of salt-grilled salmon. All are typically accompanied by an assortment of bright, crisp pickles. *Serves 4.*

3 cups cooked rice (made from 1½ cups raw rice according to master recipe, page 70); leftovers are perfect
1 tablespoon white sesame seeds
1 sheet *Asakusa nori* (dark dried laver)
Optional: 1 steamed chicken breast (page 170) OR 1 slice salt-grilled salmon (page 139); leftovers of either are fine

2–3 tablespoons chopped coriander
¼ teaspoon *wasabi* (fiery green horseradish) OR ½ teaspoon peeled and grated fresh ginger
2 cups very hot, freshly brewed *ocha* (green tea; tea making described on page 205)

Divide the rice among 4 deep bowls. Dry roast the sesame seeds until golden (page 16 for details), crush them coarsely in a *suribachi* or blender, then sprinkle some over each bowl of rice.

Dry roast the laver by waving it back and forth over direct medium heat for about 1 minute. Fold and tear the crisp sheet into 20 small rectangles and place 5 of them on each of the bowls of rice.

If making *tori cha-zuké,* shred the steamed chicken fine and garnish each bowl with some of the shreds. If making *shaké cha-zuké,* remove skin and bones from cooked fish, break it into small chunks, and divide the fish among the 4 bowls.

Garnish each individual portion with some chopped coriander and either a small dab of fiery horseradish or a small mound of ginger. Pour ½ cup of very hot tea over each bowl and serve immediately.

お
か
ゆ

SWEET RICE PORRIDGE WITH RED BEANS *(Okayu)*

A good way to use leftover rice, this porridge is pleasantly sweet and makes a nice snack by itself. Or serve it with Salt-Grilled Fish or Chicken in lieu of plain rice. *Serves 4.*

⅓ cup *sasagé mamé* (small dried red beans)

2–2¼ cups cold water

¼ teaspoon salt

1½–2 cups cooked rice (leftovers are perfect)

4 *omochi* (glutinous rice cakes), optional

Scant ¼ cup sugar

Bring several cups of water to a rolling boil and add the beans, a few at a time to keep the water at a rapid boil. After all the beans have been added, reduce the heat slightly to maintain a steady simmer. Cook the beans for 30–40 minutes, or until tender but not mushy, adding more water if necessary to keep the beans covered all the time. Drain the cooked beans.

In a large saucepan, combine the water, salt and rice and stir. Bring it to a boil over high heat, then adjust to maintain a simmer. Cook the porridge for 10 minutes, stirring frequently. For extra volume and a pleasant texture contrast, add soft rice cakes. (If your rice cakes are very hard or crusty, soften them first in a separate saucepan with warm water.) Stir in the drained red beans, heat all through for 1 minute, then serve immediately. Sprinkle the sugar over the porridge as you eat.

おむすび

RICE SANDWICHES *(Omusubi)*

For the most popular picnic lunch in Japan, triangular rice "sandwiches" are stuffed with a variety of fillings and garnished with roasted black sesame seeds or strips of roasted dried laver. Blocks of Thick Sweet Omelet (page 152) go well with rice "sandwiches," and sharp, bright-colored pickles round out the meal. *Serves 2–3.*

2½ cups cooked, still warm rice (made from 1¼ cups raw rice according to master recipe, page 70)

Scant ½ teaspoon salt

Filling A:

3 tablespoons *katsuo bushi* (dried bonito flakes)

½ teaspoon soy sauce

Filling B:

umé-boshi (pink-tinted pickled plums)

Garnish:

½ tablespoon dry-roasted black sesame seeds OR ½ sheet dry-roasted *Asakusa nori* (dark dried laver)

Season the warm rice with salt and toss it gently with a wooden spoon. Divide the rice into 6 portions. Now prepare your fillings and garnishes. Mix the dried bonito flakes with soy sauce for filling A. Remove the pits from the pickled plums for filling B. Dry roast the black sesame seeds in a heavy skillet, then transfer them to a small bowl. Dry roast the dried laver for 1–2 minutes (details for both on page 16). With a knife or scissors, cut the laver into 3 long strips.

Have a bowl of cold water nearby and dampen your hands whenever necessary to prevent the rice from sticking to them. Take one of the 6 portions of rice and form it into a ball with cupped hands. Make an indentation in the center and fill it with one third of filling A or B (1, 2). Work the rice into a ball again, closing over the filling (3). Open the palm of your bottom hand, keeping your thumb rigid and slightly higher than the other fingers. This will help shape one side of the triangle (4). Press down with your other hand to flatten the ball. Rotate the flattened ball at one-third turns to form the other two sides of the triangle. Exert gentle pressure while shaping the stuffed rice into a triangle. Garnish the rice sandwich with a strip of roasted laver (5), or with a sprinkling of black sesame seeds. Repeat the process to make 5 more stuffed and garnished triangles.

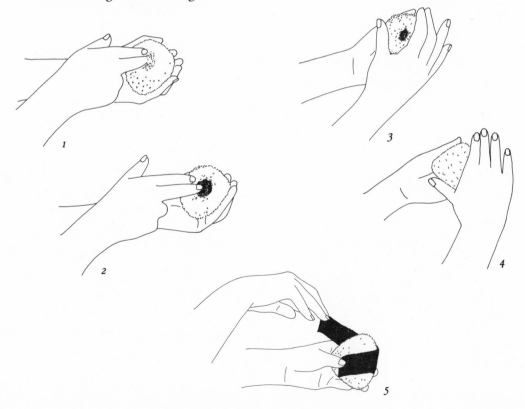

いなり寿し SUSHI STUFFED PILLOWS *(Inari-zushi)*

This is sweet vegetarian *sushi* enjoyed by adults and youngsters alike. Serve it alone or in combination with *sushi* rolled in laver (next recipe) and garnish your platter or lunchbox with red pickled ginger or other sharp, bright pickles. *Serves 3–4.*

4–6 slices *abura agé* (fried bean curd)
½–⅔ cup *dashi* (Basic Soup Stock, page 55)
¼ cup sugar
3–4 tablespoons soy sauce
2 tablespoons *saké* (rice wine)
2 cups cooked, still warm rice (made from 1 cup raw rice according to master recipe, page 70)

3–3½ tablespoons *sushi su* (seasoned vinegar)
½ tablespoon white sesame seeds
1–2 tablespoons chopped *subasu* (Sweet and Sour Lotus Root, page 175) AND/OR *amazu shōga* (pink pickled ginger)

Quickly blanch the slices of fried bean curd in boiling water to remove excess oil. Drain the slices and pat them dry with paper towels. While they are still warm, cut each slice in half, across its width. Place a slice of the bean curd on the open palm of one hand and slap down on it with the other. From the cut edge, gently pry open the fried bean curd to form a deep pocket or bag. Repeat this slap-and-pry procedure for each of the remaining pieces.

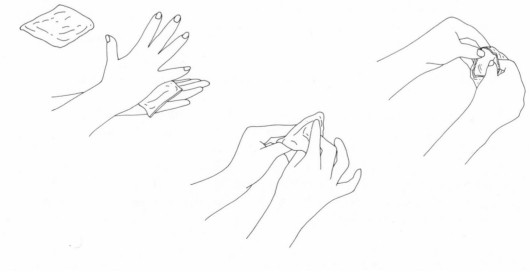

In a wide-mouthed saucepan, combine ½ cup of
the stock, all the sugar, 3 tablespoons of the soy sauce
and all the rice wine. Heat until the sugar has melted.
Place the bean curd bags in the saucepan in no more
than a double layer and simmer them for 6–7 minutes
over medium heat. If the bags look in danger of
scorching, add a bit more stock and soy sauce. Use a
"dropped" lid (*otoshi-buta,* described on page 12) for
best results. Or simmer uncovered but frequently ladle
the liquid over the bags. Let the bags cool to room
temperature in the saucepan before draining them of
excess liquid.

Sprinkle the rice with the seasoned vinegar and
toss it gently with a wooden spoon while fanning it
with a stiff fan or piece of cardboard. This helps cool
the rice to room temperature while avoiding
condensation from the steam. Dry roast the sesame
seeds (see page 16 for details) and toss them into the
rice. Add the chopped lotus root and/or pickled ginger
and toss them with the rice. Dampen your hands
slightly with cold water, and divide the seasoned rice
into 8–10 balls. Stuff each of the bean curd bags with
one of these balls.

Arrange the *sushi*-stuffed pillows, seams down, on
a large platter and serve them at room temperature.
They can be made many hours in advance and kept in
a cool spot, but do not refrigerate them.

巻き寿し SUSHI ROLLED IN LAVER *(Maki-zushi)*

These thin rolls of *sushi,* made with a variety of fillings, are light and delicate. Here
are two popular vegetarian versions: one contains strips of sweet braised gourd *(nori
maki)*, the other crisp cucumber slices garnished with sesame and fiery horseradish
(kappa maki). Good in a lunchbox by themselves or with *sushi*-stuffed pillows, they
could be served for dinner, too, with Salt-Grilled Fish (page 138) and blocks of Thick
Sweet Omelet (page 152). *Maki-zushi* rolls can also be an indoor treat served with hot
miso soup. *Makes 8 rolls to serve 4–6.*

2 cups cooked, still warm rice (made from 1 cup raw rice according to master recipe, page 70)

3½ tablespoons *sushi su* (seasoned vinegar)

Gourd strip filling *(nori maki)*:

8 six- or seven-inch strips *kanpyō* (dried gourd)
½ cup *dashi* (Basic Soup Stock, page 55)
Scant 2 tablespoons soy sauce
2 tablespoons sugar
1½ teaspoons *mirin* (syrupy rice wine)

Cucumber filling *(kappa maki)*:

½ tablespoon white sesame seeds
½ small unwaxed cucumber
¼ teaspoon *wasabi* (fiery green horseradish)

---

4 sheets *Asakusa nori* (dark dried laver)

Garnish:

¼ cup *béni shōga* (red pickled ginger)
    AND/OR *amazu shōga* (pink pickled ginger)

Sprinkle the rice with the seasoned vinegar and toss it gently with a wooden spoon while fanning with a fan or stiff piece of cardboard. This helps cool the rice to room temperature while avoiding condensation from the steam. Dip your hands in a bowl of acidulated water (1–1½ cups cold water and 1–2 tablespoons rice vinegar) and form the rice into 8 small balls. Cover with a damp cloth until ready to use.

Soak the dried gourd strips in warm water to cover for about 10 minutes. In fresh boiling water, blanch the gourd strips for 2–3 minutes and drain them. Rinse under running cold water with scrubbing motions and squeeze dry. In a small saucepan, combine the soup stock, soy sauce, sugar and syrupy rice wine. Stirring, bring it to a boil. Reduce the heat and add the gourd strips. Simmer for 12–15 minutes or until nearly all the liquid has evaporated. Remove from heat and let the braised gourd cool to room temperature.

Dry roast the sesame seeds until golden (details on page 16) and set them aside in a small bowl. Slice the cucumber diagonally and then lengthwise to make julienne strips. If using powdered horseradish mix ¼ teaspoon of the powder with ⅛ teaspoon cold water. Mix thoroughly, cover with a cloth and let it stand for 5–6 minutes. If using horseradish paste from a tube, squeeze out ¼ inch into a deep dish and cover it with a cloth until ready to use.

Just before making the *sushi*, dry roast the laver, one sheet at a time (details on page 16). Cut each sheet in half, yielding 8 pieces approximately 4 by 7 inches each.

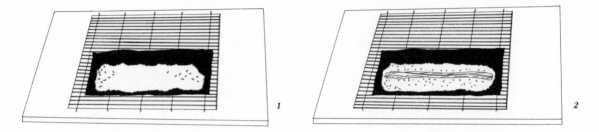

You will need a bamboo mat called a *sudaré* to roll the *sushi*. Place a single piece of laver on your *sudaré*. Then dip your hands in the acidulated water to prevent the rice from sticking to them, and take one of the 8 rice balls and spread it over two-thirds of the laver (*1*). Lay 2 strips of braised gourd horizontally across the middle of the rice (*2*). Lift up the edge of the *sudaré* closest to you and flip it over the filling (*3, 4, 5*). Press down firmly and continue to roll the cylinder of *sushi* away from you (*6, 7*). Remove the first rolled *sushi* to a dry, flat surface and make three more rolls in the same way, using the remaining braised gourd.

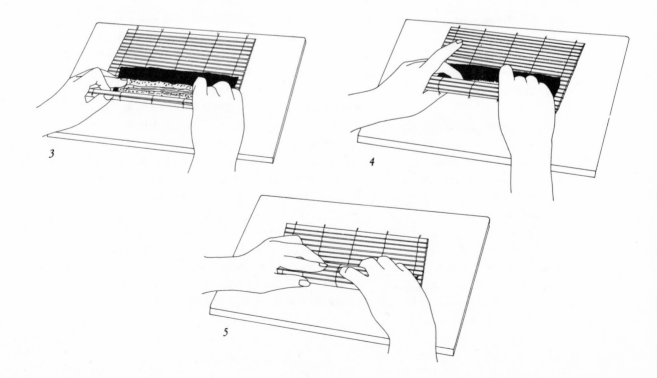

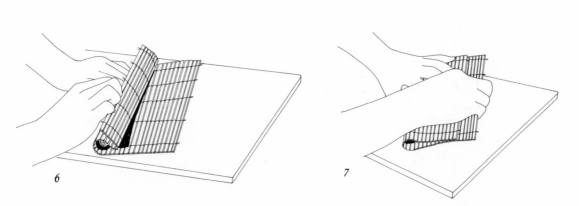

6

7

Now make the cucumber-filled *sushi*. Lay a sheet of laver on your bamboo mat and with damp hands spread one ball of rice evenly over two-thirds of it. Using the tip of your finger, paint a horizontal line across the middle of the rice with one-quarter of the horseradish. Arrange one-fourth of the cucumber slices over the horseradish line and sprinkle with one-fourth of the sesame seeds. Again, lift the edge of the bamboo mat closest to you up and over the filling. Press down firmly to seal and continue to roll the cylinder of *sushi* away from you. Remove this roll and make three more just like it with the remaining ingredients. Cut each roll of *sushi* into 6 pieces, using a very sharp wet knife. Insert the tip of the knife first, then, pushing down and away from you, continue to cut, using the base of the blade. Do not saw back and forth.

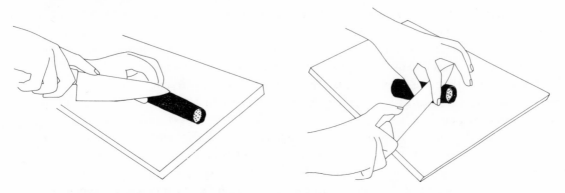

Arrange the *sushi* pieces, some standing, others lying on their sides, on a large serving platter, and decorate with pickled ginger. Serve at room temperature. This dish may be made several hours in advance and kept in a cool spot. Cover loosely with wax paper. Do not refrigerate it, though, as the laver becomes soggy and the rice unpleasantly hard.

かにちらし寿し

SCATTERED CRAB SUSHI *(Kani Chirashi-zushi)*

This is a spectacular dish, both colorful and delicious. Tartly seasoned rice is tossed with pink pickled ginger, crabmeat, freshly roasted sesame and laver, and heaped upon a large platter. Then bright yellow ribbons of omelet, pure white slices of Sweet and Sour Lotus Root, braised black mushrooms, tart red fancy crabmeat and crisp green snow peas are scattered on top. Most of these things can be prepared hours or even days in advance and assembled at the last minute, making this perfect party fare. *Serves 6–8.*

2½ cups raw rice	3–4 eggs, prepared 1 at a time according to recipe for Thin Sweet Omelet, page 151
Scant 3 cups water	
⅓ cup *sushi su* (seasoned vinegar)	
3 tablespoons *amazu shōga* (pink pickled ginger)	20–25 slices Sweet and Sour Lotus Root, made according to recipe on page 175
10 ounces canned, frozen or fresh cooked crabmeat	
3–4 tablespoons lemon juice	7–8 braised *shiitaké* (black Oriental mushrooms), prepared according to recipe on page 129
2 tablespoons white sesame seeds	
1 sheet *Asakusa nori* (dark dried laver)	¼ cup *béni shōga* (red pickled ginger)
	8–10 snow peas

Wash the raw rice until the water runs clear, then cook it according to the master recipe on page 70 using a scant 3 cups of water. Transfer the rice while still warm to a wooden bowl. The Japanese use a *handai* (illustration and details on page 38), or a large, unvarnished wooden salad bowl. Pour the seasoned vinegar, a little at a time, over the rice. Toss gently with a wooden paddle while fanning with a fan or stiff piece of cardboard. This helps cool the rice to room temperature while avoiding condensation from the steam.

Finely mince the pink pickled ginger and toss it into the rice. Pick over the crabmeat to remove all cartilage; pour a little lemon juice over it and let stand for at least 5 minutes. Squeeze out the crabmeat and set aside any fancy red leg meat (or at least one-third of the lump meat) for scattering on top. Gently toss the remaining two-thirds of the crabmeat into the rice. Dry roast the sesame seeds (page 16 for details) and toss them into the rice, too. Dry roast the sheet of laver (same page), then fold and crumble it in a clean, dry cloth. Sprinkle the laver flakes over the rice and gently toss with a wooden spoon. Now mound the rice on a large serving platter.

Cut the thin sweet omelet into long, thin ribbons and scatter them over the mound of seasoned rice. Drain the slices of lotus root of excess sweet and sour sauce and scatter them over the egg ribbons. Slice the cooked black mushrooms into julienne strips and scatter them over the garnished rice. Then scatter the reserved crabmeat over the rice. If the red pickled ginger you purchased is in slices or knobs, cut it into julienne strips and scatter these over the rice, too. Just before serving, blanch the snow peas for 1 minute in salted water, then refresh them in cold water. Pat the snow peas dry and slice them diagonally into julienne strips. Scatter these over the rice.

Serve at room temperature. Leftovers may be loosely covered and kept in a cool spot for one day. Do not refrigerate the *sushi*.

五目寿し ASSORTED VEGETARIAN SUSHI *(Gomoku-zushi)*

This makes a very impressive main course at a luncheon or dinner. Like crab *sushi*, all the many little things that go into this dish can be prepared hours or even days in advance. Assemble just before your company arrives—or even better, before their very eyes. *Serves 6–8.*

2½ cups raw rice
Scant 3 cups water
⅓ cup *sushi su* (seasoned vinegar)
5 large dried *shiitaké* (black Oriental mushrooms), soaked in warm water for 20 minutes, then sliced in julienne strips
½ cup carrot cut in julienne strips
½ cup *gobō* (burdock root) OR boiled bamboo shoots cut in julienne strips

20–25 slices Sweet and Sour Lotus Root, made according to recipe on page 175
2–3 eggs, prepared 1 at a time according to recipe for Thin Sweet Omelet, page 151
⅓ cup *béni shōga* (red pickled ginger) cut in julienne strips
¼ pound fresh string beans

Follow instructions in the preceding recipe for making rice.

Cook the strips of mushroom, carrot and burdock or bamboo shoots according to the recipe for simmered vegetables on page 129, then toss into the seasoned rice and gently mix for even distribution. Mound the rice on a large serving platter.

Decorate one-quarter of the surface with slices of well-drained Sweet and Sour Lotus Root. Slice the omelet into thin ribbons approximately ⅛ inch wide and 1½–2 inches long, and scatter them over another quarter of the surface of the rice. Decorate yet another quarter of the surface with the red pickled ginger.

Cook the string beans in boiling salted water until barely tender (3–4 minutes). Drain the beans and plunge them into cold water to stop the cooking process. Drain again, pat, and slice on the diagonal into julienne strips. Just before serving decorate the final quarter of the platter with them. Prolonged contact with vinegared rice will turn the green beans an unattractive brown. Serve at room temperature. Leftovers may be loosely covered and kept in a cool spot for one day. Do not refrigerate the *sushi*.

鯖
寿
し
MACKEREL LOAVES (*Saba-zushi*)

Here seasoned rice is topped with silver-and-blue-streaked marinated mackerel to make an impressive luncheon or dinner main course. The fish must be salted or marinated overnight; instructions for both methods are included.

Though uncooked, the final dish keeps quite well for a day at room temperature. In fact, this mackerel loaf is the refined version of a very primitive method of food preservation, namely salting, and is probably the oldest known kind of *sushi* there is. It is particularly favored in the Kansai region (area around Kyoto, Nara and Osaka), though enjoyed throughout Japan. *Serves 6–8 as a main dish.*

2 whole mackerel, each weighing about 1¼–1½ pounds	3–4 tablespoons coarse sea salt

Marinade:

⅔ cup rice vinegar 5–6 tablespoons sugar	1½–2 tablespoons *usu kuchi shōyu* (light soy sauce)

About 25–30 inches *shirata konbu* (pale-green kelp), optional since availability is limited 2 cups raw rice, cooked according to the master recipe on page 70	Generous ¼ cup *sushi su* (seasoned vinegar) 8–12 sticks *hajikami su-zuké* (whole young ginger pickled in sweet and sour sauce)

Clean, dress and fillet both mackerel (pages 28–30). Salt the 4 fillets on all sides with 3 tablespoons of salt and lay them flat in a covered glass or ceramic container for 4–5 hours in a cool but unrefrigerated spot. (Or use 4 tablespoons of salt and refrigerate the fillets overnight.) Either way, there should be a considerable amount of liquid to pour off, and the flesh should be much firmer than before. Remove the small bones down the middle of each fillet with tweezers. Carefully rinse the fillets under running cold water, then gently pat them dry.

In a small saucepan, combine the ingredients for the marinade. If you are planning on marinating the fish unrefrigerated, use 5 tablespoons sugar and 2 tablespoons light soy sauce for the marinade. (If you plan to refrigerate the marinating fish, use 6 tablespoons sugar and only 1 ½ tablespoons of light soy sauce.) If you have found the pale-green kelp (difficult to obtain in some areas of the United States but well worth special ordering), put it in the saucepan also and bring the mixture to a boil. Stir to make sure all the sugar has dissolved. Remove from the heat and let the kelp and marinade cool down to room temperature undisturbed. The kelp will turn a translucent golden-toned green and impart a subtle sweetness to the marinade.

Lay the mackerel fillets flat, skin side up, in a single layer if possible, in a glass or ceramic casserole or deep dish. Pour cooled marinade over the fish, cover and let them marinate for 2–3 hours at room temperature (or overnight in the refrigerator).

About 1 hour before shaping the loaves, cook the rice and season it with the *sushi su*. Fan the rice to cool it down as you toss gently with a wooden paddle or spoon. With damp hands, form 8 balls from the seasoned rice. Lay a damp cloth over these if you are not going to use them immediately. (The rice can be held for about 1 hour this way.)

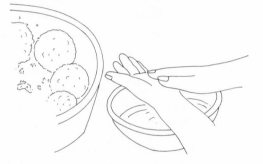

Remove the fish fillets from their marinade and peel off the thin, transparent outer skin from each piece. Peel from the head to the tail. Arrange the fillets' backs to each other, tails to right, heads to left, and cut them diagonally as shown. Now reverse the top and bottom pieces on the right-hand side. Not only will this make

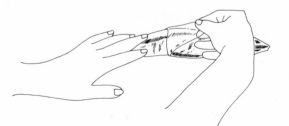

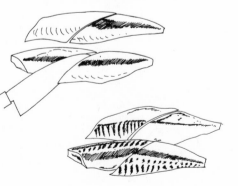

for an attractive design on the finished loaf, but it helps to even out the overall thickness of the fish fillets. Trim the right- and left-hand sides for neater loaves. (Either eat up these end pieces, or slice them very thin and toss them with thinly sliced, lightly salted, then squeezed-out cucumbers for an interesting hors d'oeuvre or side dish for another meal, which can be kept refrigerated for up to two days.)

Ideally, to shape the loaves you should have the following equipment on hand: a *sudaré* (slatted bamboo mat), some *sarashi* (white linen cloth), and four sheets of *také no kawa* (bark from bamboo, sold especially for wrapping such dishes as these). If not, you can still make do with a white napkin and either clear plastic wrap or aluminum foil, some stiff cardboard and rubber bands. If you do have the bamboo bark, soak 4 pieces of them in water for 15–20 minutes, remove a thin strip from each sheet to use as a tie and then pat the sheets dry with paper towels. *Sarashi* cloth or table napkins should be soaked in slightly acidulated water for 2–3 minutes, then wrung out very well. The *sudaré* mat should be dry, and so should your work surface.

Place the *sudaré* mat flat on your work surface and lay the damp cloth over it. Or, if you haven't a mat, lay the cloth directly on a small cutting board. Arrange one block of mackerel (two diagonally fitted pieces), skin side down in the middle of the cloth *(1)*. With damp hands, take two balls of rice and place one at each end *(2)*. Push and coax the rice with your hands to cover the mackerel fillets entirely *(3)*. Try to maintain a rectangular shape from the start. Bring the cloth and mat up over the rice

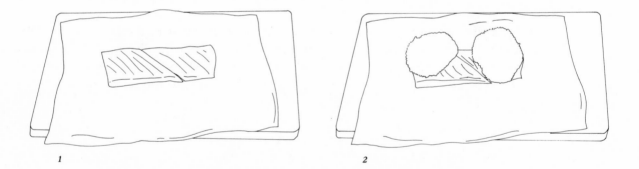

1   2

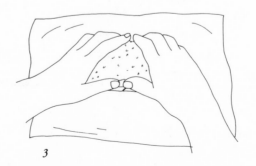

3

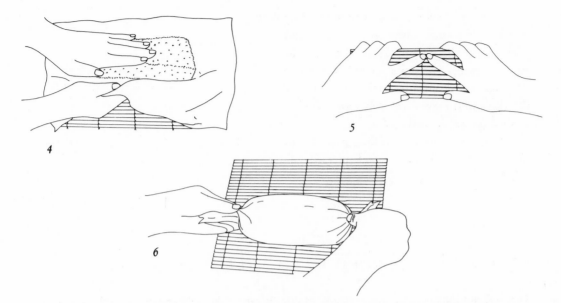

to help form a straight line and sharp-edged block *(4, 5)*. Twist the ends of the cloth gently to help shape these sides *(6)*. Open the cloth, and if you're using damp bamboo bark, place it over the fish and rice loaf. Now flip the loaf over and peel off the cloth *(7)*. The bark will be on the bottom with the fish fillets on top (8). Or, use clear wrap, foil or damp linen cloths in lieu of the bamboo bark and transfer the loaf in the same manner. If you have kelp, cut it to match the length of your mackerel block and lay it across the top of the fish. Tie up the mackerel loaf snugly in bamboo bark *(9)* or place stiff cardboards on top and bottom of loaves wrapped in plastic wrap, foil or cloth. Secure the cardboard with rubber bands and add light pressure evenly on top—a 1-pound book or two is fine. Repeat the shaping and wrapping procedure to make 3 more loaves.

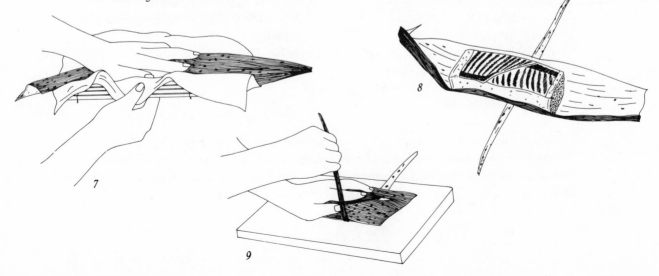

Let them set for at least 2 hours and up to 6 hours *unrefrigerated*. Unwrap the loaves and, with a very sharp damp knife, slice each loaf into 5–6 pieces . Avoid a sawing motion and dampen your knife after each cut. Reassemble the slices into loaves and lean 2 or 3 sticks of pickled ginger against each of them. Or, if the sticks of ginger are unavailable, garnish your platter with sliced red and pink pickled ginger.

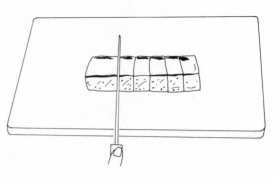

にぎり寿し RICE OVALS TOPPED WITH SALMON *(Nigiri-zushi)*

Throughout Japan, and increasingly in the West, *sushi* restaurants are filled with patrons devoted to ovals of vinegared rice topped with fresh raw fish—a delicacy known as *nigiri-zushi*. The necessity of using impeccably fresh fish and seafood, plus the deftness required in handling the seasoned rice, makes restaurant-style *nigiri-zushi* a difficult dish to produce at home. But here is a tasty variation that will work very well for the non-professional. A damp cloth can help to shape the rice, and I've made use of less perishable, though equally delectable, pale pink smoked salmon. These bite-size *sushi* make very nice hors d'oeuvres, and I suggest you decorate your platter with red pickled ginger and cucumber mountains (page 26) for extra color, flavor and texture appeal. *Makes 25.*

1½ cups raw rice, freshly cooked according to the master recipe on page 70
2–2½ tablespoons *sushi su* (seasoned vinegar)
½–¾ pound smoked Nova Scotia salmon, sliced thin

¼ teaspoon *wasabi* (fiery green horseradish) paste or reconstituted powder
Soy sauce for dipping, optional

While the rice is still warm, sprinkle it with seasoned vinegar, tossing lightly for even distribution. Wet your hands in cold water (some people add a few drops of vinegar to the water) to prevent the rice from sticking to your fingers, then divide the seasoned rice into 25 balls. Dampen a white handkerchief or table napkin and wring it out

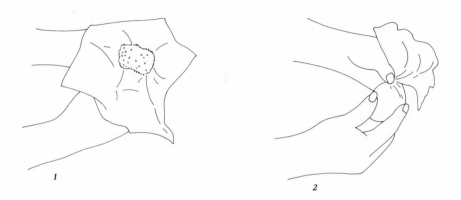

thoroughly. Place one ball of rice at a time in the center of the cloth and gather up the edges *(1)*. Twist the bag to compress the rice *(2)*. Remove the ball and, with dampened hands, press down slightly to form an oval shape *(3, 4)*. Place on a plate or tray and cover with a damp cloth to prevent the surface from hardening as you prepare the other rice ovals in the same manner.

Measure the length of your rice ovals (probably 1½ inches long) and cut enough salmon to cover each (you can always piece together a torn or shredded slice). Spread a very small amount of horseradish on the underside of each slice of salmon and drape it over the rice ovals *(5)*. Provide soy sauce for dipping, if you like.

NOTE: *Nigiri-zushi* are really best when prepared just before eating—the reason for some of the splendid performances at restaurant *sushi* bars. But the version given here can be made an hour or so in advance of your guests' arrival. Loosely cover with a damp cloth and clear wrap and place in a cool but not refrigerated spot.

ASSORTED TOPPINGS FOR RICE OVALS *(Gomoku Nigiri-zushi)*

If you have a source of absolutely fresh fish, a wide variety of toppings is possible. Lean red tuna, translucent sole or flounder, and silky squid or cuttlefish are particularly pretty and flavorful. Thin slices of bright yellow omelet make attractive toppings, too. *Serves 6–8 as appetizers, 3–4 as a main course.*

1½ cups raw rice, freshly cooked according to the master recipe on page 70
2–2½ tablespoons *sushi su* (seasoned vinegar)
¼ pound each of 2 or 3 varieties of fresh fish or seafood fillets: tuna, sole, flounder, squid, cuttlefish

2–2½-inch block of thick omelet (page 152), leftover is perfect
½ sheet *Asakusa nori* (dark dried laver)
1 tablespoon *wasabi* (fiery green horseradish) paste or reconstituted powder
¼ cup *amazu shōga* (pink pickled ginger)

Within an hour or two of serving time, prepare the rice, then season and shape it as described in the preceding recipe. Cover the ovals loosely with a damp cloth, then enclose in clear wrap. Do not refrigerate.

With the exception of the omelet, prepare your toppings as close to serving time as possible. Slice a small slab of tuna into ¼-inch-thick slices, across the grain (Basic Hold 3, page 21). Just before draping over the rice, dab a bit of fiery green horseradish on the underside of each slice.

Fillet of sole or flounder should be cut into paper-thin slices, slightly on the diagonal (*sogi-giri* cutting, page 26). Again dab the underside of each slice with a bit of horseradish before draping over the rice ovals.

Squid or cuttlefish should be cut into rectangles slightly larger than your ovals of rice. I think they look and taste better when "tied" onto the rice with ribbons of black laver. Dry roast a half sheet of laver (see page 16) and cut it with scissors into ¼-inch-wide strips. Attach as illustrated here. If making the omelet fresh, be sure it

has cooled completely before slicing it. Figure on about 5 slices for every 2 inches of thick omelet, each slice to top a single rice oval. Drape the omelet, then secure it with a thin strip of laver in the same manner as the squid or cuttlefish.

Arrange the bite-size *sushi* on a large platter or tray and garnish with pink pickled ginger. Though inedible, fresh green leaves or even plastic ones (they look like tufts of grass) can make your platter even more attractive.

Noodles

(MEN RUÍ)

Throughout the Orient, noodles are enjoyed as a snack or light meal. Lacking the prestige of rice, they are nevertheless consumed in large quantities. The Japanese eat a variety of noodles, hot and cold in soups and with dipping sauces.

Soba is the name both of a thin, beige-colored noodle and of the grain (similar to buckwheat) from which these noodles are made. Firm and slightly coarse in texture, cooked *soba* are usually served chilled and garnished with dark strips of crisp *nori* (roasted laver). A sweetened soy sauce for dipping and condiments such as *wasabi* (fiery green horseradish), grated fresh ginger and chopped scallions accompany the noodles. Occasionally, *soba* will be served hot in a garnished soup and seasoned with a blend of crushed hot spices known as *shichimi tōgarashi*.

Sōmen are very thin, pure-white noodles. For a refreshing summertime dish, they are served cold in large crystal bowls of ice water. Grated ginger, chopped scallions or *shiso* (an aromatic leaf of the beefsteak plant) and a soy-based dipping sauce typically accompany *sōmen* noodles.

Udon are thick, white, slippery noodles, which are served in a hot, hearty soup. Garnished with a variety of vegetables and slices of fish sausage *(kamaboko)*, fried bean curd *(abura agé)*, batter-fried shrimp *(tempura)* or poached eggs, these noodles make a filling snack indeed. In the northern parts of Japan, *udon* are often added to the flavorful broth resulting from *nabé mono* (stewlike, one-pot cookery).

The Japanese have adapted Chinese stir-fried noodles into a dish known as *yaki soba*. Shredded pork, cabbage and soft egg noodles are sautéed on a griddle. Seasoned with a spicy, dark sauce and garnished with chopped red pickled ginger and flakes of green laver, *yaki soba* is a colorful and aromatic dish.

Sapporo (the largest city of Hokkaidō island) is famous for its Chinese-style soup noodles, known as *ramen*. A large bowl of these is sure to warm you on even the most blustery of winter days. By the way, noodle eating in Japan, as in most of the Orient, is a noisy affair. Slurping sounds are perfectly acceptable; in fact, they are

96

equated with full enjoyment and are a compliment to the chef. So don't hesitate to show your appreciation if you're in proper company.

Storage and Cooking Instructions

Japanese noodle products are packaged and marketed in a number of forms, and unfortunately the labeling and cooking instructions in English on the package are not always clear. Since storage and cooking times are determined by whether the noodles are fresh, dried or instant rather than by type (buckwheat, egg, etc.), let's look at different kinds of Japanese noodles you're apt to encounter.

First there is *nama,* which means "raw" or "uncooked," and also "fresh." These noodles are dusted in flour and haven't been treated by heat. They are highly perishable and should be eaten within 2–3 days of purchase. (Occasionally *nama* noodles have been frozen for transport but are sold defrosted; never refreeze them.) You will find them packaged in mounds or bundles of about 6 ounces (each intended as a single portion) in the refrigerator or freezer section of large Oriental groceries. (I've included one recipe for making your own fresh thick white noodles.)

To cook, bring a large pot of water to a boil over high heat. Add the noodles all at once and stir occasionally. Cook for 2–3 minutes for *ramen* (thin yellow, "Chinese" soup noodles), 3–4 minutes for *soba* (thin beige buckwheat noodles), and 10–12 minutes for *udon* (thick white noodles). Timing should begin once the water has returned to a boil, and the water should be kept boiling the entire time. Drain the noodles and rinse them thoroughly under running cold water. If the noodles are to be eaten hot, just before serving place them in a deep strainer and lower into a pot of plain boiling water for 30–40 seconds. Lift the strainer from the pot and let the noodles drain for a few moments.

There are also fresh noodles which have already been cooked and drained, then refrigerated or frozen. They are even more perishable than uncooked fresh noodles and should be eaten within a day or two of purchase unless kept frozen.

Yaki soba (thin yellow noodles for stir-frying), *chūka soba* or *ramen* (thin yellow noodles for soups or salads), *soba* (thin beige buckwheat noodles), and *udon* (thick white noodles) will be found in the freezer or refrigerator section of most large Oriental groceries. They are packaged in mounds, each intended as a single portion. The weight of each portion varies with the type of noodle, but generally they are 6–8 ounces each. Never refreeze any fresh noodle product. Just before using, precooked fresh noodles should be blanched in rapidly boiling water for 10–15 seconds, then drained thoroughly.

Dried noodles are brittle. They have a shelf life of several years and are readily available throughout the United States. *Sōmen* (thin white noodles to be served cold) are available only dried; other types of noodles, though probably more flavorful if purchased fresh, are fine dried for most recipes. Most packages of dried noodles contain several smaller bundles of about 3–4 ounces each, and these are intended as single portions. Larger packages that are not subdivided are meant to serve 4–5.

Fresh-dried noodles are cooked by the *sashimizu* ("add water") technique. This is thought to help the dried noodle cook through to its core without becoming soggy.

Fill a large pot three-quarters full with fresh cold water and bring it to a boil over high heat. Add the noodles, scattering them over the surface. If the noodles are too long for your pot, hold one end in the boiling water first to soften them, then swirl the remainder in. Stir occasionally to prevent sticking. When the water has returned to a rolling boil, add one cup of fresh cold water. Continue to cook over high heat until the water comes to a boil again. Add a second cup of fresh cold water. Let the water boil again. For *sōmen* (thin white noodles) this should suffice. Test a strand in a cup of cold water; it should be translucent but still firm.

For cooking *soba* (thin beige buckwheat noodles) continue to cook for 3–4 minutes after the second addition of water. Test a few strands. If not cooked through, add a third cup of cold water, let it return to a boil and then drain. For *udon* cook 5–6 minutes after the second addition of water. Test, and if not cooked through, add a third cup of cold water. Again, let it come back to a boil before draining.

Fresh-dried *sōmen*, *soba* and *udon* should be well rinsed under cold water after cooking. Drain the noodles again, and if they are to be used in a hot soup, just before serving place them in a deep strainer and lower them into boiling water for 20–30 seconds. Lift out and let the noodles drain.

Most "instant" noodles come packaged in individual portions with packets of powdered soup mix included. Although the instructions suggest that the soup mix be added directly to the pot after the noodles have been cooked for 3–5 minutes, I think it's better to drain the noodles and mix the powder with fresh boiling water.

Some instant noodles come in Styrofoam cups to which boiling water is added directly. Cover the cup, wait 3 minutes, stir and eat. Some instant noodles are quite tasty, but cannot compare with fresh or even fresh-dried products. The instant-noodle boom, though, can no longer be ignored. Not only does every supermarket in the larger metropolitan areas of Japan devote at least one aisle to instant noodles, but there probably isn't a country store in the whole archipelago that doesn't stock at least three or four different brands. The craze has hit the grassroots of the nation, and this despite an abundance of excellent fresh-made noodles at restaurants which supply take-out orders and/or home delivery. Ease in shipment and relatively long shelf life of most instant noodles have influenced the import-export trade and the Japanese have flooded the world market. It is easy to find several types and brands in even the smallest Oriental grocery in the United States.

One final note: for some strange reason, most noodle products are labeled in English as "alimentary paste" or "Japanese-style alimentary paste." Fear not . . . these are merely noodles.

❖

HANDMADE THICK WHITE NOODLES *(Té Uchi Udon)*

手打ちうどん

The recipe given here is basically my mother-in-law's (a noodle maker par excellence!) and after tasting them I think you'll agree they're well worth the trouble of making. Serve them in either Fox Noodles (page 102) or Moon-Viewing Noodles (page 103), both of which are soup-and-noodle combinations. Or add them to the flavored broth resulting from any of the one-pot *nabé mono* on pages 110–118.

Nisshin, a large brand name in Japan, has packaged a combination of unbleached flours under the name *té uchi udon senyō komugiko* ("flour especially made for handmade noodles") that is far superior to ordinary flour for this purpose. It is increasingly available at larger Oriental groceries in the West. Do try to find some and use it. If not, make do with all-purpose unbleached flour. *Makes about 4 servings.*

1 tablespoon salt
Generous ⅔ cup warm water

3 cups *udon* flour (plus up to ½ cup for hands, pin and board)

Add the salt to the warm water and stir until dissolved. Put the flour in a large bowl and pour in the salty water. Stir lightly until the mixture is crumbly. Exerting a bit of pressure, form the dough into a ball and place it in a plastic bag to rest for about 30 minutes (or refrigerate it for several hours).

Since great strength is required to make such a stiff dough more pliable, most Japanese use barefoot stamping power in lieu of hand kneading. Sandwich the dough between two large sheets of plastic or place it in the center of a very sturdy plastic bag. Stand barefoot on the plastic and stamp with the whole of your foot, not just the heel. Turn frequently as you stamp until the dough is flat. With your hands, fold the dough into a ball again. Repeat the stamping and folding several times until the dough is smooth and satiny. Finally, stamp the dough out in an oval shape of a uniform ¼-inch thickness. All of this will take about 4–5 minutes for an adult female of average size and weight. If foot stamping is not your style, you'll have to hand knead 10–15 minutes before palm pressing the dough to an equivalent smoothness and thickness. Of course mechanical kneading with a dough hook or pasta machine is possible—but I find the resulting noodles dense and lacking in that wonderful handmade texture.

Transfer the dough to a large lightly floured board or table top. Alternating vertical and horizontal strokes, roll and stretch the dough into a large oval. Japanese rolling pins have no handles and are much longer and narrower than American ones. Use the longest pin you have and try to roll the dough out to ⅛ inch thick, 1 foot wide and at least 1½ feet long. If this is impossible with your pin, cut the dough in half and roll out two narrower, long pieces. (If you don't plan on using all the rolled-out dough immediately, wrap some in plastic wrap and refrigerate it for up to 3 days, or freeze it for up to 2 weeks. Let the dough return to room temperature before sprinkling it generously with flour.)

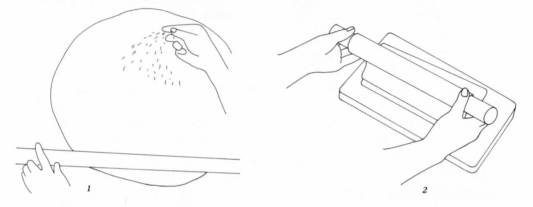

Sprinkle the rolled-out dough liberally with flour *(1)*. Then, letting the dough fall off the rolling pin, fold it somewhat like a fan, making 4 or 5 folds *(2)*. Use a long, sharp knife to cut the dough into ¼-inch-thick ribbons. Use the entire cutting edge of the knife, starting with the tip and working into the base of the blade *(3)*. Use quick, light movements to cut into the dough and away from yourself. Do not saw back and forth. Dust the noodles with flour again before lifting from the board *(4)*.

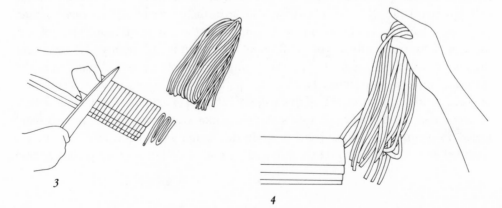

To cook the noodles, bring a very large pot of water to a rapid boil. Lightly shake off excess flour clinging to the noodles before adding them to the pot. Cook for about 10 minutes, keeping the water at a boil the entire time. Test a noodle in cold water: it should be translucent and firm but with no hard core. Drain the noodles, rinse them under cold water and drain them again.

うどんのかけ汁 HEARTY SOUP FOR THICK WHITE NOODLES
(Udon No Kaké-jiru)

This is a deeply colored and flavored broth that is particularly suited to thick white noodles. Unlike the more delicate stock made from bonito shavings, this soup freezes well. *Yields a generous quart of soup.*

⅔ cup broken pieces dried *shiitaké* OR 4–5 large whole dried *shiitaké* (black Oriental mushrooms)

5–6 inches *konbu* (kelp for stock making)

1½ quarts cold water

15–18 *niboshi* (dried sardines for stock making)

2½–3 tablespoons soy sauce

1½ tablespoons sugar

½ teaspoon *saké* (rice wine)

Place the dried mushrooms and kelp in a large pot of cold water. Bring the water to a boil rapidly, discard the kelp, and reduce the heat to a simmer. Cook the stock uncovered for 15 minutes.

Break off and discard the heads of the dried sardines (they tend to be bitter), add the bodies to the pot, and continue to cook for another 10 minutes.

Strain the stock through a cloth-lined colander, discarding the mushrooms and fish. Season the dark broth with soy sauce, sugar and *saké*.

Serve with thick white noodles in either of the following two recipes.

きつねうどん

FOX NOODLES *(Kitsuné Udon)*

The Japanese have many fanciful names for their dishes. This one refers to the garnish of fried bean curd; the golden brown is called "fox-colored." *Serves 4–5.*

3–4 slices *abura agé* (fried bean curd)

Cooking broth for bean curd:

⅓ cup *dashi* (Basic Soup Stock, page 55)	1 tablespoon soy sauce 1 tablespoon *mirin* (syrupy rice wine)

¼ pound fresh spinach OR collard greens 1 recipe fresh *udon* noodles (pages 97, 99) OR 1 scant pound fresh-dried *udon* noodles, cooked according to instructions on page 98	1 quart Hearty Soup (preceding recipe) 4–5 slices *kamaboko* (commercially prepared fish sausage), optional ¼ teaspoon *shichimi tōgarashi* (7-spice hot pepper)

Cut each slice of bean curd in half or thirds and blanch the pieces in boiling water to remove excess oil. Drain and pat dry. In a small saucepan, combine the stock, soy sauce and syrupy wine to make a cooking broth. Simmer the bean curd slices for 4–5 minutes in the broth.

Wash and trim the spinach. Blanch it in boiling salted water to cover for about 1 minute or until bright green and barely wilted. Drain the spinach and refresh it under cold running water. Drain again and squeeze out any excess liquid. Cut the spinach into 1-inch lengths and arrange them in 4–5 small bundles.

To assemble, place freshly cooked noodles in 4 or 5 deep bowls. Place 2–3 pieces of braised bean curd and a bundle of spinach on top of each bowl of noodles. Adding a slice of fish sausage makes this a more filling dish. Pour piping-hot soup over all and sprinkle with a pinch of 7-spice hot pepper. Serve immediately.

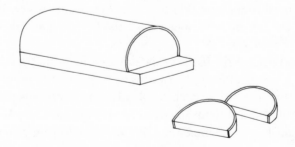

月見うどん

MOON-VIEWING NOODLES *(Tsuki Mi Udon)*

Another poetic dish . . . Here, the poached egg resembles the full moon. *Serves 4–5.*

4–5 eggs
Fresh *udon* noodles (pages 97, 99) OR 1
    scant pound fresh-dried *udon*
    noodles cooked according to
    instructions on page 98

1–2 scallions, chopped
1 quart Hearty Soup (page 101)

Poach the eggs in lightly salted water with the lid of your saucepan slightly askew. The Japanese like their eggs quite loose, in fact barely set at all, with only a hazy film covering the yolk. If you like, you can poach your eggs more firmly. Use a circular form, if you have one, to ensure a pretty, round shape.

   Divide the freshly cooked noodles among 4 or 5 bowls. Sprinkle some of the scallions on each portion and pour boiling-hot soup over all. Float a poached egg on top of each portion, being careful not to break the yolk in transfer. Serve immediately.

天ぷらそば

SOUP AND NOODLES WITH BATTER-FRIED SHRIMP *(Tempura Soba)*

Crisp fried shrimp and soft buckwheat noodles in a rich amber broth make a very nice light meal. You can make use of leftover shrimp *tempura* if you reheat them first in a preheated 250-degree oven for about 7–8 minutes. The soup can be made several days in advance and refrigerated, or frozen for up to 1 month. *Serves 3–4.*

Soup:

3½ cups *dashi* (Basic Soup Stock,
    page 55)
3 tablespoons soy sauce, preferably
    usu kuchi shōyu (light soy sauce)

3 tablespoons *mirin* (syrupy rice wine)
⅓ cup OR 1 small pack (5 grams) *katsuo
    bushi* (bonito flakes)

3–4 portions fresh *soba* (buckwheat
    noodles), cooked according to
    instructions on page 97, OR 10–12
    ounces fresh-dried *soba*, cooked
    according to instructions on
    page 98

6–8 fried shrimp *tempura* (page 157);
    leftovers are fine if reheated first
8–10 stalks *mitsuba* (trefoil) OR coriander
½ teaspoon *shichimi tōgarashi* (7-spice
    hot pepper) OR 1 teaspoon grated
    fresh ginger

To make the soup, bring the stock to a simmer in a small saucepan. Season with the soy sauce and syrupy wine, then stir, and cook for 1–2 minutes. Remove the saucepan from the heat and add the bonito flakes. Let them float to the bottom naturally, stir them up and let them settle again. Strain the broth through a cloth-lined strainer, discarding the bonito flakes. Return the soup to the saucepan and keep it piping hot unless you're making it for future use.

If you plan on reheating leftover shrimp *tempura,* do so while you boil your noodles. If you're going to fry the shrimp just for this dish, cook and drain your noodles first (you can always reheat your noodles, if they get too cold waiting, by swirling them in a pot of boiling water for a few seconds, then draining them). Chop the trefoil or coriander coarsely, and grate your ginger if you'll be using it.

To assemble this dish, divide the cooked noodles among 3 or 4 deep bowls. Pour very hot soup over the noodles to barely cover them, and top each portion with 2 fried shrimp. Garnish with some chopped trefoil or coriander, and sprinkle on a bit of the 7-spice hot pepper powder, or add ginger. Serve immediately.

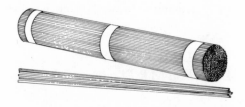

PORK AND NOODLES IN A SOY-FLAVORED BROTH (*Shōyu Aji Ramen*)

しょう油味ラーメン

Sapporo (capital city of the northern island of Hokkaidō) is famous for its thin yellow Chinese-style soup noodles, called *ramen.* The Japanese have thought up many tasty variations on the basic theme, and this one makes particularly good use of meat and stock left over from making Oriental Pork Pot Roast. *Serves 4–5.*

4–5 portions *ramen* (Chinese-style soup noodles) OR *chūka soba* (thin yellow noodles), 8 ounces per portion if fresh and 3 ounces if fresh-dried; cooked according to instructions on page 97 or 98

¼ pound fresh spinach OR collard greens

1 quart clarified stock from making Oriental Pork Pot Roast (page 120)

8–10 thin slices cooked meat from the pot roast

¼ teaspoon *sansho* (Japanese fragrant pepper)

Divide the cooked noodles among 4 or 5 deep bowls. Blanch the spinach or collard greens in boiling salted water to cover for 1 minute and drain. Rinse under cold water and drain again, squeezing out all excess water. Chop the greens coarsely, and garnish each bowl of noodles with some. Then heat the clarified pork stock until it is very hot and pour it over the noodles, barely covering them. Cut the cooked pork into julienne strips and scatter them on top of each bowl of soup noodles. Finally, sprinkle a bit of Japanese pepper over all and serve immediately.

味噌あじラーメン CHICKEN AND NOODLES IN MISO-THICKENED SOUP *(Miso Aji Ramen)*

Chicken and noodles in soup are a universally winning combination and the Japanese version is particularly nice, I think. They make theirs with a rich meaty broth that is thickened with aromatic bean paste and garnished with sesame seeds and chopped scallions. *Serves 4–5.*

4–5 portions *ramen* (Chinese-style soup noodles) OR *chūka soba* (thin yellow noodles), 8 ounces per portion if fresh and 3 ounces if fresh-dried; cooked according to instructions on pages 97 or 98
1 quart clarified Oriental Chicken Broth (page 56)

2–3 tablespoons *Shinshū Ichi miso* (medium bean paste)
¼ pound cooked chicken breast*
1–2 scallions, chopped
1 tablespoon dry-roasted white sesame seeds

Divide the cooked noodles among 4 or 5 deep bowls. In a saucepan, bring the chicken stock to a simmer and in a separate bowl dissolve the bean paste in a few tablespoons of the hot stock. Stir the dissolved bean paste into the saucepan. Pour the hot soup over the noodles to barely cover them.

Shred the cooked chicken breast with your fingers into thin strips (the irregular surfaces absorb more of the flavorful soup than flat slices would), and garnish each bowl of noodles with some. Sprinkle chopped scallions and roasted sesame seeds over all and serve immediately.

*The cooked chicken used in this recipe could be leftovers from making steamed or boiled chicken. Or it could be a breast freshly poached in the stock before the *miso* paste is added.

焼
き
そ
ば

SPICY STIR-FRIED NOODLES *(Yaki Soba)*

Spicy stir-fried noodles, called *yaki soba,* are one of many outdoor festival treats in Japan. Neighborhood shrines and temples have frequent *Matsuri* carnivals, and booths selling masks, toys, trinkets, soft drinks, cotton candy, grilled corn, squid and griddle-fried *yaki soba* line the entranceways. The recipe given here is a meatier version than most found in Japan, but it should still bring back memories to those who've sampled the "real thing." *Serves 4.*

4 portions (about 6 ounces each) of precooked fresh *yaki soba* noodles
½ pound lean butt of pork, sliced into extra fine julienne strips
2–3 tablespoons vegetable oil
1 cup coarsely shredded cabbage OR 1 cup mixed cabbage and onions

2 teaspoons *saké* (rice wine)
Pinch of salt
4–5 tablespoons *Wooster Sōsu* (dark, spicy Japanese version of Worcestershire sauce)

Garnish:

1 teaspoon *ao nori* (green laver flakes)
1 teaspoon chopped *béni shōga* (red pickled ginger)

Rinse the noodles in boiling water, drain them and set them aside.

In a large skillet or wok, sauté the pork in 1–2 tablespoons of oil over high heat, stirring frequently. When the meat is no longer pink, add the cabbage or cabbage and onions. Continue to stir-fry the mixture 1–2 minutes more or until the vegetables have softened a bit. Season with *saké* and salt and toss well to distribute.

Add the remaining tablespoon of oil and reduce the heat slightly. Toss in the noodles and stir-fry all for a minute or two. Season with the dark sauce and continue to cook for another minute. Serve the noodles hot, garnished with green laver flakes and chopped red pickled ginger.

ざ
る
そ
ば

COLD NOODLES WITH LAVER *(Zaru Soba)*

This is a hot-weather snack traditionally served in boxes lined with bamboo-slatted mats called *zaru*. If you haven't any, drain your noodles extra well and serve them mounded on chilled flat glass plates. *Serves 3–4.*

Dipping sauce:

1½ cups *dashi* (Basic Soup Stock,
   page 55)
3 tablespoons soy sauce, preferably *usu*
   kuchi shōyu (light soy sauce)

1½ tablespoons sugar
1 tablespoon *mirin* (syrupy rice wine)

3–4 portions (each about 6 ounces)
   fresh *soba* (buckwheat noodles)
   OR 10–12 ounces fresh-dried *soba*

½ sheet *Asakusa nori* (dark dried
   laver

Condiments:

¼ cup chopped scallions
2–3 tablespoons grated fresh ginger

1–2 teaspoons *wasabi* (fiery green
   horseradish)

Combine the dipping sauce ingredients in a small saucepan and heat through, stirring to dissolve the sugar. Chill the sauce well.

Prepare the noodles according to instructions on page 98 for fresh and page 97 for fresh-dried. Drain the noodles very well before mounding them on 3 or 4 small *zaru* mats or plates.

Dry roast the laver over direct medium heat for 1 minute or so. Fold it several times and crumble it in a clean, dry cloth. Sprinkle some of the crumbled laver over each mound of noodles. Serve the noodles at room temperature with individual cups of dipping sauce. Provide condiments in a serving dish or in separate small dishes, to add to your dipping sauce at the table. Dip your noodles, a few at a time, and eat.

素
麺 COLD THIN NOODLES *(Sōmen)*

These noodles are usually served on ice in large crystal bowls with matching cups for dipping sauce. The tinkling of ice against glass adds another cooling dimension to this hot-weather dish. *Serves 4–5.*

Dipping sauce:

1½ cups *dashi* (Basic Soup Stock,
   page 55)
3½ tablespoons soy sauce, preferably
   usu kuchi shōyu (light soy sauce)

2 tablespoons sugar
1½ tablespoons *mirin* (syrupy rice
   wine)

4–5 bundles (each about 4 ounces) *sōmen* (thin white wheat noodles), cooked according to instructions on page 98	Ice cubes

Garnishes:

1 small unwaxed cucumber, unpeeled, cut in thin rounds	⅓ cup canned *mikan* (sliced Japanese oranges), drained

Condiments:

1 tablespoon grated fresh ginger
1 tablespoon finely chopped fresh *shiso* (aromatic green leaves of beefsteak plant), when available; if not, 1 teaspoon finely chopped fresh mint OR coriander

In a small saucepan, combine the ingredients for the dipping sauce. Heat it, stirring, until the sugar melts. Chill the sauce.

Put a few ice cubes in a bowl of cold water and add freshly cooked and drained noodles. Let them chill for 2–3 minutes before draining them again.

Put several ice cubes in each of 4 or 5 deep glass bowls. Add cold water to fill the bowls one-third full. Divide the noodles among the bowls and add a few more ice cubes to each if you wish. Garnish with some cucumber rounds and *mikan* slices and serve immediately with dipping sauce in individual bowls and condiments.

To eat, add whatever condiments you wish to your dipping sauce. Lift out noodles, dip them in the sauce and slurp.

冷
し
中
華

COLD CHINESE-STYLE NOODLE SALAD
(Hiyashi Chūka)

For a colorful and flavorful summer lunch, serve this noodle salad with chilled barley tea (page 205) and fresh fruit for dessert. I've kept the braised mushrooms as an optional ingredient here because they are a bit troublesome to make from scratch. But any leftovers from another day will be a welcome addition for color, texture and flavor. *Serves 3–4.*

3–4 portions *ramen* (Chinese-style soup
noodles) OR *chūka soba* (thin yellow
noodles), 8 ounces per portion if
fresh and 3 ounces if fresh-dried;
cooked according to instructions on
page 97 (fresh) or 98 (dried)
5–6 slices boiled ham

1 unwaxed cucumber, unpeeled
2 thin omelets, prepared according to
recipe on page 151
2–3 braised *shiitaké* (black Oriental
mushrooms) prepared according to
recipe on page 129; optional

Dressing:

2–3 tablespoons white sesame seeds
1½ tablespoons superfine sugar
4 tablespoons soy sauce
1½ tablespoons rice vinegar
¼–⅓ cup *dashi* (Basic Soup Stock,
page 55) OR water

1–1½ tablespoons sesame oil
¼ cup finely minced scallions
2–3 tablespoons very finely minced
fresh ginger

Cook the noodles according to the instructions on page 97 or 98 and chill them for
30 minutes. Divide and mound the noodles in 3 or 4 plates with flanges or shallow
soup bowls. Slice the ham, cucumber, omelets and mushrooms into julienne strips.
Alternate clusters of each, leaning them against the noodles teepee fashion.

Just before serving, make the dressing: dry roast the sesame seeds (see page 16 for
details) and transfer them while still warm to a *suribachi* or blender. Crush the seeds
to release their aroma and add the sugar, soy sauce, vinegar and stock one at a time,
blending well after each addition. Stir in the sesame oil, scallions and ginger. Pour
the dressing over the noodle salads and serve.

Braised and Simmered Foods

(NI MONO)

Tender, moist and intensely flavored, braised and simmered foods are the mainstay of Japanese cooking. Sometimes vegetables, meat, or seafood are lightly sautéed first, while at other times the ingredients are simmered from the start in variously seasoned shallow liquids. In most cases the cooking broth is allowed to reduce entirely and a final few moments of exposure to high heat semi-glazes the food.

Here also are the one-pot dinners, called *nabé mono*. Most of these dishes are meant to be prepared at the table, and the justly famous Braised Beef and Vegetables known as *sukiyaki* leads the list. Lesser known, but equally delicious are the seafood, pork and chicken *nabé mono* that follow. Then there are slow-simmering stews, a meaty pot roast, a poached and pungently sauced fish dish and several meat and vegetable combinations to provide you with a variety of main-course possibilities. Sweet but spicy chicken livers and bite-size beef and scallion rolls make lovely hors d'oeuvres. Finally, there is a selection of cooked fresh and dried vegetables that make wonderful side dishes to steamed, grilled or fried meat and fish courses.

❖

BRAISED BEEF AND VEGETABLES *(Sukiyaki)*

すき焼き

Well known and loved in the West, this Japanese dish is enjoyed in its native land in the cold winter months when friends and family gather together around the *kotatsu*, a table-and-heating unit all-in-one that creates a wonderfully cozy atmosphere. Even without the added warmth of legs under the *kotatsu* blanket, *sukiyaki* is sure to take the chill out of you on the most blustery winter day. The recipe here is for the Tokyo version of this famous dish. If uncooked eggs are not your thing, just forget about them. *Serves 6–8 with lots of hot white rice and assorted pickled vegetables.*

1½ pounds well-marbled beef sirloin

3–4 leeks

2 cakes *yaki-dōfu* (grilled bean curd)

1 can or package *shirataki* ("white waterfall"; gelatin-like noodles)

½ pound *hakusai* (Chinese cabbage) OR *moyashi* (bean sprouts)

¼ pound *shungiku* (chrysanthemum leaves)

¼ pound fresh mushrooms

Large piece of beef suet

½–⅔ cup soy sauce

¼–⅓ cup *saké* (rice wine)

½ cup *dashi* (Basic Soup Stock, page 55)

Up to ¼ cup sugar

6–8 fresh eggs

Partially freeze the meat to ensure ease in slicing it thin. Paper-thin slices about 2 inches square are ideal. Trim the leeks and use the white parts, cutting them on the diagonal into ¼-inch-thick slices. Drain the cakes of grilled bean curd (they come packed in water) and cut each in half lengthwise, then cut each half across 3 times to make 16 bite-size blocks. Drain the can or package of gelatin-like noodles and cut them into approximately 6-inch lengths. Rinse and pat dry the cabbage, cut it into 1-inch-thick wedges and slice the wedges across into 2-inch pieces. Or rinse and drain the bean sprouts, discarding any discolored ones. Rinse and pat dry the chrysanthemum leaves, trim off any roots or flowering buds and cut long stalks into 5–6-inch lengths. Wash, pat dry and trim off the stems of the mushrooms. Flute them if you wish, or slice them in half, if large.

Place all of the above ingredients and the piece of suet on a large platter or tray and bring it to the table. Also have ready a small pitcher or bowl of soy sauce, another of rice wine, a third of soup stock and a fourth of sugar. These will be used while cooking. For each person, have a small individual bowl into which a fresh uncooked egg has been dropped. The egg is beaten lightly at the table and used as a dipping sauce for the braised meat and vegetables.

Heat a heavy skillet on a table-top cooking unit and melt the suet in it, oiling the surface to prevent the meat from sticking. Lay one-third of the meat and leeks in the skillet. Sear the meat; remove and discard the suet. Then push the meat over to make room for one-third of the cabbage (or bean sprouts) and mushrooms. Season the foods with one-third of the soy sauce, rice wine, sugar and stock. Lower the heat to maintain a steady simmer, add some gelatin-like noodles, and cook the meat and vegetables for 3–4 minutes. Add one-third of the chrysanthemum leaves, cook for another minute, then let everyone start to help himself to whatever he wants. Replenish the skillet with half of the remaining ingredients, adding the chrysanthemum leaves at the last minute, and cook as you did before. Eat, then cook the remaining meat and vegetables in the same manner.

かき鍋 OYSTER POT WITH BEAN BROTH *(Kaki Nabé)*

Oriental vegetables and pale, plump oysters are simmered in a broth thickened with dark pungent bean paste. Thin, threadlike slivers of fresh ginger are scattered across the pot in the last few minutes of cooking to add a final aromatic touch. Prepare this dish at the table—an attractive ceramic dish with a lid is particularly good—and serve it with hot white rice and a tart green salad or rice-bran pickles. *Serves 4–5.*

1 pound fresh shucked oysters
1 cake *tōfu* (bean curd)
½ cup *shirataki* ("white waterfall";
　gelatin-like noodles)
3 leeks
¼ pound *shungiku* (chrysanthemum
　leaves)
8–10 inches *konbu* (kelp for stock
　making)

4–5 cups water
¼ cup *Sendai miso* (dark fermented bean
　paste)
2 tablespoons sugar
2 tablespoons *saké* (rice wine)
1-inch knob fresh ginger

Rinse and pat dry the oysters. Drain the bean curd and cut it in half lengthwise, then across 3 or 4 times to yield 8–10 bite-size blocks. Blanch the gelatin-like noodles in boiling water for 30 seconds, drain and let them cool to room temperature naturally. Cut across the clump of noodles once or twice for easier eating later. Rinse the leeks and trim them, leaving some of the green on if tender; then cut on the diagonal into ½-inch slices. Rinse the chrysanthemum leaves and trim the stems, discarding any flowering buds. Cut the stalks in half if more than 7–8 inches long. Arrange all these ingredients attractively on a large platter or tray.

Using 6–7 inches of the kelp and all the water, make a weak broth. Discard this kelp after the water comes to a rolling boil and strain the broth into a pitcher that you can bring to the table. Place the rest of the kelp at the bottom of the pot you will use for final cooking. In a small saucepan, combine the bean paste, sugar and wine and stir over medium heat until the sugar dissolves. Mound the seasoned bean paste on the kelp in the middle of your cooking pot.

Just before cooking, peel the knob of ginger and slice it very thin. Then stack these slices and cut them into threadlike slivers. Place these in a small pile on your platter of ingredients.

At the table, put half the oysters, blocks of bean curd and leeks in the pot around the mound of bean paste. Pour half of the kelp broth over all and bring it to a boil over moderate heat. Skim off the froth, lower the heat to maintain a simmer, and cook for 2–3 minutes. Add half the chrysanthemum leaves and scatter half the ginger threads over the top and let simmer for another minute. Each person picks from the pot what he wants, scooping up a bit of bean paste from the center for a more pungent effect.

Replenish the cooking pot with the remaining oysters, leeks, bean curd and all the gelatinous noodles, then pour in more kelp broth. Simmer, skimming occasionally, for 4–5 minutes. Add the rest of the chrysanthemum leaves and ginger for the last minute or two of cooking. Each person helps himself to oysters and vegetables. Strain the bean paste-thickened broth to make a tasty soup to end the meal (or save it for the next day, if you prefer).

水
炊
き
PORK AND VEGETABLE POT WITH CLEAR BROTH *(Mizutaki)*

An inviting array of vegetables and thinly sliced pork are brought to the table and cooked in a clear delicate broth. Bite-size pieces are scooped from the communal pot and dipped into individual bowls of a piquant lemon-and-soy sauce or a fiery grated radish condiment. *Mizutaki* makes a perfect family or company dinner on a chilly day, served with hot white rice and assorted pungent pickles. *Serves 4–6.*

1½ pounds lean boneless pork loin
1 cake *yaki-dōfu* (grilled bean curd)
5–6 scallions with green tops intact
¼ pound fresh button mushrooms
1 small carrot
½ pound *hakusai* (Chinese cabbage)
¼ pound *shungiku* (chrysanthemum leaves) OR dandelion greens OR fresh spinach

1 lemon, cut into wedges
¼–⅓ cup soy sauce
2–3 inches *daikon* (Japanese white radish)
1 *tōgarashi* (dried hot red pepper)
6 inches *konbu* (kelp for stock making)
1 quart fresh cold water

Partially freeze the pork to facilitate cutting, and slice it into paper-thin slices about 2 inches square. Drain the grilled bean curd (it invariably comes packaged in water) and slice it once lengthwise, then across 3 or 4 times to yield 8–10 bite-size blocks. Trim the scallions and cut them into 2-inch lengths. Wash and pat dry the mushrooms, then trim off and discard the stems; slice the mushrooms in half. Scrape the carrot and cut it into decorative flower shapes (page 25) or into ¼-inch-thick rounds. Rinse the cabbage, drain and cut it into 1-inch-thick wedges. Cut each wedge across into 3 sections. Rinse the chrysanthemum leaves well under cold running water, trim the bottoms of the stems and cut off any flowering buds. If the stalks are very long, cut them in half. Pat the leaves dry. Arrange all these ingredients and the lemon wedges attractively on a large platter or tray.

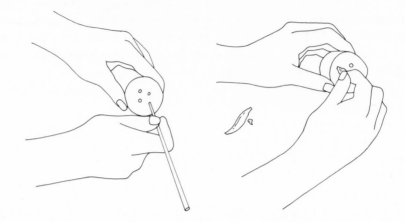

Divide the soy sauce among 4–6 small bowls—one for each person. Peel the radish and poke several holes in it. Then break open the dried red pepper pod and remove all the seeds. Stuff pieces of the red pepper into the holes you made in the radish and grate it. The white will be flecked with red and the mild radish is given a fiery accent. (The Japanese call this particular condiment *momiji oroshi* or "autumn maple leaves.") Drain off any liquid from grating and mound the fiery radish in a shallow bowl. At the table each person can add lemon juice and/or radish to taste to his own bowl of soy sauce.

Make a clear broth from the kelp and water, discarding the kelp once the water has come to a boil. Lower the heat slightly and start adding the ingredients from your platter. Begin with half the pork, adding it 1 slice at a time. Next, toss in half the carrots and mushrooms. Let these cook, partially covered, for 3–4 minutes, then add half the scallions, cabbage and grilled bean curd and cook for another 3–4 minutes. Each person helps himself to bits of meat and vegetables, dunking these pieces lightly into his own dipping sauce before eating. Replenish the cooking pot with the remaining meat, carrot slices, and mushrooms. After 3–4 minutes add scallions, cabbage and bean curd. Continue to cook for another 3–4 minutes, then add the chrysanthemum leaves and cook them about 1 minute or until barely wilted. Remove the pot from the heat and let everyone pick out whatever he wishes to eat.

NOTE: You can strain the broth remaining in the large pot and use it instead of plain water for cooking other vegetables. And *mizutaki* is just as delicious made with chicken instead of the pork.

鳥 CHICKEN AND VEGETABLE POT
鍋 WITH DARK BROTH *(Tori Nabé)*

Bite-size pieces of chicken are simmered with an interesting assortment of vegetables in a sweetened dark stock. No dipping sauces here—the pot is rich and flavorful just as it is. The Japanese love to add soft rice cakes or cooked thick white noodles to this pot after all the chicken and vegetables have been eaten, and I'm sure you'll enjoy it this way, too. Or serve hot white rice on the side to eat throughout the meal. A tossed green salad or salt-pickled vegetables would complement the menu nicely. *Serves 4–6.*

3–4 chicken breasts, skinned and boned
3–4 scallions
2–3 leeks
1 cake *yaki-dōfu* (grilled bean curd)
1–2 clumps *énokidaké* (small fragrant white mushrooms on tall slender stalks); fresh are marvelous, but canned are fine, too
8–10 inches *gobō* (burdock root); fresh is preferred
¼ pound *shungiku* (chrysanthemum leaves) OR fresh spinach

Optional: 4–6 *omochi* (glutinous rice cakes) OR 1 pound cooked *udon* (thick white noodles)
3 cups *dashi* (Basic Soup Stock, page 55)
5 tablespoons *usu kuchi shōyu* (light soy sauce)
1½ tablespoons regular soy sauce
2 tablespoons *mirin* (syrupy rice wine)
2 tablespoons sugar

Slice the chicken breasts into thin, bite-size pieces. Trim the scallions and leeks, then cut them into 2-inch lengths. Drain the grilled bean curd (it usually comes packed in water) and cut it in half lengthwise, then across 3 or 4 times to yield 8–10 bite-size blocks. Rinse the mushrooms under cold water and trim off the dark yellow and brown roots (attached to fresh mushrooms). Peel or scrape fresh burdock root, cut it into shavings (page 25), and soak them in cold water for a few minutes before draining. Or drain canned burdock root and blanch it for 10 seconds then drain again and cut it into shavings. Rinse and towel dry the chrysanthemum or spinach leaves, then trim off any roots and/or flowering buds. If the stalks are longer than 4–5 inches, cut them in half. If you've decided to add glutinous rice cakes to your pot, soak them in a bowl of water to ensure softness. Or, if using noodles, cook and drain them well. Arrange all your ingredients attractively on a large platter or tray and bring it to the table.

In a large pot, combine the basic stock, soy sauces, syrupy rice wine and sugar. Heat while stirring to melt the sugar. Bring the seasoned broth to a boil, then lower the heat slightly to maintain a steady simmer. Add half the chicken slices, scallions, leeks, bean curd, mushrooms and burdock root, and simmer for 4–5 minutes. Add half the green leaves, cover and cook for another minute or two. Have everyone help himself to what he likes, then replenish the pot with the remaining chicken and vegetables and cook them as you did before. When all has been eaten, drain your rice cakes and add to the dark broth. Simmer for 1–2 minutes until very soft and stretchy. Give each person 1 rice cake and ladle some of the dark soup over it. (Or add cooked and drained noodles to the pot and heat them through for a minute, serving some to each person with the soup from the pot.)

お
で
ん   FISH DUMPLING STEW (*Oden*)

This is a slow-simmering pot that can cook for as little as 30 minutes or as long as several hours. Reheated, even days later, it tastes just as delicious. Serve *oden* as a main course with lots of hot white rice and a variety of colorful pickled vegetables. *Serves 4.*

Fish paste for making dumplings:

½ pound white-meat fish fillets (flounder, sole or halibut is particularly good)	1 tablespoon cornstarch
	1½ tablespoons beaten egg
	Scant ½ teaspoon salt
1 tablespoon all-purpose flour	

2-inch piece of *gobō* (burdock root)	2 tablespoons *saké* (rice wine)
8 small shrimp with shells intact	½ cake *konnyaku* (pearly-toned gelatinous cake)
1–2 tablespoons vegetable oil for hands and plate	4 inches *daikon* (Japanese white radish)
Oil for deep frying	4 *ganmodoki* (vegetarian patties, page 163), optional for extra volume; leftovers are perfect.
1–2 quarts *dashi* (Basic Soup Stock, page 55)	
1–2 tablespoons soy sauce	1 tablespoon prepared hot mustard
2 tablespoons *mirin* (syrupy rice wine)	

It is a very simple matter to make the basic fish paste in a food processor, blender or even a meat grinder. (The traditional Japanese method is to chop the fish fine, then grind it in a serrated mortar.) Coarsely chop the fish fillets and feed them into your machine (if using a meat grinder, put it through twice) and continue to mash and grind the fish until it forms a smooth, glossy mass. Add the flour and cornstarch and turn on your machine for a few seconds to blend it in. (If you are using a meat grinder, transfer the ground fish to a bowl and beat in the remaining ingredients with a fork or whip.) Add the egg and salt and blend again.

Peel the burdock root, cut it lengthwise into 4 strips, and soak them in a small bowl of cold water for a few minutes while preparing the shrimp. Remove the shells of the shrimp, leaving the tail sections intact. Devein, then score the underbelly lightly to prevent them from curling up when frying. Pat dry the burdock strips and the shrimp.

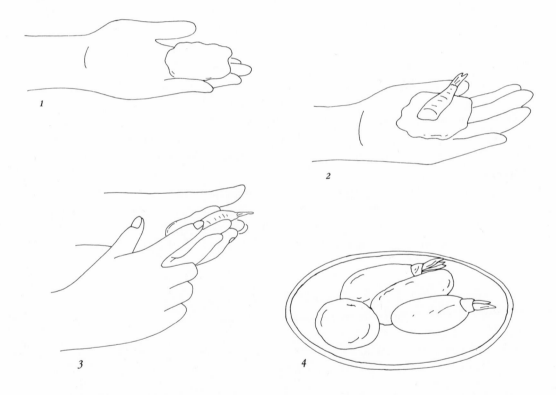

Lightly oil a plate, then your hands. Scoop up about 1–1½ tablespoons of the fish paste and form a small patty *(1)*. On some patties lay a strip of burdock, on others a shrimp and roll the patties to enclose the filling *(2, 3)*. The burdock root should be completely covered by the fish mixture (to prevent discoloration when frying), but the shrimp tails should be left sticking out one end. As you finish each dumpling lay it on the oiled plate *(4)*

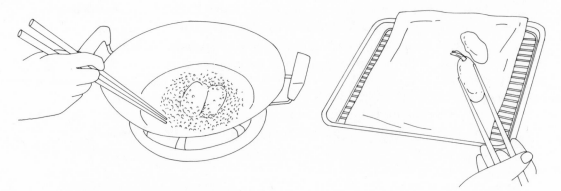

Heat your oil for deep frying to a medium temperature (300–325 degrees F.) and fry the filled fish dumplings, a few at a time, until golden and cooked throughout (about 5 minutes). Drain them well on paper towels.

Season 1 quart of the soup stock with 1 tablespoon soy sauce, the syrupy rice wine and regular rice wine. Bring the soup to a boil, reduce the heat to barely maintain a simmer and add the fried fish dumplings. Cover with a dropped lid and cook for at least 30 minutes or, if you have the time, for an hour and a half. Add more soup stock, seasoned with soy sauce, as necessary to keep the dumplings covered at all times.

Cut the *konnyaku* cake into 4 squares, then cut each of these in half diagonally to make 8 small triangles. Peel the radish and cut 4 one-inch-thick slices. Cut these into half moons or quarters. Add the vegetables and vegetarian patties to the dumplings for the last 15–20 minutes of cooking. Serve mustard on the side for dabbing.

小かぶと鳥肉だんご STEWED TURNIPS AND CHICKEN BALLS
(Kokabu To Toriniku Dango)

Here is a very tasty combination of seasoned ground chicken and turnips, stewed in a faintly sweet broth and garnished with lemon peel. *Serves 4–6.*

1 dried *shiitaké* (black Oriental mushroom)	2 teaspoons *saké* (rice wine)
1 pound ground uncooked chicken	1 teaspoon sugar
½ beaten egg	1 teaspoon soy sauce
2 teaspoons cornstarch	6–8 small white turnips, with their
1 teaspoon grated fresh ginger	leaves OR ¼ pound fresh spinach OR
½ teaspoon salt	collard greens if turnip leaves are
	unavailable

Stewing liquid:

2⅓ cups *dashi* (Basic Soup Stock,   ½ teaspoon salt
    page 55)   1 tablespoon sugar
1 tablespoon *mirin* (syrupy rice wine)   1 tablespoon soy sauce

---

Peel from ½ lemon

Cover the dried mushroom for 15–20 minutes with warm water to which a pinch of sugar has been added. Rinse the mushroom under cold water, remove and discard the stem and squeeze out excess liquid. Chop the mushroom into very fine dice.

In a bowl, combine the ground chicken, egg and cornstarch. Add the diced mushroom and season the meat mixture with ginger, salt, rice wine, sugar and soy sauce. Mix all thoroughly and dampen your hands with water before making 10–12 balls from the soft meat mixture.

Peel the turnips and cut them in half. Select 12–15 of the prettiest leaves and blanch them in boiling salted water for 30 seconds. They should be bright in color and only barely wilted after blanching. Drain the blanched leaves and squeeze out any excess moisture. Cut into 1–1½-inch lengths.

Combine the stewing liquid ingredients in a deep pot and, stirring occasionally, bring it to a boil. Drop the chicken balls, one at a time, into the boiling liquid. Swirl and stir the liquid to prevent sticking. When all the balls have become firm and white, reduce the heat to maintain a simmer. Add the turnip pieces and simmer, covered with a dropped lid (or uncovered, ladling liquid over frequently), for 10–15 minutes. Add the blanched leaves during the final minute of cooking. Cut the lemon peel into 4–6 decorative shapes (*matsuba* cutting, page 25) and float them on top of the stew just before removing the pot from the stove. Serve warm or at room temperature.

GLOSSY PORK AND PUMPKIN STEW
(Butaniku To Kabocha No Tsuya Ni)

豚肉とかぼちゃのつや煮

This is a simple dish to make, perfect on those autumn days when bright, plump pumpkins make their way to market. The average Jack-o'-lantern is about 4 pounds, so if you get one that size, you'll use only a quarter of it for this recipe. Serve the stew with a green salad—spinach with Sesame Seed Dressing (page 182) would be a good Oriental choice—tart, crisp pickles and lots of hot white rice. You may be tempted to reduce the amount of sugar in this recipe; please don't. The sugar is added in two stages, for flavor and gloss, and the resulting stew isn't nearly as sweet as you might imagine. *Serves 4–6.*

1–1½ pounds lean pork butt

1 tablespoon vegetable oil

2½ cups *dashi* (Basic Soup Stock, page 55)

Scant ¼ cup sugar

2 tablespoons *saké* (rice wine)

1 pound pumpkin

3 tablespoons soy sauce

1 tablespoon *mirin* (syrupy rice wine)

Cut the pork into 1–1½-inch cubes and sauté them in a deep pot in the oil until browned. Pour off any excess oil before adding 2 cups of the stock, half the sugar and 1 tablespoon of the rice wine. Skim off any froth that may come to the surface, then use a dropped lid or partially cover and simmer for 45 minutes.

Peel the pumpkin, remove any seeds, and cut it into pieces approximately the same size as the pork. Add the pumpkin pieces to the pot with ½ cup more stock, raise the heat and skim the surface of any froth. Reduce the heat to maintain a simmer and add the remaining sugar and rice wine. Cook for 5 minutes and add the soy sauce. Cook for 10–15 more minutes or until the pumpkin is tender but not mushy. Before serving, add the syrupy rice wine and cook for 1 more minute over high heat.

豚肉のまる煮 ORIENTAL PORK POT ROAST *(Butaniku No Maru Ni)*

This tender, slow-simmered pot roast is sure to become a family favorite. Served hot or cold, sliced thick or thin, it is absolutely delicious. The braising juices are as flavorful as the meat itself and can be thickened with a little cornstarch to make a tasty gravy. You can also make it into a rich, amber aspic, or enjoy it as a soup with Chinese-style noodles. *This recipe yields 15–20 slices and about 1 quart soup. Serves 4.*

1½–2 pounds boneless pork loin roast

1½ tablespoons vegetable oil

1½ cups water

¼ cup soy sauce

⅓ cup *saké* (rice wine)

5–6 slices fresh, peeled ginger (each approximately 1 × 2 × ¼ inches)

2–3 leeks OR 5–6 scallions, cut into 2-inch lengths

½ teaspoon salt

3 whole black peppercorns

In a sturdy dutch oven, brown the pork evenly in the oil over medium-high heat. Add the water, soy sauce and rice wine and reduce the heat to maintain a slow simmer. Add the ginger and leeks or scallions (use green and white parts of either), salt and peppercorns, and partially cover the pot.

Braise the pork, turning it occasionally, for 1½–2 hours. Add more water when necessary to make sure the meat is at least half covered by liquid throughout the cooking. Remove the roast and slice it. (For paper-thin slices, wait until the meat has cooled to room temperature, then chill it for an hour before cutting.) Strain the braised liquid and discard all solids.

鯖 MACKEREL IN BEAN SAUCE *(Saba No Miso Ni)*
の
味
噌
煮

This pungent bean sauce garnished with fresh ginger is perfect with firm-fleshed mackerel. Here the fish is blanched and poached, then simmered in a fast-reducing sauce. The result is tender, richly flavored fish that would be particularly good served with hot white rice and a cold, tart vegetable salad. *Serves 4.*

4 small mackerel fillets, about 2–3 ounces each, with skin intact	Small knob of fresh ginger (about size of thumb)
2 teaspoons salt	5 tablespoons *Sendai miso* (dark bean paste)
5–6 inches *konbu* (kelp for stock making)	4 tablespoons sugar
½ cup water	2 tablespoons *saké* (rice wine)

Rinse the fish fillets gently under water and pat them dry. Sprinkle the salt over the fillets and let them marinate for 10–15 minutes. Use tweezers to remove any small bones.

Bring a pot of water to a rolling boil. Blanch the salted fillets until they are firm and white, and quickly remove them. Gently rinse off any scum that might be clinging to the fish.

In a small saucepan prepare the poaching liquid. Place the kelp in ½ cup water and bring it to a boil. Discard the kelp and remove the pan from the stove. Peel and grate half the ginger, squeezing the gratings to obtain about 2 teaspoons ginger juice. Add the ginger juice to the kelp liquid.

Arrange the blanched fillets in one layer, skin side up, in a wide pot or skillet. Pour the poaching liquid over the fillets and simmer them, partially covered, for 2–3 minutes over very low heat.

Combine the bean paste, sugar and rice wine in a small saucepan, and, stirring constantly, cook over medium heat for a minute or so. Add the bean sauce and stir gently to mix. Cook for 3–4 more minutes over medium heat; the sauce should be glossy and reduced by more than half.

Peel the remaining ginger and cut into very thin threads. Soak these in a small bowl of cold water for 5 minutes before draining them well.

Serve the fish warm, or at room temperature, well napped with the dark bean sauce and garnished with a small tuft of yellow ginger threads.

いか
めし

STEWED STUFFED SQUID *(Ika Meshi)*

This is one of the few Japanese dishes requiring a great deal of time to cook: several hours from start to finish. But it's not difficult to make, and the stewed squid will keep nicely in the refrigerator for 2–3 days. It can be reheated in just a few minutes.

In the northern provinces of Japan, stewed stuffed squid find their way into many a box lunch. You might like them for lunch or dinner with either a clear Egg Drop Soup (page 58) or a *miso*-thickened one. An assortment of colorful pickles or a vinegary tossed green salad would be nice, too. *Serves 4.*

⅓ cup uncooked rice

⅓ cup uncooked *mochi-gomé* (glutinous rice)

4 small whole squid, each weighing about ½ pound

Cooking liquid:

3–4 cups water

⅓ cup *saké* (rice wine)

⅓ cup soy sauce

2 tablespoons sugar

Measure out your rice and glutinous rice and combine them in a strainer. Wash the rice until the water runs clear or the starchy residue will make the final dish sticky and gummy. Let the rices soak in water to cover for at least 30 minutes. Drain just before ready to use. (The combined rices will have swollen to nearly a cup by now and will be snowy white.)

Remove the innards of a squid, reserving its legs but discarding the intestinal tract and ink-filled "sac." Remove the cartilage from inside the body; leave the tail "flaps" intact. Rinse the body well inside and out but leave the skin on and pat the squid dry. Now repeat this entire procedure for the other 3 squid.

Trim off the suction cups from the legs. Coarsely chop the legs (there should be about 1 cup in all). Loosely fill each squid with rice until three-quarters full, then stuff in one-quarter of the chopped leg pieces and close each sac with a toothpick. (The legs act as a plug to keep the rice from falling out.) If you like, make shallow decorative slits on the body.

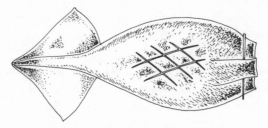

In a pan just barely large enough to hold the 4 squid (they shrink quite a bit with cooking) combine the ingredients for the cooking liquid. Lay the 4 stuffed squid in the pan and simmer on the lowest flame possible for 1½–2 hours, adding a bit more water if it looks in danger of scorching. Use a dropped lid if you have one, or if not, ladle the simmering liquid frequently over all surfaces. Whether you're using a dropped lid or not, turn the stuffed squid about every 30 minutes or so. Let the squid cool to room temperature in the pan. Remove all toothpicks and slice each squid into 5–6 rounds. If you prefer to eat your squid warm, wrap each in foil and steam for 2–3 minutes.

FINE-CRUMB CHICKEN (*Soboro Ni*)

そぼろ煮

Here, ground chicken is braised in a fast-reducing, intensely seasoned broth; the result is a rich-colored, crumbly meat of varied uses. A popular lunchbox food in Japan, fine-crumb chicken is spread over cooked white rice and garnished with bright yellow strips of thin omelet and some greenery—a few blanched snow peas or string beans, perhaps.

There are many exciting ways to adapt this simple yet flavorful dish to a Western-style meal, too. Try stuffing tomatoes with it, or rolling some up in crisp lettuce leaves. Fine-crumb chicken makes tasty open-faced sandwiches, and it is also very nice to use as a filling for a fluffy omelet. *Makes about 1 cup.*

½ pound lean, finely ground uncooked
   chicken
2 tablespoons *saké* (rice wine)
1½ tablespoons soy sauce

2 teaspoons sugar
1½ tablespoons water OR *dashi* (Basic
   Soup Stock, page 55)

In a skillet, combine all the ingredients and stir using several chopsticks (or a fork or two) to break up any large clusters of meat, and to distribute the seasonings evenly.

Cook the meat and seasonings, uncovered, over medium heat, stirring constantly, for about 5 minutes. Most of the liquid should be reduced by this point, and the meat should be rich-colored and crumbly in appearance. Shaking the skillet with one hand and stirring with the other, cook the fine-crumb chicken over high heat for a minute or two more or until it is dry and all the liquid has been reduced.

Serve warm or at room temperature. Do not chill it, though, before serving as this will change the texture in an unattractive way. Any leftover chicken may be refrigerated for up to 3 days, but be sure to reheat it slightly before using.

揚げ福袋 **TREASURE BAGS** *(Agé Fuku-bukuro)*

Treasure Bags are brimming with a variety of good-tasting things. Fried bean curd is stuffed with meat and vegetables, then tied up with ribbons of gourd and simmered in a seasoned stock. Three or 4 Treasure Bags make a substantial single portion. Rice, soup, pickles and a tart salad would round out the meal nicely. *Makes 12 bags.*

6 slices *abura agé* (fried bean curd)
3–4 small dried *shiitaké* (black Oriental mushrooms)
1–1½ cups *shirataki* ("white waterfall"; gelatin-like noodles)
12 six- to eight-inch ribbons of *kanpyō* (dried gourd)

½ small carrot, cut into short, extra fine julienne strips to yield approximately ¼ cup
¾ pound ground lean chicken meat
¼ cup green peas

Simmering stock:

¼ cup strained mushroom liquid
2–2½ cups *dashi* (Basic Soup Stock, page 55)

4 tablespoons soy sauce
2½ tablespoons sugar
1 tablespoon *saké* (rice wine)

Quickly blanch the slices of fried bean curd in boiling water to remove excess oil. Drain the slices and pat them dry with paper towels. While they are still warm, cut each slice in half, across its width. Place a slice of the bean curd on the open palm of one hand and slap down on it with the other. From the cut edge, gently pry open the fried bean curd to form a deep pocket or bag. Repeat this slap-and-pry procedure for each of the remaining pieces.

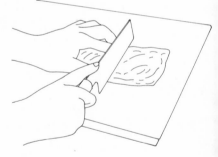

Cover the dried mushrooms for 15–20 minutes with warm water to which a pinch of sugar has been added. Reserve the mushroom liquid for use in the simmering stock. Rinse the mushrooms under cold water, squeeze them dry, remove and discard the stems, then slice into extra fine julienne strips.

Drain a small can or bag of gelatin-like noodles (it will measure about 1 cup). Cut them into approximately 2-inch lengths and blanch them for 1 minute in rapidly boiling water. Drain, and allow the noodles to cool to room temperature naturally.

Cover the dried gourd strips with warm water to which a pinch of sugar has been added. Allow at least 10–15 minutes for the gourd to soften. Rinse the softened strips under cold water with a slight scrubbing motion and squeeze them dry.

Combine sliced mushrooms, cooled noodles, julienne carrots, chicken meat and peas in a large bowl. Stuff each fried bean curd with one-twelfth of this filling *(1)*. Gather up the open end of each bag and tie it closed with a ribbon of gourd *(2–4)*.

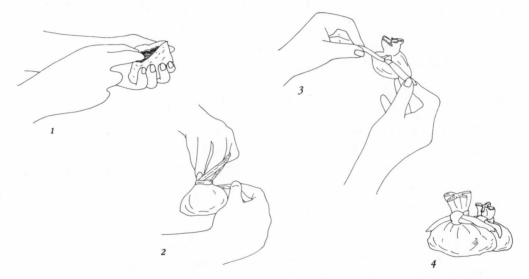

Make the simmering stock in a deep saucepan that is wide enough to hold all the bags in a single layer. Combine the mushroom liquid and basic stock and heat through before seasoning with the soy sauce, sugar and rice wine. Add the bags, ties facing up, to the simmering stock. For best results simmer, covered with a dropped lid. Or simmer uncovered but frequently ladle the stock over the bags as they cook. Simmer for 12–15 minutes over medium heat. If the ribbons of gourd are still white, turn the bags upside down and simmer for 3–5 more minutes. Serve the Treasure Bags warm, or at room temperature, with a bit of the stock ladled over each. These bags can be prepared up to 2 days in advance. Refrigerate but never freeze the cooked bags and reheat them in the stock just before serving.

牛
肉
と
新
じ
ゃ
が
い
も
の
煮
物

BEEF AND NEW POTATO STEW
(Gyūniku To Shinjagaimo No Ni Mono)

Some very familiar ingredients here are prepared in a decidedly different way. The Japanese typically serve small portions of this stew with hot white rice, assorted pickled vegetables, and perhaps a clam or fish soup. *If you wish to follow suit, the recipe will serve 4. If intended as a main course with perhaps only a tossed green salad on the side, it will serve 2.*

10–12 small (1–1½ inches in diameter) new potatoes
¾–1 pound boneless, well-marbled sirloin tips
6–8 snow peas

2 cups *dashi* (Basic Soup Stock, page 55)
3 tablespoons sugar
3½ tablespoons soy sauce
1½ tablespoons *saké* (rice wine)

Scrub the potatoes, scrape off the skins, then steam them until barely tender (about 7–8 minutes). Cut the meat into paper-thin slices (partially freezing beforehand will help) about 2 inches square. String the snow peas and cut each in half, slightly on the diagonal. Blanch them in boiling salted water for 20–30 seconds, then drain immediately.

   Combine the soup stock, sugar, soy sauce and rice wine in a small pot, stirring to dissolve the sugar. Add the steamed potatoes and simmer them, preferably with a dropped lid, until lightly colored (about 6–7 minutes). Add the meat, separating the slices as you place them in the pot, and continue to cook for 2–3 minutes. Add the blanched snow peas and simmer for 1 more minute, then serve.

炒
り
鳥

BRAISED CHICKEN CUBES
AND VEGETABLES *(Iri-dori)*

Here is a truly fabulous dish of varied tastes and textures. Cubes of crunchy, woodsy burdock root, tender chicken, smooth *konnyaku* and colorful sweet carrot are braised in a faintly sweet soy broth and finished off with a pinch of fiery hot spices. In Japan, this chicken and vegetable dish frequently shares the limelight with blocks of Thick Sweet Omelet (page 152) on a Japanese picnic lunch menu. Serve it warm at a Western brunch with scrambled eggs and toast or at dinner over a bed of hot rice with a tossed green salad. *Serves 4–6.*

¼ cup *gobō* (burdock root), peeled and diced into ¼-inch cubes

½ cake *konnyaku* (gelatinous cake made from a tuber vegetable)

1 large chicken breast, skinned and boned

1½ tablespoons vegetable oil

⅓ cup carrot, peeled and diced into ¼-inch cubes

3 tablespoons soy sauce

2½ tablespoons sugar

2 teaspoons *saké* (rice wine)

⅛ teaspoon *shichimi tōgarashi* (7-spice hot pepper)

If using fresh burdock root, soak the pieces in cold water to cover for 5 minutes, then drain them well. If using canned burdock root, blanch the pieces for 30 seconds in boiling water, then drain.

Cut the *konnyaku* into ¼-inch cubes and blanch them for 1 minute, then drain. This will remove the slightly unpleasant (but entirely normal) odor that this vegetable has. It will make it more porous, too, for better absorption of cooking flavors later.

Cut the chicken into pieces approximately the same size as the vegetables.

Over medium heat, sauté fresh burdock root for 1–2 minutes in vegetable oil until it becomes slightly translucent. Then add the carrots and, stirring, sauté for another 1–2 minutes (if using canned burdock root, sauté it with the carrots). Add the *konnyaku* and continue to sauté for another minute before adding the chicken. Continue to cook, stirring, until the chicken has turned white (about 2 minutes). Season with the soy sauce, sugar and rice wine and cook for 4–5 minutes. The braising liquid will be frothy and bubbly.

When nearly all the liquid has been reduced, increase the heat to very high and shake the pan vigorously to insure a well-glazed effect. Remove from the heat, sprinkle the hot spices over all and toss well.

SPICY BRAISED LIVERS *(Réba No Tsukuda Ni)*

レ
バ
ー
の
佃
煮

Here is a delicious hors d'oeuvre, served warm or cold. It can be made several days in advance and refrigerated, making it particularly good party fare. *Serves 4–6.*

¾ pound chicken livers

1½ cups water

1 teaspoon salt

1 teaspoon ginger juice, extracted from peeled and grated fresh ginger

4–5 scallions

1 tablespoon vegetable oil

1 tablespoon *saké* (rice wine)

1 tablespoon *mirin* (syrupy rice wine)

1½ tablespoons soy sauce

1 teaspoon sugar

⅛ teaspoon *shichimi tōgarashi* (7-spice hot pepper)

Trim and cut the livers into bite-size pieces. Combine the water and salt in a small bowl and soak the liver pieces for about 20 minutes. Remove and pat them dry with paper towels or a cloth.

Prepare the ginger juice by peeling and grating a knob of fresh ginger. Squeeze the gratings to release the juice. Cut the scallions into ½-inch pieces, using only the firm, white part of the vegetable.

In a skillet, sauté the livers in vegetable oil over medium-high heat. Add the scallions and ginger juice as the livers begin to change color. Continue to sauté for a few more minutes, stirring frequently. Add the rice wine, syrupy rice wine, soy sauce and sugar, and lower the heat. Stir for even distribution of seasonings, and simmer for 5–6 minutes, uncovered, or until most of the liquid has been reduced.

For a glazed effect, return the skillet to very high heat and shake and toss the livers in the fast-reducing liquid. Sprinkle on a pinch of hot spices and serve.

ねぎ巻き GLAZED BEEF ROLLS *(Négi Maki)*

Scallions wrapped in thin sliced beef are braised in a sweetened soy sauce, then garnished with crushed sesame seeds to make a perfectly wonderful hors d'oeuvre. Serve these rolls hot or at room temperature. *Makes 16 bite-size pieces.*

¼–½ pound lean beef, sliced paper thin
8–10 scallions
1 tablespoon vegetable oil
2 tablespoons soy sauce
1½ tablespoons sugar

1 tablespoon *saké* (rice wine)
1 tablespoon *dashi* (Basic Soup Stock, page 55) OR water
1 teaspoon sesame seeds

Cut the beef into 8 slices, each approximately 6 inches long and 2 inches wide. Trim the scallions of their roots and any wilted tops before cutting them into 2-inch lengths. Make 8 bundles of scallions, using some of the green tops and white bottoms. Wrap each bundle tightly in a strip of meat and secure with a toothpick or string.

Heat the oil in a skillet and sauté the beef rolls over high heat, shaking the pan frequently to brown them on all sides. Add the soy sauce, sugar, rice wine and stock or water, and lower the heat slightly. Braise the rolls in the foaming liquid, turning them occasionally, for 3 minutes. Remove the pan from the heat and remove toothpicks or strings. Continue to braise, shaking the pan, for 2 minutes or until nearly all the sauce is reduced. Put the rolls on a plate, then cut each across in half.

In a clean dry skillet, dry roast the sesame seeds until golden and coarsely grind them. Sprinkle the crushed seeds over the beef rolls just before serving.

う
ま   # SWEET SIMMERED ORIENTAL
煮   # VEGETABLES (Uma Ni)

Black mushrooms, carrots and bamboo shoots are the classic combination of vegetables to be simmered in a sweetened soy broth. Served at room temperature as a side dish to almost any chicken or fish entrée, these vegetables are moist, tender and incredibly flavorful. The mushrooms alone, prepared in the same manner, find their way into a number of seasoned rice and noodle dishes, too. *Serves 4–6.*

5 large dried *shiitaké* (black Oriental mushrooms)	⅔ cup reserved mushroom liquid
1 carrot	1 teaspoon *saké* (rice wine)
2 small whole boiled bamboo shoots	2 tablespoons sugar
1 cup *dashi* (Basic Soup Stock, page 55)	1½ tablespoons soy sauce
	1 teaspoon *mirin* (syrupy rice wine)

Soften the black mushrooms for 20 minutes in 1 cup warm water to which a pinch of sugar has been added. Strain the mushroom liquid and reserve ⅔ cup of it. Rinse the mushrooms thoroughly and squeeze them dry before removing and discarding the stems. Cut the mushrooms in halves or quarters.

Scrape the carrot and cut it obliquely (see page 27 for cutting instructions) into 8–10 pieces. Drain the bamboo shoots and rinse them under cold water before slicing them vertically into ¼-inch-thick wedges. Each piece will look like a hair comb (in fact the name for this cut in Japanese is *kushi-gata* or "comb shape"). Occasionally some white grainy material lodges between the "teeth" of the "comb." Rinse it away with cold water.

Combine the basic soup stock, reserved mushroom liquid and rice wine in a saucepan and bring it to a boil. Add the mushrooms, carrots and bamboo shoots and reduce the heat to maintain a simmer. For best results in simmering, use a dropped lid, otherwise baste frequently. Simmer the vegetables for 3 minutes before adding the sugar. Cook for another 7–8 minutes or until the liquid has been reduced by about half. Add the soy sauce, cook for 3–4 more minutes and then add the syrupy rice wine. Cook over high heat, shaking the pan, for 30–40 seconds. Let the vegetables cool to room temperature in the saucepan before serving. By the way, these vegetables keep well, refrigerated, for 2–3 days.

NOTE: Peeled, obliquely cut (page 27) and blanched *gobō* (burdock root), braid cut (page 24) and blanched *konnyaku* (a pearly-toned, gelatinous cake made from a tuber vegetable) or halved water chestnuts are also very good prepared in the same way, either singly or in combination with the other vegetables.

切り干し大根 BRAISED RADISH RIBBONS *(Kiri-boshi Daikon)*

Here shredded dried Japanese white radish is braised in a sweet soy broth, yet its flavor, aroma and texture are strangely reminiscent of sauerkraut. That's probably why so many Westerners familiar with this Japanese dish like to serve it with corned beef, baked ham or pork chops. On a Japanese menu, it's very nice with fish or poultry. *Serves 4–6.*

1 cup dried *kiri-boshi daikon* (shredded
    sun-dried Japanese white radish)
½ tablespoon vegetable oil
¾ cup *dashi* (Basic Soup Stock,
    page 55)

1½ tablespoons sugar
1½ tablespoons soy sauce
2 teaspoons *saké* (rice wine)

Rinse the dried shredded radish in a colander and squeeze out any excess moisture. Put the rinsed radish in a small pot with warm water to cover and bring it to a rolling boil. Remove from the heat and let the radish soak for 5 minutes before draining it. Again, squeeze out any excess moisture. The radish should be soft and pliable now.

Sauté the softened radish in the oil over medium heat for 1–2 minutes, stirring frequently. Add the soup stock and seasonings, stir to mix well, and lower the heat slightly. Cover with a dropped lid if you have one, or use a regular lid but leave it askew. Braise, stirring occasionally, till nearly all the cooking liquid has been reduced (about 10 minutes). Serve warm or at room temperature. Any leftovers will keep well 3–4 days if covered and refrigerated.

きんぴら BRAISED BURDOCK ROOT AND CARROT *(Kimpira)*

Thin slivers of two flavorful root vegetables are sautéed and simmered in a fast-reducing, sweetened soy sauce. Mounded on individual small plates and garnished with a sprinkling of white sesame seeds, this makes a very nice side dish to Cold Steamed Chicken (page 170), Salt-Grilled Fish (page 138) or Thick Sweet Omelet (page 152). *Serves 2–3.*

12–15 inches *gobō* (burdock root)
½ small carrot
1 tablespoon vegetable oil
1 tablespoon *saké* (rice wine)

1 tablespoon sugar
2 tablespoons soy sauce
½ teaspoon white sesame seeds

Scrape burdock root (if canned, drain and peel) and cut it into thin slivers (see page 25, *sasagaki* cutting). Soak the slivers for 5–10 minutes in a bowl of fresh cold water (or blanch slivers of canned burdock), then drain them. Scape the carrot and cut it into thin slivers just like the burdock.

In a skillet, heat the oil and sauté the vegetables over high heat. Cook, stirring constantly, for about 2 minutes, then pour in the rice wine. Reduce the heat, add the sugar and, stirring, braise the vegetables for 1 minute. Add the soy sauce, stir, and braise until all the liquid is reduced (about 5 minutes) and the vegetables are a deep, glistening golden brown. Mound on small plates and serve warm or at room temperature, garnished with the sesame seeds.

ひじきの煮物 ## BRAISED SEA VEGETABLE *(Hijiki No Ni Mono)*

Most Westerners agree that *hijiki* is the tastiest sea vegetable used in Japanese cuisine. Black and lustrous, its licorice-like flavor combines well with sweet carrot strips. The Japanese often add thin ribbons of fried bean curd to this dish for extra volume and texture contrast. Either way, this makes a colorful and flavorful side dish to any meal. *Serves 4–6.*

½ cup dried *hijiki* (black sea vegetable)	½ cup *dashi* (Basic Soup Stock, page 55)
1–2 small carrots	⅔–¾ cup if including fried bean curd
½ slice *abura agé* (fried bean curd), optional	1 ½ tablespoons sugar
	1 ½ tablespoons soy sauce
1 tablespoon vegetable oil	1 teaspoon *saké* (rice wine)

Soak the dried black sea vegetable in warm water to cover for about 15–20 minutes. Since it will soften and swell to many times its original volume, use a fairly large bowl. Rinse in cold water and drain. Cut into approximately 1-inch-long pieces and pat them dry. Peel the carrot and cut it into julienne strips. If using fried bean curd, pour boiling water over it to remove excess oil. Pat the bean curd dry with paper towels before slicing it crosswise into thin ribbons.

Heat the oil in a skillet and sauté the sea vegetable and carrot strips, stirring constantly, for about 2 minutes. Add the soup stock and seasonings, and braise the mixture over moderate heat for 15–18 minutes (if using fried bean curd, add it after 10–12 minutes) or until most of the liquid has been reduced. Serve warm or at room temperature. Any leftovers will keep well for 3–4 days covered in the refrigerator.

筍 FRESH BOILED BAMBOO SHOOTS *(Takénoko)*

Springtime is time for bamboo shoots—a tender yet crunchy vegetable with an elusive aroma all its own. Haunt your local source of fresh Oriental vegetables from late March through May. Select fairly small shoots weighing about 1 pound each. Damp earth should still be clinging to the outer leaves, and a faint musky odor is no cause for alarm. There should be no mold, however, anywhere on the shoot. *A single untrimmed 1-pound shoot will yield about ½–⅔ pound, which should serve 4–6, depending upon what recipe you choose.*

1–2 small fresh bamboo shoots, each
    weighing about 1 pound
4–6 cups cold water

⅓ cup *nuka* (rice bran powder)
1–2 *tōgarashi* (dried hot red pepper)

Peel away a few of the outer leaves of the shoots and rinse to remove any soil (*1*). Cut each top slightly on the diagonal (*2*), and trim the base of each straight across (*3*). Slash each shoot lengthwise, but do not cut in deeply (*4*).

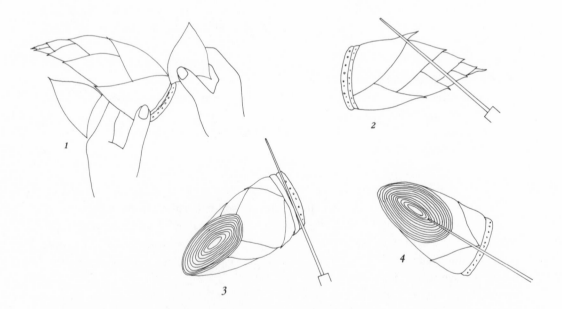

Place the bamboo shoots in a saucepan with the water, rice-bran powder and red hot pepper. Bring the water to a boil, then reduce the heat to maintain a steady simmer. Cook the shoots for 45–50 minutes, or until a wooden pick passes easily through the thick core. Let the shoots cool to room temperature in the liquid. Now peel away and discard all the outer leaves and with a knife trim off any large pebbly bumps at the base of each shoot.

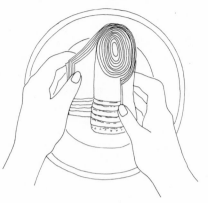

Fresh-boiled bamboo shoots should be stored in cold water to cover in the refrigerator. Change the water every day. They will maintain maximum flavor for the first 2 days, but won't spoil for 5 or 6.

筍 の 土 佐 煮 BAMBOO SHOOTS SIMMERED IN AMBER BROTH *(Takénoko No Tosa Ni)*

Subtly seasoned and colored by smoky bonito flakes, these bamboo shoots make a very nice side dish to a fish, chicken or egg entrée. Fresh boiled bamboo shoots make this dish especially good, though canned shoots are nice prepared this way, too. *Serves 4.*

1–2 bamboo shoots (about 1 pound in all), trimmed and boiled fresh or canned
1½ cups *dashi* (Basic Soup Stock, page 55)

2 tablespoons soy sauce
1 tablespoon *mirin* (syrupy rice wine)
½ cup *katsuo bushi* (bonito flakes)

Drain the bamboo shoots and slice them lengthwise into ¼-inch-thick "combs" (*kushi-gata* cutting described and illustrated on page 26). If any white material clings between the "teeth" of the "combs," rinse it away under cold water.

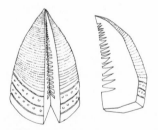

In a saucepan, combine the soup stock, soy sauce and syrupy rice wine. Add the bamboo shoots and simmer them over moderate heat for 10–15 minutes, or until they are very tender and little of the broth remains. Use a dropped lid if you have one, or leave a regular lid askew. Sprinkle half of the bonito flakes over the shoots, remove the saucepan from the heat and let it cool uncovered to room temperature. Remove the bamboo shoots to your serving platter or individual small shallow bowls. Strain the broth and pour it over the shoots. Just before serving, garnish by sprinkling the remaining bonito flakes over the bamboo shoots.

千
切
り
煮
つ
け

BRAISED CELERY STRIPS *(Sengiri Nitsuké)*

Celery is a fairly recent addition to the Japanese diet, and here it is imaginatively combined with pork, ginger and roasted sesame. Served hot or at room temperature, a small mound of braised celery strips makes a nice accompaniment to fish, chicken or egg dishes. *Serves 3–4.*

2–3 ounces boneless pork loin	½ tablespoon white sesame seeds
½ teaspoooon ginger juice, extracted from grated fresh ginger	1 tablespoon vegetable oil
	2 teaspoons soy sauce
2 teaspoons *saké* (rice wine)	1 teaspoon sugar
3 large stalks celery	¼ teaspoon salt

Partially freeze the meat to make cutting easier, and slice the pork into paper-thin slices. Cut these across the grain into thin strips approximately 2 inches long. Combine the ginger juice and rice wine and toss the pork in it, letting it marinate while you cut the celery and roast the sesame seeds.

Remove any leaves from the celery stalks, then cut them into 2-inch strips. Cut each 2-inch piece lengthwise into thin (about ¼-inch) strips. In a clean, dry skillet dry roast the sesame seeds until they are golden, then transfer them to a small dish.

Heat the oil in a skillet and sauté the pork strips over high heat, stirring constantly for 30–40 seconds, or until no longer pink. Add the celery to the skillet and sauté, tossing and stirring, for a few moments before seasoning with the soy sauce, sugar and salt. Lower the heat and braise for 2 minutes or until nearly all the liquid has been reduced. Sprinkle the sesame seeds over all and toss to distribute.

大
根
の
炒
め
煮

GOLDEN BRAISED JAPANESE WHITE RADISH
(Daikon No Itamé Ni)

Here is a simply delicious way of bringing out the natural flavor of Japanese white radish—even when it's slightly wilted and 3 or 4 days old. Sweet, mellow and rich-colored, braised radish makes a nice side dish to serve with almost any fish or meat. *Serves 3–4.*

7–8 inches *daikon* (about ¾-pound Japanese white radish)	2 tablespoons sugar
½ tablespoon vegetable oil	1 tablespoon *saké* (rice wine)
¾ cup *dashi* (Basic Soup Stock, page 55)	1½ tablespoons soy sauce

Peel the radish and cut it into ¾-inch-thick rounds. In a skillet large enough to hold the slices in a single layer, sauté the radish in the oil over medium heat for 1–2 minutes. Turn the slices over and continue to sauté them for another minute.

Add ½ cup of the stock and all the sugar and rice wine. Lower the heat and simmer for 5 minutes, then add the rest of the stock and the soy sauce. Turn the slices over and continue to simmer, using a dropped lid if you have one, for about 5 minutes. Turn the slices and cook for another 3–4 minutes or until nearly all the braising liquid is reduced. Serve hot, or at room temperature.

茄子の利休煮　BRAISED EGGPLANT IN SESAME AND BEAN SAUCE (Nasu No Rikyū Ni)

Tender chunks of eggplant braised in a dark, smooth, pungent sauce are garnished with freshly roasted white sesame seeds to make a memorable vegetable accompaniment to Salt-Grilled Fish (page 138), steamed chicken or a fluffy omelet. *Serves 4.*

¾-pound eggplant
3 tablespoons vegetable oil
⅓ cup *dashi* (Basic Soup Stock, page 55)
2½–3 tablespoons *Sendai miso* (dark bean paste)

2 tablespoons sugar
1½ tablespoons *saké* (rice wine)
2 teaspoons white sesame seeds

Remove the stem and peel the eggplant unless you are sure the skin will not be tough (Japanese miniature eggplants are very sweet with tender skins; if you can find them, just quarter them). Cut the eggplant into ½-inch cubes and sauté them in the oil over high heat, stirring, until translucent. Pour in the soup stock, lower the heat to barely maintain a simmer, and cook for 5 minutes. If you have a dropped lid, use it; if not leave a regular lid askew, stirring occasionally.

In a small saucepan over low heat combine the bean paste, sugar and rice wine, stirring until smooth, with the sugar completely dissolved. Stir this thick sauce into the simmering eggplant and cook for 2 more minutes.

Dry roast the sesame seeds (page 16) until they are golden. Transfer them to a *suribachi* and grind them coarsely, or turn them out on a dry cutting board and cut them (as you would mince parsley) to release their aroma. Fold half the sesame seeds into the eggplant mixture, before removing from the heat.

Enjoy the eggplants warm or at room temperature. Just before serving, garnish with the remaining sesame seeds.

五
目
豆
煮

BEANS AND ASSORTED VEGETABLES
(Gomoku Mamé Ni)

The Japanese make extensive use of soybeans in their cuisine, and here those nutritious beans are cooked until tender, then simmered in a lightly seasoned broth with a variety of vegetables. The key to flavorful dried-bean cookery is long, gentle simmering, and this is one of the few Japanese dishes requiring many hours of cooking. The final dish keeps well, though—for up to a week if refrigerated. Beans and Assorted Vegetables is versatile; serve it with any grilled or steamed fish, chicken or egg dish. Or enjoy it with a Western-style platter of cold meats. *Serves 4.*

Brine for soaking beans:

3 cups cold water
¼ teaspoon salt

⅓ cup *daizu* (dried soybeans)
5–6 cups cold water (for cooking)
2 large dried *shiitaké* (black Oriental mushrooms)
½ cup warm water, with a pinch of sugar
¼ cup carrot, cut in ¼-inch dice
7–8 inches softened *konbu* (kelp; leftovers from stock making)*

¼ cup liquid from soaking black mushrooms
1¼ cups *dashi* (Basic Soup Stock, page 55)
2 tablespoons soy sauce
2 tablespoons sugar
1 tablespoon *mirin* (syrupy rice wine)

In a saucepan, combine 3 cups cold water with ¼ teaspoon salt and heat it through, stirring to dissolve the salt. Let the brine cool to room temperature, then soak the dried beans in it for 8 hours or overnight. Drain the beans, place them in a saucepan with several cups of fresh cold water, and bring to a boil over moderate heat. Skim off any froth, reduce the heat to maintain a simmer, and cook the beans until they are tender (about 1½–2 hours). Add more water as necessary to keep the beans from sticking and burning. When the beans are done, drain them well.

Soak the dried mushrooms for 20 minutes in ½ cup warm water to which a pinch of sugar has been added. Rinse the mushrooms, remove and discard their stems and dice them. Peel and dice the carrots. Strain the mushroom liquid, reserving ¼ cup of it.

*If not using leftover kelp that is already soft, place dried kelp in a small saucepan with water to cover. Bring the water to a boil, then remove the pot from heat. (By the way, this kelp broth could be used in lieu of the basic *dashi* stock in this recipe).

Cut the softened kelp into ¼-inch-wide strips, then across into small squares.

In a saucepan, combine the mushroom liquid, basic stock, soy sauce, sugar and syrupy rice wine, and heat it, stirring, to dissolve the sugar. Add the beans and vegetables and simmer over medium-low heat for 15–20 minutes or until nearly all the liquid has been reduced. For superior flavor, simmer with a dropped lid; if unavailable, ladle the seasoned stock over the cooking beans and vegetables frequently.

Serve warm or at room temperature.

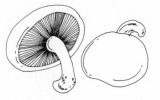

Grilled and Skillet-Grilled Foods

(YAKI MONO)

The word *yaki* means to "sear with heat" and the Japanese consider grilled, broiled and skillet-grilled (what we would call "pan-fried") foods to be of the same nature. Seafood, fish, vegetables, meat, poultry and eggs are all "seared with heat" in the Japanese kitchen. With skewered or net-grilled foods there is often little or no seasoning used before cooking. Instead the grilled food is dipped into a variety of highly seasoned sauces later at the dinner table. The major exception is glaze-grilled food, for which a sweet soy-based sauce is brushed lavishly in the final moments of grilling. The Japanese also marinate fish steaks in a sweetened *miso* (fermented soybean paste) before grilling or broiling them.

Both marinated and unseasoned meats are skillet-grilled as you'll discover in Gingery Pork Sauté and Skillet-Grilled Beefsteaks and Vegetables.

Finally, there are two skillet-grilled omelets—one thin and crêpelike, the other thick and cakelike.

❖

塩
焼 Salt-Grilled Fish *(Shio Yaki)*

Perhaps one of the oldest known methods of food preparation in Japan, salt grilling still remains a distinctive part of Japanese cuisine. Coarse salt is sprinkled on small whole eviscerated fish or fish steaks, which are then grilled over very hot coals. A simple dipping sauce of lemon and soy sauce brings out the subtle flavor of the fish. If you have a bit of Japanese white radish left over from another use, grate it and add it to the dipping sauce. It will add a sharp, crunchy accent. Trout, snapper, swordfish, salmon and mackerel are particularly well suited to salt grilling.

138

切り身 FISH STEAKS *(Kirimi)*

Serves 4.

4 small salmon or swordfish steaks,
    each weighing about ¼ pound
2 teaspoons coarse salt
Lemon wedges

2–3 inches *daikon* (Japanese white
    radish)
Soy sauce

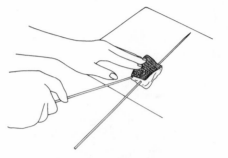

Salmon steaks may be skewered and suspended above, or grilled directly on, a net several inches from intense heat. Skewered fish are more attractive, though a bit more trouble to prepare than net-grilled ones. Details on both methods and necessary equipment appear on pages 32 and 8. Either way, wash and pat dry the salmon steaks and lightly salt them on both sides just before grilling.

If there is skin covering part of one side, this should be the "right" side, the one to be presented face up on the final dish. If the skin merely borders the thickness of the steak, you may choose either side for final presentation. Grill the right side first, for 5–6 minutes. Turn and grill for another 3–4 minutes. If using skewers, twirl them frequently to prevent sticking. When finished grilling remove the skewers immediately. Serve the fish warm or at room temperature with lemon wedges and grated radish, and provide small dishes of soy sauce, too. Each person makes his own dipping sauce by adding lemon juice and radish, to taste, to the soy sauce.

姿焼 WHOLE FISH *(Sugata Yaki)*

Serves 4.

4 small whole trout
1–1½ tablespoons coarse salt

Lemon wedges, soy sauce
1 unwaxed cucumber, optional

Whole fish look and taste better when skewered, though they may be grilled on a net if skewering equipment is unavailable.

Eviscerate and skewer the fish (see pages 29 and 32) just before grilling. Whole grilled fish requires two saltings: one decorative layer for fins and tail, and one for overall seasoning. For each fish, take ¼ teaspoon or more of salt between thumb and forefinger and press it onto the tail. Take more salt and make the back fin stand up as you press the salt on it. Then salt the fins near the gills. When the fish is cooked, these areas will be dry with a shimmering white crust. Now lightly salt the entire fish.

Grill the fish, right side first, for 7–8 minutes. Twirl the skewers frequently from the start to prevent the fish from sticking as it cooks. Turn the fish and grill it for 4–5 more minutes.

Remove the skewers immediately and serve the fish warm or at room temperature with lemon wedges and soy sauce. The Japanese often serve salt-grilled whole fish on long rectangular plates. The fish is from the sea and appears to be swimming, and often something stolid from the land, such as cucumber "mountains," is chosen as a garnish. If you wish to follow suit, cutting instructions appear on page 26.

鳥
肉
の
塩
焼

SALT-GRILLED CHICKEN BREASTS
(Tori Niku No Shio Yaki)

This is a simple, succulent chicken dish that adapts itself easily to both Western and Japanese menus. Serve it with rice or potatoes, assorted pickles or a tossed green salad, and maybe a braised vegetable on the side. *Serves 4.*

4 small boned chicken breast halves, each weighing about ¼ pound	½ tablespoon salt
	½ lemon, cut into wedges
1 tablespoon *saké* (rice wine)	

Sprinkle the chicken breasts with rice wine and let them stand for a few minutes. Preheat your broiler or grilling unit to high. Now sprinkle the breasts with salt and place them on a net or rack so that the skin faces the source of heat and is about 2–2½ inches from it. (Skewering the breasts first will help to prevent shrinkage.) Broil or grill the chicken for 3–4 minutes. If the skin is only barely colored, continue to grill for another 7–8 minutes. Or, if the skin looks slightly charred, lower the heat and cook for another 5 minutes. Turn the chicken breasts over and continue to cook for 3–4 minutes. The chicken should be cooked through but still very juicy. Serve warm or cold with lemon wedges.

海
老
の
串
焼

SKEWERED SALT-GRILLED SHRIMPS
(Ebi No Kushi Yaki)

A splash of wine and a sprinkling of salt are all that are needed to bring out the sweetness of fresh shrimps. Keep the shells on while cooking; the shrimps will be juicier and brighter that way. If you want, you could peel off the shells for your guests before serving them with lemon wedges and soy sauce for dipping. *Serves 4 as an hors d'oeuvre.*

12 jumbo shrimps (with shell and tail intact)	1 teaspoon coarse salt
1 teaspoon *saké* (rice wine)	½ lemon, cut into wedges
	2–3 tablespoons soy sauce, for dipping

Wash and pat dry the shrimps. Skewer them curled on parallel skewers to form a crescent. Insert the first skewer through the head and tail; place the second skewer through the belly. Preheat your grilling or broiling unit to high (about 400 degrees). Now sprinkle wine, then the salt, over the shrimps and cook them immediately. Grill or broil for 2 minutes, then turn the shrimps over and grill for just another minute or two. Don't overcook; when the salt is crusted and the shells dry and opaque, the shrimps are done. Remove them from the skewers while they are still hot. Serve warm or at room temperature.

か
き
の
港
焼

SEAPORT-STYLE GRILLED OYSTERS
(Kaki No Minato Yaki)

A delightful appetizer from the sea. Here the grilled oysters are garnished with roasted paper-thin black seaweed, hence the name *minato* or "seaport" style. *Serves 5–6.*

¼ teaspoon salt	1½ tablespoons soy sauce
2 dozen oysters, shucked	1 sheet *Asakusa nori* (dark dried laver)
1½ tablespoons *saké* (rice wine)	1 small lemon, cut into wedges

Sprinkle the salt over the oysters and let them stand for a few minutes before rinsing them with cold water. Pat the oysters dry and marinate them for 2–3 minutes each in first the *saké*, then the soy sauce.

For every 6–8 oysters you will need 2 very sharp, thin skewers (metal are preferable, but if you are using bamboo, soak them in cold water for 15 minutes beforehand). First skewer the hard, muscular end of each oyster, then run a parallel skewer through the soft belly.

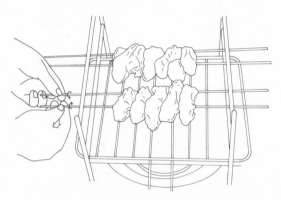

Grill or broil the oysters for 1–2 minutes, twirling the skewers frequently to prevent sticking. Turn once halfway through. They should be cooked through, but still juicy. Remove the oysters from the skewers immediately.

Dry roast a sheet of laver (page 16) and crumble it in a dry cloth, then sprinkle over the oysters. Serve warm or at room temperature with lemon wedges.

焼茄子 GRILLED EGGPLANT *(Yaki Nasu)*

These eggplants are delectable served with almost any fried or braised meat, fish or poultry dish. Choice in the final seasoning—a sprinkling of dried bonito, a small mound of grated ginger, or a dab of mustard—lets you suit your own mood or menu. *Serves 4–5.*

4–5 whole small eggplants (no larger than 5 inches long and 4 inches in diameter at the thickest spot)

⅓ cup *dashi* (Basic Soup Stock, page 55)
1 teaspoon soy sauce
½ teaspoon *mirin* (syrupy rice wine)

Final seasonings:

2–3 tablespoons finely shaved *katsuo
bushi* (bonito) OR 1–1½ tablespoons
grated fresh ginger OR 1–1½
teaspoons commercially prepared
hot mustard

Lay the eggplants on a net over direct heat. Grill them over medium heat for about
10–15 minutes, turning them several times. The skin will wrinkle and the pulp soften.
Peel or scrape away the skin with a dull knife to expose the tender yellowish pulp
beneath. The Japanese like to keep the stems attached, but you can slice them off if
you prefer before transferring each eggplant to a small shallow bowl.

In a small saucepan, combine the soup stock, soy sauce and syrupy rice wine and,
stirring, bring it to a simmer. Ladle a little of this sauce over each eggplant. If you
want to serve the dish cold, chill it now and garnish just before serving. Choose any
1 of the 3 final seasonings suggested above and garnish the top of each eggplant with
a bit of it. To eat, scrape the seasoning off the top and stir it into the sauce surrounding
the eggplant.

手
羽
肉
の
照
り
焼

GLAZE-GRILLED CHICKEN WINGS
(Téba Niku No Teri Yaki)

Grilled and glazed with a sweet soy sauce, this chicken dish has wide appeal. Serve
it either hot or cold with a tossed green salad and hot white rice. *Serves 4.*

12–16 meaty chicken wings
½ teaspoon salt

Teri yaki sauce:

¼ cup soy sauce   1–2 tablespoons sugar
¼ cup *mirin* (syrupy rice wine)

Lightly salt the chicken wings on all sides, then spread them out on a rack or net.
Heat your broiling or grilling unit to high and cook the chicken wings for 6–8
minutes, flipping them over once halfway through. Meanwhile, in a small saucepan,
combine the *teri yaki* sauce ingredients and heat them through, stirring. Continue to
cook the sauce for a minute or two until it thickens.

Dip the chicken wings, one at a time, into this sauce and return them to the rack or net. Now lower the heat slightly and continue to grill or broil for another 4 minutes. Dip the wings again into the *teri yaki* sauce and cook for a final 2–3 minutes.

ほ
た
て
貝
の
照
り
焼

GLAZE-GRILLED SCALLOPS *(Hotatégai No Teri Yaki)*

Succulent bay scallops glazed with a sweetened soy sauce make a wonderful appetizer or side dish. *Serves 4–6.*

¾ pound bay scallops, shelled
1½–2 tablespoons *saké* (rice wine)

Teri yaki sauce:

¼ cup soy sauce   2 tablespoons sugar
¼ cup *mirin* (syrupy rice wine)

Rinse the scallops and pat them dry on paper towels before marinating them for 10 minutes in the rice wine.

Thread the scallops on several skewers. If using bamboo ones, soak them first in cold water for 15 minutes. Grill or broil the scallops 2 inches from the source of heat for 3–4 minutes, turning the skewers over once after a minute or so.

In a small saucepan, combine the *teri yaki* sauce ingredients. Stirring, simmer the sauce for 3–4 minutes or until it begins to thicken slightly.

Using a pastry brush, paint the partially grilled scallops with the *teri yaki* sauce on all sides. Continue to grill the scallops for another minute before brushing on more sauce. Grill for another ½ minute, then remove the scallops from the heat. Serve hot or at room temperature.

焼
鳥

SKEWERED CHICKEN GRILL *(Yaki Tori)*

Here sizzling, succulent chicken bits and scallions are glazed with a sweet soy sauce in their final moments of grilling. Popular in its native land as a grownup's snack, it can also make a heartier main course if served with a *miso*-thickened soup, hot white rice, tart salad and assorted pungent pickles. *Serves 4 as a main dish; serves 6–8 as an hors d'oeuvre.*

½ pound chicken meat (dark and light) 6–7 scallions
 with skin but no bone
½ pound chicken livers, trimmed of
 any fat or membrane

Glazing sauce:

½ cup soy sauce   1 tablespoon *saké* (rice wine)
3 tablespoons sugar   2 tablespoons *mirin* (syrupy rice wine)

¼ teaspoon *shichimi tōgarashi* (7-spice
 hot pepper), optional

You will need about 20 short (6-inch) bamboo skewers or 6 or 7 longer metal brochettes. If you plan to use bamboo, soak them in water for 15 minutes. Preheat your grill or broiler.

 Cut the chicken into 1- or 1½-inch cubes and the scallions into 1 or 1½-inch lengths. Cut the livers into approximately the same size. Thread pieces of chicken and scallion alternately on the skewers or brochettes, beginning and ending with a piece of chicken. Now make up some liver skewers in the same way.

 Grill or broil the skewered chicken and livers 3–4 inches from medium-high heat for 3–4 minutes. Turn and continue to grill for 5–6 minutes.

 Meanwhile, in a small saucepan, combine the soy sauce, sugar, rice wine and syrupy rice wine and simmer, stirring, for 5–6 minutes until the sauce thickens a bit. Then lightly brush some of this glazing sauce on the grilling chicken and livers and continue to grill for a minute or so until the sauce begins to dry. Now brush on more sauce frequently and lavishly and grill for a final few minutes. Sprinkle on a pinch of the 7 hot spices just before serving for a sharper flavor.

蒲 GLAZED GRILLED EEL *(Kabayaki)*
焼

In Japan, this succulent, aromatic dish is served in the summertime, since it is thought to be just the thing for reviving strength sapped by the heat. In fact, there is a special day for eel eating called *Doyo No Ushi No Hi*. Calculated by the lunar calendar, it comes sometime in July and is invariably the hottest day of the year. Glazed Grilled Eel tastes best when laid upon a bed of snowy white rice (pour any remaining sauce over eels and rice) and served with assorted crisp pickles. Fill out the menu with tart Red and White Salad (page 173) or Eggplant Salad with Tart Sesame Dressing (page 184) and a clear Egg Drop Soup (page 58). *Serves 3–4.*

2 eels, filleted but not skinned (total
    weight about 1 pound)

Glazing sauce:

2–3 tablespoons soy sauce   2–3 tablespoons sugar
2–3 tablespoons *saké* (rice wine)

¼ teaspoon *sansho* (Japanese fragrant
    pepper)

Trim the fillets into 6–8 slices, each measuring about 4½–5 inches in length. Take 2 slices of the same length and arrange them skin side down next to each other on your board. Insert 2 or 3 skewers as illustrated. Repeat the skewering procedure for the remaining fillets.

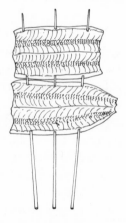

Inside a steamer, stand the skewers at an angle so that the eel does not touch the sides or bottom rack of the pot. Steam the eel for 10–15 minutes (the longer time for those who prefer their eel very tender). Remove the skewers and grill or broil the eel several inches from moderately high heat until the skin and flesh begin to color (about 5–6 minutes). Remember to twirl the skewers from the start to prevent sticking.

In the meantime, combine the ingredients for the glazing sauce in a small saucepan, and cook for 3–4 minutes, stirring.

With a pastry brush, paint the glazing sauce lavishly on both sides of the grilling eel. Continue to cook for 8–10 more minutes, glazing the eel with more sauce every minute or so and flipping the skewers frequently. Remove the skewers immediately (twirl the skewers as you remove them to keep the eel from falling apart) and sprinkle the flesh side with Japanese pepper.

いかの松かさ焼

"PINE-CONE" SQUID *(Ika No Matsukasa Yaki)*

Golden squares of nubbly, tender squid look like pine cones and taste divine. They make an unusual and attractive hors d'oeuvre. *Serves 6–8.*

2–3 fillets of squid (about 1½ pounds)
1–2 tablespoons soy sauce
1–2 tablespoons *mirin* (syrupy rice
     wine)

1 teaspoon black sesame seeds, dry
     roasted

Lay the triangular-like fillets flat on the board, inner surface down. (If you're having trouble deciding which side is the inner one, look closely for ridges; these indicate where the cartilage used to be on the inside of the body.) With a very sharp knife score the outer surface of the squid with many shallow cuts in a crosshatch design.

Remove the skin from tail to head if this has not already been done, and slit open the conical body. If you have leg and tail "flaps" left over from filleting a whole squid, trim off the suction cups from the legs and either salt grill the squid pieces on a net and serve them with lemon wedges and soy sauce or use them in place of shrimp in the fish dumpling recipe (page 116).

Marinate the squid in soy sauce for 10–15 minutes. Reserving the soy sauce for later use, remove the squid and skewer each fillet with 3 skewers. Grill or broil over moderately high heat until the squid becomes opaque and the nubbly design from the crosshatching becomes fairly obvious (about 1–2 minutes). Twirl the skewers in place, then flip over the squid and grill or broil the nontextured side for 1–2 minutes. Now

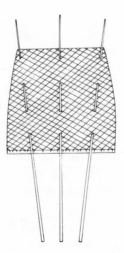

add the syrupy rice wine to the reserved soy sauce and brush this glaze frequently and lavishly over both sides of the grilling squid for 3–4 minutes. Remove the skewers immediately and sprinkle the textured side of the squid with dry-roasted black sesame seeds. Cut the fillets into bite-size squares and serve the squid warm or at room temperature.

魚
の
味
噌
漬
焼

MISO-MARINATED FISH GRILL
(Sakana No Miso-zuké Yaki)

Brown and crusty outside, mellow sweet and moist inside, this marinated fish is absolutely delicious. Since this fish could be marinated for as little as 8 hours or as long as 72, it's a nice recipe to keep in mind when you shop at the fish market. If you see a special on snapper, porgy or halibut, buy some and put it in the *miso* marinade for the next day or several days after that.

Although the marinade never touches the flesh of the fish, the unique tenderizing and aromatic flavoring quality of the *miso* is at work. The cooking aromas alone are enough to evoke fond memories in anyone who has ever lived in Japan. *Serves 2–3.*

2–3 fish steaks, each no thicker than ½
    inch; porgy, sea bream, red snapper
    and halibut are particularly good
    prepared this way

Marinade:

1–1½ cups (a 300- or 500-gram bag)
    Saikyō miso (light bean paste)
½ tablespoon *saké* (rice wine)

2–3 tablespoons *mirin* (syrupy rice
    wine)

Combine the *miso,* rice wine and syrupy rice wine well in a glass, ceramic, foil or enamel-lined flat container just large enough to hold the fish steaks in a single layer. Wrap the fish in a dry linen cloth (or a double thickness of surgical cotton gauze or a triple thickness of cheesecloth) and bury it deep in the *miso* marinade before covering your container with clear wrap. Marinate the fish for at least 8 hours at room temperature or up to 72 hours in the refrigerator.

Just before grilling, remove and unwrap the fish steaks. The flesh will have taken on a luminous golden cast and may be a bit slippery. Skewer the fish (page 32) and grill or broil it, with the skin 2–2½ inches from the heat, for 7–8 minutes. Use fairly low heat. Even so, the outside will brown quickly and may even char a bit. Turn the fish over and continue to grill or broil for 5–6 more minutes. Remove the skewers while the fish is hot. Serve the fish warm or at room temperature.

NOTE: The *miso* marinade may be used 3 or 4 more times within a month. After removing the fish from the marinade, drain off any accumulated liquid. Stir the paste and store it in the refrigerator in a covered glass, ceramic or enamel-lined container.

しょうが焼 GINGERY PORK SAUTÉ *(Shōga Yaki)*

I absolutely adore fresh ginger, and so do the Japanese, who use it in so many ways. Here its pungent aroma and flavor make this pork dish particularly appealing. Serve the dish with hot white rice, a clear soup and assorted sharp pickles or a green salad. Any leftover meat makes fine sandwich fillings, especially when accompanied by crisp lettuce leaves or cucumber slices. *Serves 4.*

¾ pound lean pork	2 tablespoons soy sauce
½ teaspoon peeled and grated fresh ginger	¼ pound fresh snow peas OR *hakusai* (Chinese cabbage)
1 tablespoon *saké* (rice wine)	2 tablespoons vegetable oil

Slice the meat bacon-thin (partially freezing the pork makes slicing easier). Make a marinade from the ginger, rice wine and soy sauce, and add the pork slices, one at a time to make sure they are evenly coated. Marinate the meat, turning occasionally, for 10–15 minutes.

Wash and pat dry the snow peas and string them if necessary. Or cut the cabbage across the stalks, into ¼–½-inch strips, rinse under cold water and drain well.

Heat the oil in a heavy cast-iron skillet and, separating the slices, sear the pork over medium heat in 2 or 3 batches if necessary until the color changes. Flip the slices over and sear again, removing them as they change color. Set the meat aside and sauté the snow peas or cabbage with fast stirring, flipping motions, adding a drop more oil to the skillet if necessary. Sauté the vegetables for 1–2 minutes (they should still be crisp) then transfer them to individual plates.

Return the pork all at once to the skillet, with whatever marinade and juices remain from the first searing. Sauté the pork over high heat, turning frequently, until it is well cooked and glazed (about 2–3 minutes). Serve the pork with the vegetables, either warm or at room temperature.

NOTE: After cooking, the skillet will look discouragingly encrusted with marinade. Just soak it immediately after using for at least 10 minutes before scrubbing it clean.

鉄
板   SKILLET-GRILLED BEEFSTEAKS
焼   AND VEGETABLES (*Teppan Yaki*)

Paradoxically, there is little beef in the Japanese diet, yet some of the finest steaks in the world can be had in Japan. Kobe beefsteaks are justly famous—they are incredibly tender and beautifully marbelized (vastly expensive, too!). For this dish, treat yourself to a good cut and enjoy it a new way. *Serves 4.*

4 small boneless rib steaks, each ¼ inch   4 ounces fresh bean sprouts
    thick and weighing about 6 ounces   Suet or vegetable oil
2 green bell peppers OR 8 okra pods

Dipping sauce and condiments:

4–6 tablespoons soy sauce   1 *tōgarashi* (dried hot red pepper)
2–3 tablespoons *dashi* (Basic Soup   ½ small lemon or lime, cut into 4
    Stock, page 55)   wedges
2-inch piece of *daikon* (Japanese white
    radish)

Trim the steaks of any excess fat, if necessary (these trimmings can be melted down and used instead of oil). Cut the green peppers in quarters and remove the seeds or wash and pat dry the okra pods. Soak the bean sprouts in a bowl of cold water for a few moments, then drain them well. Discard any badly bruised or discolored sprouts, as these will be bitter.

Prepare your dipping sauce and condiments before cooking your meat and vegetables. Each diner should be given a small, shallow bowl. Into each bowl pour a generous tablespoon of soy sauce, thinned out with a few drops of soup stock. Peel the radish and poke several holes in it, then break open the dried red pepper pod and remove all the seeds. Stuff pieces of the red pepper into the holes you made in the radish and grate it. The white will be flecked with red (the Japanese call this condiment *momiji oroshi* or "autumn maple leaves") and the mild radish is given a fiery accent. Drain off any excess liquid that may accumulate as you grate and mound the *momiji oroshi* in a shallow bowl, surrounding it with lemon or lime wedges. When eating, each person adds lemon juice and/or fiery grated radish to taste to his own dipping sauce.

Use a heavy, cast-iron skillet, and oil it lightly. Over high heat, sear the steaks on both sides (you can lower the heat and cook a few moments longer if you like your meat medium done). The Japanese slice their steak into ½-inch-thick strips just before removing it from the skillet, which makes for easier chopstick eating later.

Remove the steak strips to a warmed platter or individual plates and lightly cover with aluminum foil to keep it warm while you cook the vegetables. Stir-fry the green peppers for 2 minutes or the okra for 3 minutes. Next stir-fry the bean sprouts for a minute, adding a bit more oil to the skillet if necessary. Serve the vegetables with the meat.

う す 焼 卵 THIN SWEET OMELET (Usu Yaki Tamago)

Crêpe-like dishes, similar to this one, may be found in many cuisines throughout the world. The Japanese make theirs in rectangular skillets and flip them with a single chopstick! For the less adventurous, round pans and spatulas can still produce lovely, bright yellow sheets of omelet. These crêpes are used to decorate many rice dishes. *Makes a single sheet.*

1 egg
1 teaspoon sugar
Vegetable oil

Beat the egg and the sugar together, trying not to incorporate air as you do so. Heat a *tamago yaki nabé* (a special rectangular metal skillet) or a 6–7-inch round skillet and barely coat the surface with oil, using a swab of paper towel. The pan should be hot enough to make a test drop of egg sizzle, but not so hot that the pan smokes. Remove the pan from direct heat and pour the egg in, all at once. Quickly tilt and rotate the pan to coat the bottom with a thin, even layer of egg. Return the pan to medium-high heat and cook the omelet until it is dry around the edges and set throughout (about 1 minute). If the omelet appears to be in danger of scorching before it has set, remove the pan from direct heat for a few seconds (placing the pan on a well-wrung-out damp cloth will help it cool quickly). Do not lower the heat as this makes the final omelet pale and greasy.

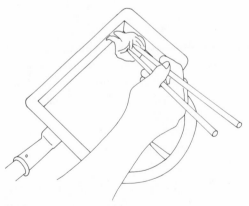

When the omelet is dry but still bright yellow, flip it. The traditional method of flipping is illustrated here: Run the tip of a chopstick around the entire outer edge of the omelet *(1)*. It should easily come away from the pan. Twist and twirl the chopstick *(2)*, working it under the sheet of egg across its width. Lift up the omelet—it is now draped across the chopstick *(3)*—and inverting top and bottom surfaces, lay the omelet down again *(4)*. Roll the egg away from you until it is flat in the pan. You can practice this with a sheet of paper and a pencil if you like.

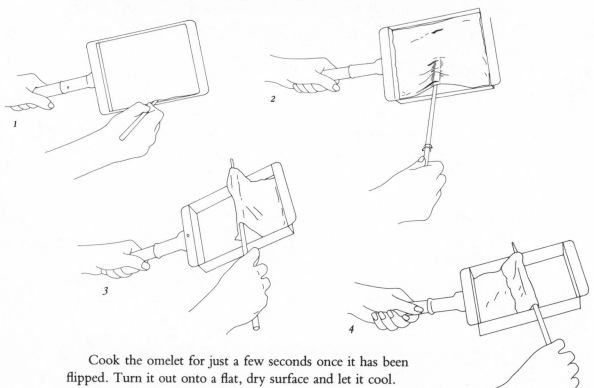

Cook the omelet for just a few seconds once it has been flipped. Turn it out onto a flat, dry surface and let it cool.

NOTE: If you wish to make more than one omelet, repeat the recipe for each additional sheet. Lightly oil your pan between omelets.

厚焼卵 THICK SWEET OMELET *(Atsu Yaki Tamago)*

This is a favorite picnic lunch with Japanese children and a most welcome side dish in an adult meal, too, when garnished with sharp, crisp grated radish. As this omelet is quite sweet, served cold, and looks somewhat like marble cake, you may want to serve it as a dessert for a Western meal. *Serves 4–5.*

⅓ cup *dashi* (Basic Soup Stock,
    page 55)
⅓ cup sugar
1½ teaspoons soy sauce

1½ teaspoons *saké* (rice wine)
½ teaspoon salt
5 eggs
Vegetable oil

Optional garnish:

¼ cup grated *daikon* (Japanese white
    radish)

½ teaspoon soy sauce

In a small saucepan, combine the basic stock, sugar, soy sauce, rice wine and salt and heat, stirring, until the sugar and salt have dissolved. Let the sweet stock cool to room temperature.

In a bowl, beat the eggs well, but try not to incorporate any air as you do so. Pour in the sweet stock and stir to blend together.

Traditionally, this omelet is made in a rectangular pan called a *tamago yaki nabé* (see page 9). If you have only a round 6–7-inch pan, it is possible, with effort, to shape a square as the omelet cooks; or cut the completed rolled omelet into slices.

Lightly oil your pan and pour in one-fourth of the seasoned egg mixture, tilting and rotating the pan to ensure an even coating. Cook the omelet over medium to medium-high heat for a few moments or until the eggs are barely set. Prick any air bubbles with a chopstick if necessary, while the egg is cooking. Fold the omelet and lightly oil the pan around it. Slide the omelet to a different part of the pan and lightly oil again. Before pouring in any more egg, push the omelet to the back of a rectangular pan or the center of a round one. Pour in a third of the remaining egg, lifting *(1)* the already set omelet lightly to allow the new layer of egg to run under it. Cook for a few moments until barely set *(2)* and fold again *(3)*.

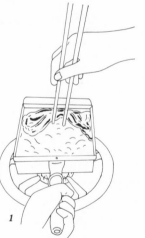

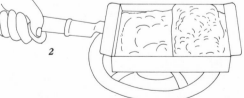

Make 2 more layers in the same manner, being particularly careful with the last folding as this determines the shape of the final dish. Once the block has been made, cook it for a few moments longer on all sides to caramelize the sugar. Turn the block out onto a flat surface and let it cool before cutting it into 8–10 small blocks.

The traditional presentation at table is 2 blocks of omelet on each individual flat dish, garnished with a small mound of grated radish. The radish should be drained of excess liquid after grating, formed into a mound and then barely colored by drizzling a few drops of soy sauce over the top. Spread a bit of radish on the sweet omelet as you're eating.

Deep-Fried Foods

(A G É   M O N O)

There is a considerable amount of deep-frying done in the contemporary Japanese kitchen, despite the fact that oils and fats were not used in the ancient traditional cuisine. Over many centuries, Japanese cooking absorbed some Chinese and European influence, and as a result today one finds several unusual deep-fried dishes. Perhaps the most famous of these is *tempura* (batter-coated fried shrimp and vegetables), which originated around the sixteenth century and owes much to the Portuguese and their fried fritters.

It is common now for Japanese cooks to deep-fry fish, shellfish, meat, poultry and vegetables, coating most foods with either a batter, breadcrumbs, flour or cornstarch before cooking them. Most Japanese fried foods are only lightly seasoned before cooking, then served later with spicy sauces or condiments. One very tasty exception to this rule, though, is marinated and twice-fried Gingery Fried Chicken.

Generally, the recipes here are suitable as main dishes in a Western meal or as featured dishes on a Japanese menu. Fried foods are nicely complemented by a crisp, vinegary green salad or an assortment of pungent pickles.

❖

龍
田
揚

CRISPY FISH *(Tatsuta Agé)*

A pale, thin crust seals in moist and tender fish, which is accented by colorful, fiery condiments and a faintly sweet amber broth. It makes an attractive and unusual main course at a Western meal or an impressive dish to be featured on a Japanese menu, with side dishes of braised vegetables, salt-pickled greens, white rice and clear soup. *Serves 4.*

4 small whole, cleaned butterfish or 8   ¼ cup soy sauce
   small smelts

Amber broth:

¾ cup *dashi* (Basic Soup Stock,
    page 55)
1½ tablespoons soy sauce (preferably
    usu kuchi shōyu, light soy sauce)

2 teaspoons sugar
1 teaspoon *saké* (rice wine)

Condiments:

1 *tōgarashi* (dried hot red pepper)
1½–2-inch piece (about 3 ounces) of
    daikon (Japanese white radish)

1 scallion, green tops only

½ cup cornstarch (preferably Japanese
    katakuriko for really crisp fish)

Vegetable oil for deep frying

Rinse out the belly cavity of each fish well, then pat dry, inside and out, with paper towels. With a sharp knife, lightly score the fleshier parts. Pour ¼ cup soy sauce over all the fish and let them marinate for 5–10 minutes while you prepare the amber broth and condiments.

In a small saucepan, combine the stock, soy sauce, sugar and wine, and heat it through, stirring, until the sugar dissolves. Keep this amber broth warm.

Break open the pod of the hot red pepper and remove all the seeds. Peel the radish and poke several small holes in it, stuffing these with slivers of the dried hot pepper pod. Then grate the stuffed radish into a bowl. The white will be flecked with red (the Japanese poetically call this condiment *momiji oroshi* or "autumn maple leaves") and the mild radish is given a very fiery accent. Chop the green parts of the scallions very fine, and set aside in a small dish.

Lift the marinating fish out of the soy sauce and dredge each thoroughly in cornstarch. Heat the oil to about 350 degrees F. (the cornstarch should sizzle immediately but not burn) and, one at a time, fry the fish. Turn once or twice while frying for 5–6 minutes. Drain the fish well on paper towels and keep the first ones warm in a slow oven while you fry the others.

On each of 4 flat plates, lay a single crispy butterfish or 2 smelts. Drain off any accumulated liquid from the fiery grated radish, and mound a small bit of it on each plate just in front of the fried fish. Sprinkle some of the chopped green scallion over the radish. In each of 4 separate shallow bowls, place some warm amber sauce. Each person stirs fiery radish and scallions to taste into his own bowl of broth, then dips the crispy fish bit by bit into this seasoned sauce.

天
ぷ
ら

BATTER-FRIED SHRIMP AND VEGETABLES *(Tempura)*

Tempura, one of the best-known Japanese dishes in the West, transforms shrimp and a variety of vegetables into delicate, crisp puffs. There are two schools of thought concerning the making of the batter; some chefs insist that just flour and water be used, and others always include some egg. It's really a matter of personal choice—the plain flour-and-water batter produces wispy, lacelike morsels, whereas the addition of egg makes for richer, more golden *tempura.* The recipe here allows for both options.

Traditionally, each diner is provided with a shallow bowl of faintly sweet amber dipping sauce, to which he can add as much grated radish and/or fresh ginger as he wishes. Wedges of fresh lemon or lime make an attractive and delicious garnish, too—squeeze a bit of juice directly on the fried *tempura.*

Unlike most Japanese main courses, this is a dish that should be served piping hot, a good reason for making it in small batches at the table if you've got the equipment. If not, keep freshly fried and drained pieces warm for up to 20 minutes in a 225–250-degree oven. *Serves 4.*

12 jumbo shrimp	2 green bell peppers OR 8 okra pods
1 small eggplant (weighing about ¼ pound)	4 fresh white mushrooms
	1 carrot

Batter:

1 cup flour (preferably low-gluten *tempura ko*)	Vegetable oil for deep frying
1 cup ice water OR 1 egg yolk, beaten, plus enough very cold water to measure 1 cup liquid	

Dipping sauce *(tentsuyu):*

1 cup *dashi* (Basic Soup Stock, page 55)	1 tablespoon *mirin* (syrupy rice wine)
3 tablespoons soy sauce (preferably *usu kuchi shōyu,* light soy sauce)	1 tablespoon sugar

Condiments:

¼ cup grated peeled *daikon* (Japanese white radish)	½ lemon or lime, cut into 4 wedges, optional
2 teaspoons peeled and grated fresh ginger	

Shell and devein the shrimp, leaving the tail sections intact. Lightly score the underbelly to prevent the shrimp from curling when fried. Remove the stem and cut the eggplant in half across its width, and then each half into 4 pieces lengthwise. Cut each of these 8 wedges into a fan shape (see page 27). Cut each green pepper into quarters, lengthwise, and remove the seeds. Or wash the okra pods well and pat them dry. Wash the mushrooms and remove and discard their stems. (Cut very large mushrooms in half.) Pat them dry. Peel the carrot and slice it into matchsticks.

Now prepare your batter: Measure the flour and place all but one tablespoon into a large bowl. Make a well in the center of the flour and pour in half of the plain ice-cold water or the egg-and-cold-water mixture. Stir with light, circular motions, incorporating about half of the flour. The batter should be slightly thinner than that used for pancakes, and small lumps are of no importance. It is better to undermix than overmix the batter.

Make the dipping sauce before frying the *tempura,* by combining the ingredients in a small saucepan and heating it through. You should have at least 1½–2 inches of oil in your pan. Heat the oil to approximately 360 degrees F. and test a bit of your batter. It should sink slightly then rise immediately, puffing out and coloring lightly.

Hold each shrimp by its tail and lightly dust it in a bit of flour. Then dip into the batter before frying it. Fry no more than 3 or 4 at one time to prevent the oil from cooling down too much. The shrimp will puff, turn golden brown and be cooked through in about 2–3 minutes. Turn the shrimp once if necessary, halfway through the frying. Drain well and skim the oil with a net skimmer to remove batter spatterings.

Coat each eggplant piece in the batter and fry, 3 or 4 at a time, skin side down, in the oil for 1 minute. Turn the pieces and continue to fry them for another minute or two until golden and cooked through. Drain well. Skim the oil again.

Pour a bit more egg liquid into the bowl and incorporate more flour to make additional batter. Dip the pepper pieces or okra pods, one at a time, in the batter and fry them (less than a minute for peppers, about 1–1½ minutes for okra). Drain well and skim the oil.

Dip the mushrooms in batter and fry them for about 1 minute. Drain them well. Add more egg liquid to make batter if needed. Toss in the carrot strips and let 4 or 5 stick together, forming several small bundles. Fry the bundles for 1½–2 minutes and drain well.

On each of 4 large individual plates (the Japanese often use woven bamboo trays) lay a sheet of plain white paper or a doily and arrange 3 shrimp, 2 eggplant pieces, 2 pepper pieces or 2 okra pods, 1 mushroom and 1–2 bundles of carrot.

Serve the *tempura* hot, providing each diner with the warm dipping sauce and condiments to be added to the sauce.

PORK CUTLETS *(Tonkatsu)*

と
ん
か
つ

Originally a "foreign" dish of Dutch extraction, these pork cutlets have been thoroughly adopted by the Japanese. Thin boneless chops are lightly breaded and deep fried, then served against a mound of very finely shredded raw cabbage. A dark, thick, spicy sauce to be poured over all provides an interesting flavor accent. *Serves 4.*

4 lean boneless pork chops, each about ⅓ inch thick
¼ cup flour, seasoned with a pinch of salt and *sansho* (Japanese fragrant pepper)
½ beaten whole egg, thinned with 1 teaspoon cold water

¾ cup coarse bread crumbs
Vegetable oil for deep frying
2 cups very finely shredded cabbage
Tonkatsu sōsu (commercially prepared spicy sauce)

Lightly dust the chops in the seasoned flour. Dip them, one at a time, in the egg wash, then coat each of them well with bread crumbs.

There should be at least 1½ inches of oil in your pan and room enough to fry 2 cutlets at once. Heat the oil to approximately 375 degrees F. and test a few bread crumbs, preferably ones with a bit of egg wash clinging to them. The crumbs should sizzle and foam, but not burn, on the surface of the oil. Fry the cutlets, 2 at a time, for about 3 minutes. Turn and fry them for another 3–4 minutes or until golden brown and cooked through.

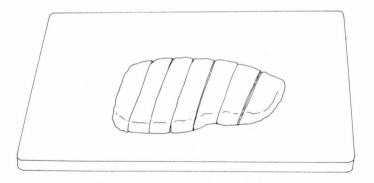

Drain the cutlets on paper towels and slice them across their width into ¼-inch strips (this is primarily for chopstick etiquette). Reassemble each cutlet, leaning it against its own small mound of shredded cabbage. Serve *tonkatsu sōsu* in a pitcher, to be poured to taste by each person.

か ら 揚 GINGERY FRIED CHICKEN *(Kara Agé)*

Marinated in a robustly seasoned soy sauce, dredged, then fried twice for extra crispness, this Japanese version of fried chicken is sure to find many Occidental fans. Serve it hot with rice, pickles and a tart salad like Red and White Salad (page 173), or cold with Spinach in Sesame Seed Dressing (page 182). *Serves 4.*

1½ pounds boneless chicken OR 2½ pounds chicken with bone
¼ cup soy sauce
¼ cup *saké* (rice wine)
1½–2 teaspoons peeled and grated fresh ginger
1 clove garlic

⅓ cup all-purpose flour
⅓ cup cornstarch
¼ teaspoon salt
⅛ teaspoon *sansho* (Japanese fragrant pepper)
Vegetable oil for deep frying
1 lemon, cut into 6–8 wedges

Cut the chicken into pieces about 1 inch square. (If you have bought it with the bone in, you must bone it first.) In a shallow bowl, combine the soy sauce and rice wine, then stir in the grated fresh ginger. Lay the clove of garlic on your cutting board and whack it with the flat side of a broad-bladed vegetable knife or Chinese cleaver. This will smash the garlic, releasing its unique aroma, and at the same time loosen the skin for easy removal. Place the smashed garlic clove in the bottom of the bowl of marinade. Add the chicken pieces and let them marinate for 20 minutes at room temperature or up to 8 hours covered and refrigerated.

Combine the flour, cornstarch, salt and pepper in another shallow bowl or pan. Lift the pieces of chicken, one at a time, from the marinade and dredge them in the seasoned flour mixture. Shake off any excess flour and remove the coated chicken to a plate, letting it stand for 5 minutes. During this time, the coating will absorb some of the marinade and the pieces will change from white to a beige color.

Heat your oil to approximately 350 degrees F. (a pinch of the dredging mixture will sizzle immediately on the surface of the oil without burning) and fry the chicken pieces, in batches of 4–5 each, for less than a minute. This first frying will seal the outer surfaces with a light-colored crust. Drain the chicken well on paper towels and lower the temperature of your oil to about 325 degrees (a pinch of the dredging mixture will sink slightly before sizzling). Refry the chicken, this time in batches of 6–7 pieces each, for 3–4 minutes. Drain the chicken again on paper towels, and serve it hot or at room temperature with lemon wedges.

茄子のはさみ揚

FRIED STUFFED EGGPLANT *(Nasu No Hasami Agé)*

Dark, sleek eggplants are slit and stuffed with a pale, seasoned shrimp filling, then dusted with cornstarch and deep-fried to make an unusually tasty dish. Fresh lemon or lime wedges make an attractive and delicious garnish. Serve the stuffed eggplant with Egg Drop Soup (page 58) and make use of the leftover yolk. String Beans in Thick Bean and Sesame Sauce (page 184) or tart Green Sea Salad (page 177) plus rice could round out the meal nicely. *Serves 4.*

Stuffing:

½ pound uncooked shrimp, shelled and deveined	½ teaspoon *saké* (rice wine)
½ teaspoon fresh ginger, peeled and finely minced	½ teaspoon cornstarch
	1–1½ tablespoons egg white

6–8 small eggplants, each no longer than 4 inches	Vegetable oil for deep frying
1–1½ tablespoons cornstarch	1 lemon or lime, cut into wedges
	Soy sauce for dipping

Pat dry the cleaned shrimp with paper towels and coarsely chop it before feeding it into a food processor, hand grinder or other mechanical device for chopping food fine. Or be more traditional and mash the chopped shrimp in a *suribachi* to a thick paste.

Season the shrimp with the minced ginger and rice wine, then sprinkle ½ teaspoon of cornstarch over all. Let it stand a few seconds, then stir it in before adding the egg white. Mix the paste well and chill it while you cut the eggplants.

Trim the tips of the eggplants before cutting each in half lengthwise. Trim off the rounded uncut sides of each piece (save one of these for testing the temperature of the oil), then slit each lengthwise to within 1 inch of the stem. Carefully open and dust the inside with cornstarch. Score top and bottom of each piece with shallow strokes. Stuff the eggplants with some of the shrimp paste and lightly dust the outside of each stuffed end with more cornstarch.

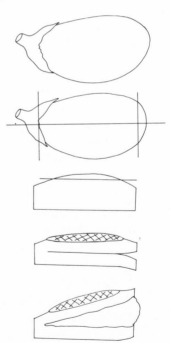

Heat your oil to approximately 350 degrees F. (a sliver of eggplant will float on the surface, the oil bubbling) and fry the stuffed eggplants 3 or 4 at a time, skin side down. Fry for about 5–6 minutes, turning the eggplants several times. Drain well on paper towels and serve hot with lemon or lime wedges. Provide each person with a small dish of soy sauce for dipping.

FRIED CHICKEN BALLS SIMMERED IN DARK SAUCE *(Tsukuné Agé Ni)*

つくね揚煮

This is an unusually seasoned meatball dish that makes a particularly nice appetizer or hors d'oeuvre, a pleasant change from Swedish meatballs at a buffet. The meatballs can be fried in advance and frozen for up to three weeks. Be sure to let them thaw completely at room temperature, though, before simmering in the dark sauce. *Makes 18–20 meatballs.*

¾ pound ground uncooked chicken

¼ teaspoon ginger juice, extracted from peeled and grated fresh ginger (page 34)

1 teaspoon *Sendai miso* (dark bean paste)

Pinch of salt

2–3 tablespoons very finely minced onion

1 teaspoon cornstarch

Vegetable oil (for hands, for deep frying)

Sauce:

¼ cup *mirin* (syrupy rice wine)

¼ cup *dashi* (Basic Soup Stock, page 55)

¼ cup soy sauce

½ teaspoon poppy seeds, optional

In a bowl, season the ground chicken with the ginger juice, bean paste, salt and onion. Mix well, then sprinkle the cornstarch over the soft mixture and let it stand for a few moments before mixing again. Lightly oil your hands to prevent the mixture from sticking to them and form 18–20 little meatballs.

In a deep pan, heat your oil to approximately 350 degrees F. and fry the meatballs in several batches. Fry each batch for 3–4 minutes, turning the balls frequently, until they are cooked through and a deep golden brown. Drain the meatballs well.

In a saucepan, combine the syrupy wine, soup stock and soy sauce, and bring it to a boil. Lower the heat and add the fried chicken balls, simmering them for 5 minutes. Turn the balls frequently as they cook. Remove from the heat and skewer 2 chicken balls on each of 9 or 10 toothpicks and lift them out of the sauce. Serve the meatballs warm or at room temperature and sprinkle a few poppy seeds over them just before serving for an extra taste, texture and color accent.

がんもどき

VEGETARIAN PATTIES *(Ganmodoki)*

These bean curd–based patties are nutritious and economical, a standard dish on Japanese vegetarian menus. I think they are best simmered in a seasoned stock, though freshly fried the patties are delicious with just a bit of grated radish or ginger and a drop of soy sauce. Use whatever vegetables you have to mix with the bean curd. Try peeled carrot; peeled, soaked, and drained burdock root or lotus root; softened *shiitaké* black mushrooms or woodtree ear mushrooms; and boiled bamboo shoots. They are all good singly or in combination with one another. Fried patties may be frozen for up to 1 month, or stored in an airtight container in the refrigerator for 3 or 4 days. *Makes 12 patties, 2–3 per serving* for a side dish with rice, *miso* soup and Green Sea Salad (page 177) or Cucumber and Celery in Apple Dressing (page 174).

1½–2 cakes *tōfu* (soybean curd), about ¾ pound
¼–⅓ cup very finely chopped vegetables
¼–½ teaspoon dry-roasted black sesame seeds
Pinch of salt

2–3 teaspoons *yama imo* (glutinous yams), peeled and grated, OR 1½–2 teaspoons egg white
Vegetable oil for deep frying

Simmering stock:

2 cups *dashi* (Basic Soup Stock, page 55) OR 2 cups liquid from soaking mushrooms (OR 1 cup of each, combined)

2 tablespoons soy sauce
2 tablespoons sugar
1 teaspoon *saké* (rice wine)

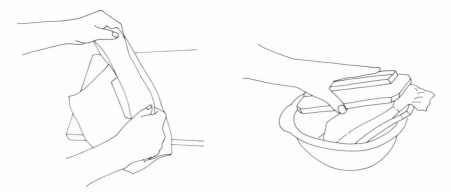

Lift the bean curd out of its storage liquid and wrap it tightly in a kitchen towel. Then place the wrapped bean curd on a flat surface at an angle in a bowl, and place a light weight (several ounces) on top. Let it drain for at least 3–4 hours and up to 12 hours. Remove the bean curd (much firmer now that excess liquid has been pressed out of it) and place it in a clean, dry towel. Gather up the edges of the towel to form a bag and gently squeeze it, mashing the bean curd as you do so.

Empty the mashed bean curd into a bowl and add the chopped vegetables and roasted sesame seeds. Hand mix well and knead for a few minutes. Sprinkle a pinch of salt over the mixture and mix it in, then add the glutinous yam or egg white to bind it all together. Continue to knead for another minute or so, then lightly oil your hands and form 12 patties from the mixture.

In several batches, deep fry the patties at medium-low (300–325 degrees F.) temperature for 2–3 minutes or until they float on the surface, well puffed. Flip them over and continue to fry for another few minutes until golden. Drain the patties well on paper towels and/or a rack.

In a saucepan, combine the simmering stock ingredients and bring to a boil, stirring until the sugar is melted. Add the fried patties and lower the heat to maintain a steady simmer. For best results, simmer with a dropped lid, or turn the patties several times so that all surfaces have a chance to absorb the seasoned stock. Cook for 5–6 minutes, or until the stock has been reduced by half. Serve warm or at room temperature, with a bit of stock ladled over the patties.

NOTE: Handling glutinous yam may irritate the skin on your hands—wear gloves when peeling and grating; use a spoon for mixing.

Steamed Foods

(MUSHI MONO)

The Japanese enjoy a wide variety of subtly seasoned steamed foods, and this section begins with two egg dishes: one a warm pudding filled with bits of shrimp, chicken and vegetables, the other a silky-smooth chilled custard. Following are two elegant side dishes—ethereal Turnip Clouds and shiny Silver Boats—both to be served piping hot. Then there is abalone steamed with a splash of wine and a pinch of salt, served with a tart soy sauce for dipping. Chicken is similarly steamed with wine and salt, but finished off very differently; plunged into an icy bath, patted dry and sauced with a creamy sesame seed dressing, the Cold Steamed Chicken is absolutely delicious. Finally, there is a tasty Fish and Noodle Casserole that is simple to prepare and makes a wonderful luncheon or light dinner entrée.

❖

茶椀蒸 STEAMED EGG PUDDING (*Chawan Mushi*)

This is a classic side dish, often part of a full-course formal dinner. Serve these puddings in small individual cups with deep-fried, braised or grilled foods. *Serves 6.*

4 eggs
1½ cups cold *dashi* (Basic Soup Stock, page 55)
¾ teaspoon salt
1 scant teaspoon *usu kuchi shōyu* (light soy sauce)
1¼ teaspoons *mirin* (syrupy rice wine)
6 small uncooked shrimp, shelled and deveined

½ small uncooked chicken breast, skinned, boned and sliced thin on diagonal (cutting instructions for *sogi-giri*, page 26)
5–6 button mushrooms, washed, trimmed and sliced thin
12 snow peas, blanched in boiling salted water

Break the eggs into a bowl and beat them well. Add the cold soup stock, salt, soy sauce and syrupy wine, and stir to combine all well. Let the egg mixture stand for a few minutes before straining it twice through an *uragoshi* (see page 33) or a fine-meshed strainer to remove all air bubbles and lumps.

In each of 6 individual heat-proof 6-ounce cups, place 1 shrimp and some chicken and mushroom slices. Pour in the strained egg mixture to fill each cup two-thirds full. Place the cups in a steamer and steam over high heat for 2 minutes, then reduce the heat to very low and continue to steam for 15 minutes. Remove the lid of your steamer, add 2 snow peas to each cup and re-cover. Steam for 20–30 seconds. Carefully remove the hot cups and serve immediately. Eat with a spoon.

卵
豆
腐

COLD EGG CUSTARD *(Tamago-dōfu)*

Cool and smooth, this custard makes a lovely side dish for a summer luncheon or dinner. *Serves 4.*

3 large eggs	Pinch of salt
⅔–¾ cup cold *dashi* (Basic Soup Stock, page 55)	Pinch of sugar
1 teaspoon *mirin* (syrupy rice wine)	Drop of *usu kuchi shōyu* (light soy sauce)

Sauce:

⅓ cup *dashi* (Basic Soup Stock, page 55)	½ tablespoon *mirin* (syrupy rice wine)
½ teaspoon *usu shōyu* (light soy sauce)	½ teaspoon sugar

Garnish:

1 teaspoon grated fresh ginger
2–3 teaspoons finely minced scallions

Break the eggs into a measuring cup and beat them until well combined. Let the foam settle a bit before reading the measurement; you should have ⅔–¾ cup beaten eggs. Pour the eggs into a bowl and measure out an equal amount of basic soup stock. Stir the eggs and stock before adding 1 teaspoon syrupy rice wine, a pinch of salt and sugar and a drop of soy sauce. Stir again to mix all well. Strain the seasoned egg mixture through an *uragoshi* (page 33) or a fine-meshed strainer into a bowl to ensure a smooth, foamless liquid.

Traditionally, the custard is steamed in a rectangular metal mold called a *nagashi-bako* (details on page 39). If you don't have one, I suggest you use individual heat-proof bowls, since removal of the cooked custard from ordinary molds is very difficult. Pour the egg mixture through an *uragoshi* or strainer into your mold or individual bowls. If you are using a metal mold, place it on several wooden chopsticks laid flat across the rack of your steamer (metal mold directly against metal rack provides too great a conduction of heat and the bottom of the custard will scorch). If you are using glass or ceramic bowls this probably won't be necessary.

Steam the custard over low heat for 10–12 minutes. Ideally your custard should have a smooth, glassy surface with no air bubbles, water spots or bumps to mar it. You can test for doneness with a toothpick; if no liquid fills the puncture point your custard is cooked.

Remove the mold or bowls from your steamer and let them cool for 5–10 minutes on a rack. If using a *nagashi-bako,* unmold the custard by lifting up the inner tray and loosening its edges with a damp knife. Slide the custard out onto a cutting board and slice it into 4 blocks. Using a spatula or knife, carefully transfer the blocks to individual deep plates or bowls (frosty glass dishes look particularly cool on a summer day).

Combine the sauce ingredients in a small saucepan and heat through until the sugar has melted. Chill the custards and sauce separately for at least 1 hour and up to 8 hours. Just before serving, pour a few spoonfuls of sauce around the blocks of custard. Or, if the sauce is to accompany individual custards still in their cups, serve it in a separate pitcher. In either case, garnish each portion with a small mound of grated fresh ginger and a sprinkling of minced scallions.

かぶら蒸 TURNIP CLOUDS *(Kabura Mushi)*

This is a delicately seasoned, elegant little side dish to serve with more intensely flavored fish or meat courses. *Serves 4.*

4 jumbo shrimp	1 egg white
3–4 white turnips	Pinch of salt

Sauce:

½ cup *dashi* (Basic Soup Stock, page 55)	Pinch of salt
¼ teaspoon *usu kuchi shōyu* (light soy sauce)	¼ teaspoon *saké* (rice wine)
	¼ teaspoon cornstarch

Garnish:

1 teaspoon *wasabi* (fiery green
    horseradish) paste or reconstituted
    powder OR 2–3 sprigs *mitsuba*
    (trefoil) or coriander

Shell and devein the shrimp, then cut each into 4–5 pieces. Divide them up among 4 small bowls (or use teacups, preferably without handles) and lay the pieces at the bottom.

Peel and grate the turnips onto a kitchen towel. Bring the corners of the towel together to form a small bag and twist the top closed, squeezing out about half the liquid. You should have approximately ½ cup grated turnip.

In a bowl, beat the egg white with the pinch of salt until soft peaks form. Add the grated turnip, mixing in gently but thoroughly.

Divide the turnip and egg-white mixture among the 4 bowls, mounding it softly to cover the pieces of shrimp. Steam the bowls of turnip clouds for 10–12 minutes.

In the meantime, season the basic stock with light soy sauce, salt and rice wine, and heat it through for several minutes. Dissolve the cornstarch in an equal amount of cold water and stir it into the seasoned stock. Cook over medium heat, stirring, until the sauce thickens slightly. Pour some of the sauce over each steamed turnip cloud. Garnish the top of each portion with either a small dab of fiery green horseradish (to be dissolved in the surrounding sauce by each diner), or chop sprigs of trefoil or coriander and scatter them over each "cloud." Serve piping hot.

 ## SILVER BOATS *(Gin-gami Mushi)*

Shiny packages of foil containing bite-size pieces of delicately seasoned shrimp, chicken and vegetables are steamed, then served very hot as a side dish with grilled or raw fish. *Serves 4.*

4 large shrimp	Pinch of sugar
½ small chicken breast, about ¼ pound	4–5 inches softened *konbu* (kelp); leftovers from stock making are perfect
2 dried *shiitaké* (black Oriental mushrooms)	¼ cup strained liquid from soaking black mushrooms
½ cup warm water	

½ teaspoon soy sauce

¼ teaspoon *saké* (rice wine)

Pinch of salt

4 ten-by-six-inch sheets of
aluminum foil

4 thin slices of lemon

Devein and shell the shrimp, leaving the tail pieces intact. Remove skin and bone from the chicken and cut it into ¼-inch-thick slices, slightly on the diagonal (see *sogi-giri* cutting, page 26). Cut each of these in half or thirds to make bite-size pieces approximately 1½ inches square. Soak the dried mushrooms in warm water to which a pinch of sugar has been added, for 15–20 minutes. Strain and reserve the soaking liquid. Remove and discard the stems from the mushrooms and slice into quarters. Soak these again in plain warm water to cover for 10 minutes. Squeeze the mushroom pieces dry and discard this secondary liquid. Season the original strained mushroom liquid with soy sauce, rice wine and salt, and stir it. Cut kelp left from stock making into 1-inch squares. Or soak dried kelp in warm water to cover for 15 minutes before cutting.

   Lay the sheets of aluminum foil on your work counter and place several pieces of kelp in the middle of each. On top of the kelp, lay a slice of lemon, 1 shrimp, several chicken slices and 2 mushroom quarters. Gather up the end pieces of foil as illustrated to form a boatlike shape. Pour in a tablespoon or so of seasoned mushroom liquid and twist top edges of foil together. Place the silver boats in a steamer and steam for 10–12 minutes. Remove with pot-holdered hands and serve immediately.

あわびの酒蒸 STEAMED ABALONE *(Awabi No Saka Mushi)*

Steamed with a minimum of seasonings, this abalone dish is delicate and tender, making it a lovely hors d'oeuvre. Prepared in this manner, it may well change the minds of many who think of abalone as rubbery and tasteless. If you can't find abalone, try steaming shucked cherrystone clams on open half shells for only 2–3 minutes. *Serves 4–6.*

2–3 fresh abalone, on the half shell, each weighing about ½ pound

1½–2 teaspoons salt

1–1½ tablespoons *saké* (rice wine)

2 tablespoons fresh lemon or lime juice

¼ cup soy sauce

Wedges of lemon or lime

Scrub the shells lightly and rinse off any sand. Trim the abalone meat of any spongy growth around the edges. Lightly salt the abalone and place them, shell down, in a steamer. Pour ½ tablespoon of rice wine over each abalone.

Over high heat, bring the water in the bottom of your steamer to a rapid boil. Adjust the heat to maintain a steady flow of steam and cook the abalone for 20–25 minutes. Test by piercing the flesh with a toothpick; the abalone should be very tender. Pour off the steaming juices and remove the abalone meat from the shells. (Rinse and save the shells if you wish to use them for serving.)

Cut the abalone, slightly on the diagonal (*sogi-giri* cut, page 26), into ⅛-inch-thick slices. Arrange the slices on a platter, or return them to their shells. Make a dipping sauce by combining the fruit juice and soy sauce, providing additional wedges of lemon or lime for those who wish. Serve warm (but do not reheat) or at room temperature.

鳥の酒蒸 COLD STEAMED CHICKEN (*Tori No Saka Mushi*)

Moist and tender, this chicken dish is sure to become a hot-weather favorite. Serve it with the sesame sauce suggested here or spicy mustard. *Serves 3–4.*

2–3 boned chicken breasts, each weighing about ⅓ pound

½ teaspoon salt

1 tablespoon *saké* (rice wine)

Ice water

1 large tomato

1 cucumber

Dipping sauce:

2 tablespoons white sesame seeds

1 scant teaspoon superfine sugar

1 teaspoon soy sauce

⅛ teaspoon sesame oil

2–3 tablespoons strained broth from steaming

Lightly salt the chicken breasts all over and lay them, skin side up, on a heat-proof plate with deep flanges. Pour the rice wine over the chicken and steam for 25 minutes.

Remove the chicken breasts from the plate, being careful not to spill the broth collected there. Plunge the chicken breasts, one at a time, into a bowl of ice water until all fat has floated to the surface of the water and the meat is cool enough to handle. Gently "wash" the chicken and remove the skin, if you prefer. Pat the chicken breasts dry and cut them, slightly on the diagonal, into thin slices (*sogi-giri* cutting, page 26).

Decorate your serving platter with tomato and cucumber slices. The Japanese have a way of cutting cucumbers into attractive thin curlicues which look particularly refreshing in hot weather. Follow the instructions for *kaminari* cutting on page 24 if you wish to follow suit. Arrange the chicken slices attractively on your platter and chill for at least 30 minutes and up to several hours.

Dry roast the white sesame seeds and grind them to a paste in a *suribachi* or a blender. Add the sugar, soy sauce and sesame oil, blending well after each addition. Strain the broth that collected on the heat-proof plate while steaming and thin the sesame sauce with about 2 tablespoons of it. Chill the sauce before serving it with the cold chicken.

白
身
の
そ
ば
蒸

FISH AND NOODLE CASSEROLE (*Shiromi No Soba Mushi*)

This makes a very nice light luncheon or dinner when served with a crisp, tart salad or an assortment of pickles. *Serves 3–4.*

¾-pound fillets of sole, halibut or flounder

¼ teaspoon salt

6–8 ounces fresh OR 2–3 ounces fresh-dried *soba* (buckwheat noodles)

½ cup *dashi* (Basic Soup Stock, page 55)

2 tablespoons *usu kuchi shōyu* (light soy sauce)

1 tablespoon *mirin* (syrupy rice wine)

1 teaspoon sugar

2–3 green scallions, chopped

Use an attractive, 2–3-quart heat-proof casserole at least 1½ inches deep. Lightly salt the fish fillets and lay them, in a single layer if possible, on the bottom of your casserole. Place dish in a steamer and steam the fish over high heat for 3–5 minutes. Carefully remove the hot casserole and pour off the accumulated liquid.

Cook the *soba* noodles according to the instructions on page 97 or 98. Drain the noodles, rinse them under cold water and drain them again. Lay the cooked noodles over the fish.

In a small saucepan, combine the soup stock, soy sauce, syrupy rice wine and sugar. Stirring, heat it until the sugar melts. Pour the broth over the noodles and fish and resteam for 2–3 minutes over medium heat.

Garnish the casserole with chopped scallions and serve immediately.

Mixed, Sauced
and Tossed Foods

(S U N O M O N O / A É M O N O / S A S H I M I / A N K A K É)

The Japanese eat an exciting variety of mixed, dressed and sauced foods. You'll find
some of them are uncooked seafood and fish dishes, and these are known as *sashimi*
or "fresh slices." Occasionally marinated, more often not, *sashimi* is served with
aromatic and decorative garnishes and soy sauce for dipping. Whether cooked or
uncooked, the dishes in this section make delectable appetizers, side dishes and salads
to serve with either a Western or Japanese meal.

    I've started with a recipe for a basic sweet and sour sauce used in most *su no mono*
("vinegared things") and several tart and refreshing vegetable, fruit and seafood salads
follow that. Then come the *aé mono* ("mixed things") and *sashimi,* in which vegetables
and seafood, both cooked and raw, are combined with some very interesting salad
dressings and dips. Sesame seeds, walnuts and soybeans in several guises play a major
role in seasoning. Finally, *an kaké* ("thickly sauced" foods) are represented by two
vegetable and meat combinations and a classic raw tuna and potato dish.

❖

甘酢 SWEET AND SOUR SAUCE *(Amazu)*

This is a simple, basic sauce to be used in many recipes. It will keep for weeks
refrigerated in a covered glass or ceramic container. *Makes about ½ cup.*

½ cup rice vinegar
¼ cup sugar
¼ teaspoon salt

Combine the ingredients listed above in a small saucepan. Stirring with a wooden
spoon, cook the sauce over low heat until the sugar and salt melt. Allow the sauce
to cool to room temperature before using or storing it.

紅
白
な
ま
す

RED AND WHITE SALAD (*Kōhaku Namasu*)

In Japan, red and white are the colors of felicity, and dishes combining these are thought to be particularly festive. Here the deep orange tones of the carrot and dried apricot provide the "red," while the snowy *daikon* radish provides the "white." This vegetable and fruit salad is a classic in its native land, commonly served at the New Year. It could easily accompany grilled fish or roasted poultry any time of the year, though. *Makes about 1 cup to serve 3–4.*

¼ teaspoon salt
Generous ⅔ cup *daikon* (Japanese white
    radish) peeled and cut into fine
    julienne strips
Scant ¼ cup carrot, peeled and cut into
    fine julienne strips

2–3 dried apricots, sliced into fine
    julienne strips
Peel from ¼ of a lemon, sliced into
    fine julienne strips
⅓ cup *amazu* (Sweet and Sour Sauce,
    preceding recipe)

Lightly salt the cut raw vegetables, each in its own bowl. Let the vegetables stand for 5 minutes before squeezing out and discarding all accumulated liquid. Combine the slightly wilted carrot and radish and toss in the apricots and lemon peel. Pour the sweet and sour sauce over the vegetables and fruit and allow the mixture to marinate for at least 30 minutes or up to 3 days if covered and refrigerated.

    To serve, drain the vegetables and fruit of all excess sweet and sour sauce. For a particularly attractive presentation hollow out 6–8 lemon halves and fill them with the salad. Serve chilled or at room temperature.

な
め
こ
の
み
ぞ
れ
和
え

SLIPPERY MUSHROOMS IN SLEET SAUCE
(*Naméko No Mizoré Aé*)

Here is a dish that combines several tastes and textures that may well be new to you. Slippery, earthy mushrooms float in a sweet and sour sauce to which grated radish adds a sharp, crunchy accent. The Japanese like to eat this dish with salt-grilled fish though it could be served with roasted poultry, too. *Serves 4–6.*

¾ cup canned *naméko* (slippery
    mushrooms), drained
2 tablespoons soy sauce
¼ cup peeled, grated *daikon* (Japanese
    white radish)

¼–⅓ cup *amazu* (Sweet and Sour
    Sauce, page 172)

Blanch the slippery mushrooms in boiling water for about 1 minute and drain them. Pour the soy sauce over the mushrooms and let them marinate for about 10 minutes.

Place the grated radish on a clean kitchen towel, and gather up the edges to enclose the radish in a small bag. Twist and squeeze lightly. Run it under cold water for a few seconds and then squeeze out all liquid again. Empty the contents of the bag into a small bowl. Add sweet and sour sauce, a few spoonfuls at a time, until the grated radish is barely suspended in it and takes on the appearance of semi-melted snow.

Drain the mushrooms of any excess soy sauce and toss them in the sleet sauce. To serve, mound about 2 tablespoons of the mushrooms in sleet sauce on small individual plates. Serve chilled or at room temperature.

CUCUMBER AND CELERY IN APPLE DRESSING *(Kyūri No Ringo Aé)*

きゅうりのりんご和え

Here is a tart and crunchy salad that goes very well with poultry and fish. Serve it on a bed of lettuce leaves, if you like. *Serves 2–3.*

1 cucumber, preferably unwaxed	½ red Delicious apple
1 stalk celery	1½–2 tablespoons chilled *amazu* (Sweet
Pinch of salt	and Sour Sauce, page 172)

Dice the cucumber into ¼-inch cubes, peeling it first if it is waxed. Slice the celery lengthwise into 3–4 strips, then across into ¼-inch pieces. Lightly salt the cut vegetables, then prepare the dressing.

Spread a clean, dry, white linen handkerchief or napkin on your cutting board. Peel and core the apple, then grate it onto the spread cloth. Work quickly to prevent discoloration. Lift up the edges of the cloth and let some of the juice drain out before transferring the grated apple to a glass bowl. Add chilled sweet and sour sauce to taste and stir to distribute the apple gratings.

Squeeze the salted cucumber and celery pieces lightly and drain off any accumulated liquid. Toss the vegetables in the apple dressing and serve chilled or at room temperature.

酢
ば
す

SWEET AND SOUR LOTUS ROOT *(Subasu)*

Whenever I see fresh lotus root, I buy it and make a large batch of *subasu*. These crisp, white, tart-yet-sweet slices add interest to so many foods. Traditionally a part of many vinegared rice dishes, they are particularly delicious tossed into a Western salad and make a decorative and flavorful garnish to grilled fish or poultry. *Subasu* is relatively simple to make (perhaps the hardest task is finding fresh lotus root) and will keep, if refrigerated, for several months. Neither the fresh vegetable nor the marinated one should be frozen, though. Dried lotus root is a bit easier to find but unfortunately cannot substitute in this recipe. Fresh lotus root is in season in the spring and fall, so look in your favorite Oriental market for it then. *Makes about 30 slices.*

1 small fresh lotus root, weighing
  about 6 ounces
1½ cups cold water

2 tablespoons rice vinegar
½–¾ cup *amazu* (Sweet and Sour
  Sauce, page 172)

Peel the lotus root and cut it into very thin round slices. To prevent discoloration, drop the slices immediately into a ceramic or glass bowl filled with acidulated water (made from 1½–2 cups cold water and 2–3 tablespoons rice vinegar). Soak the lotus root in the acidulated water for at least 5 minutes before rinsing under cold water.

   In an enamel or glass saucepan combine the water and rice vinegar called for in the list of ingredients. Bring this acidulated water to a boil and cook the lotus root slices for 2–3 minutes (they will still be crisp). Drain the cooked lotus root well and marinate the slices in sweet and sour sauce to cover, in a glass or ceramic container. Marinate the slices for at least 2 hours. Before serving, drain the lotus root slices of excess sauce.

   For longer storage, use a glass jar sealed with paraffin or a tight-fitting lid. Because lids sometimes rust around the rims, it is a good idea to cover the jars first with plastic wrap. Always use a clean utensil to extract slices. Be sure that there is enough sweet and sour sauce to cover what's left (exposure to the air will cause discoloration and spoilage). Keep the jars refrigerated.

黄
身
酢
和
え

TART YELLOW SAUCE *(Kimizu Aé)*

This is a velvety egg sauce for napping boiled seafood and green vegetables. Piquant in flavor and smooth in texture, it combines beautifully with chunks of lobster meat, crabmeat, shrimp, squid or octopus and thin-sliced cucumber rounds, fresh cooked asparagus or string beans. *Yields about ¼ cup; use about 1 tablespoon per serving.*

3 egg yolks
3 tablespoons *amazu* (Sweet and Sour
    Sauce, page 172)

Combine the yolks and 2–2½ tablespoons of the sweet and sour sauce. Stir with a wooden spoon until it is well mixed.

    The cooking of this sauce is a bit tricky. Strong, direct heat is necessary to ensure gloss and vivid color, though it increases the danger of scorching and curdling. The Japanese resolve this by stirring the sauce constantly and cooking it at repeated short intervals over a medium-high flame. In the interim they cool the saucepan on a damp towel. The rhythm is something like 10 seconds heat then 5 seconds rest on the damp towel. It should take no longer than 1–1½ minutes for the sauce to thicken to the consistency of loosely scrambled eggs. Don't worry about lumpiness at this stage.

    Let the sauce cool for a minute or two before transferring it to a dry, white linen towel or a table napkin. Gather up the ends of the towel to enclose the thick sauce in a small bag *(1)*. Twist the bag, forcing the sauce through the weave of the cloth *(2)*. Scrape off the smooth, thick yellow sauce from the outside of the bag (lumps will have smoothed out) and place in a small bowl *(3)*. Thin it to the consistency of heavy cream with the remaining sweet and sour sauce. Tart yellow sauce will keep well for 1–2 days, refrigerated and covered.

    Chill the yellow sauce, seafood and vegetables separately. Assemble your salad just before serving: a mound of pink-tinted seafood, a bundle of verdant vegetables, and a dollop of bright yellow sauce.

1

2

3

きゅうりと若布の酢の物

GREEN SEA SALAD (*Kyūri To Wakamé No Su No Mono*)

This healthful salad combines crisp cucumbers and soft, slippery *wakamé* (lobe-leaf; a kind of sea vegetation) in a tart dressing. Young, tender tangles of *wakamé* are harvested in the early spring and the Japanese love to eat this salad on the first warm days of the year. *Serves 3–4.*

1 ounce tangle dried *wakamé* (lobe-leaf)	2 teaspoons sugar
4 tablespoons rice vinegar	1 cucumber, preferably unwaxed
3 tablespoons soy sauce	¼ teaspoon salt

Soak the lobe-leaf tangle in a large bowl of warm water for 20–25 minutes. It will soften and expand to many times its original volume. Rinse the softened vines under cold water, then pat dry. Remove and discard any tough stems, and chop the lobe-leaf coarsely.

In a small saucepan, combine the vinegar, soy sauce and sugar, and heat it, stirring, until the sugar melts. Chill the dressing.

Peel your cucumber, if it is waxed, before slicing it in half lengthwise. If the seeds are very large or numerous, scrape them out. Place the cucumber flat on the board and slice thin. Lightly salt it and let it stand for a few minutes before gently squeezing the slices. Drain off any excess liquid before combining the cucumber slices with the chopped lobe-leaf. Pour the chilled dressing over all and toss. Serve chilled or at room temperature.

変り昆布巻

MARINATED FISH ROLL (*Kawari Konbu Maki*)

Use flounder, fluke, sole, sea or striped bass to make this unusually attractive and delicious appetizer. Save some kelp from stock making (covered in plastic wrap it will keep in the refrigerator for 3–4 days) and the next time you're in the fish market ask for a small piece of the freshest fillet they have. Make up a fish roll—it will keep quite nicely for 4–5 days—and slice off a few pieces at a time. *Serves 3–4.*

Dashi konbu (kelp for stock making); a piece 10–12 inches long and 3–4 inches wide when softened	About 1½ cups rice vinegar
	Peel from ¼ lemon OR small knob of fresh ginger (about the size of your thumbnail)
4–5 ounces very fresh fillet of fish	
½ teaspoon salt	Soy sauce for dipping, optional

If you have a broad piece of kelp left over from stock making, that is perfect. Place it in a pot with a quart of cold water. Bring the water to a boil rapidly, then remove the pot from the heat. Let the kelp sit in the broth until it is cool enough to handle. (Save this broth and use it in lieu of regular *dashi* stock in other recipes.) If you are using a dried piece of kelp, let it cook for 2 minutes before removing the pot from the heat.

Lay the fish fillet on a flat dish and lightly salt all surfaces. Put the fish aside for 10–15 minutes and you'll notice a bit of liquid has accumulated. Pat this away gently with paper towels. Cut the fillet in half, lengthwise, slightly on the diagonal. Now lay the two pieces side by side in a small, shallow dish and pour in enough rice vinegar to cover the pieces entirely. Let the fish marinate for at least 30 minutes, but not more than 1 hour, at room temperature.

In the meantime, cut the lemon peel into the thinnest possible slivers. Or peel the ginger and slice it as thin as you can. Pile these slices up, then cut them into very thin threads.

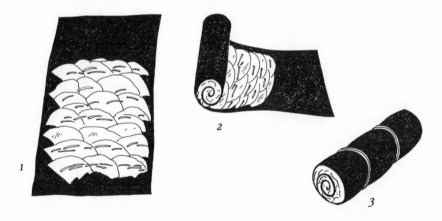

Lift the fish from the rice vinegar, reserving the vinegar for later. Place the fish on a cutting board and, using the sharpest knife you have, cut very thin slices on the diagonal. The outer surfaces of the fish will have already turned opaque from contact with the vinegar; the inner surfaces may still be translucent. Move the slices to a corner of your board and wipe your cutting surface dry before laying down the broad ribbon of kelp. Now arrange the slices of fish on the kelp, leaving a ½-inch border *(1)*. Scatter lemon peel or ginger threads over the fish. Roll the kelp and fish tightly *(2)* and tie up the roll securely at both ends with string *(3)*. You may find the rolling a bit difficult the first time because of the slippery nature of the kelp. You can always dismantle the roll, wipe the kelp with toweling, and start again. You'll get the knack of it after one or two tries, I'm sure. Cut the roll in half if necessary to fit it into a wide-mouthed glass or ceramic container just large enough to accommodate the roll or rolls with 1 inch of head space. Pour the reserved rice vinegar over and add more if necessary to cover the roll or rolls completely. Cover your container and marinate for at least 3 hours at room temperature or 8 hours in the refrigerator.

Just before serving, lift the roll or rolls from the marinade. Insert decorative toothpicks evenly spaced about ⅓ inch apart along the roll. Now remove the string. With a very sharp knife, slice between the toothpicks to make bite-size pieces. Serve the rolls chilled or at room temperature, with soy sauce for dipping, if you wish.

CUTTLEFISH IN PINK DRESSING *(Ika No Masago Aé)*

いかの真砂和え

Satiny ribbons of raw cuttlefish dressed with salty cod roe make very elegant and unusual hors d'oeuvres. This dish requires the very freshest cuttlefish but once made will keep well for several days, refrigerated. *Serves 4–5.*

1 small fresh cuttlefish or squid, filleted (about ½ pound)	½ teaspoon salt
1 tablespoon *saké* (rice wine)	1 fresh cod roe (about 3 ounces)

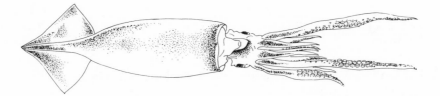

Remove the skin from tail to head and slit open the conical body of the cuttlefish or squid if this hasn't already been done. Cut off the tail "flaps" and reserve these with the legs trimmed of any suction cups. These squid or cuttlefish bits and pieces are good salt-grilled on a net and served with lemon wedges and soy sauce.

Lay the triangular-shaped fillet on your board and sprinkle half the rice wine and all the salt over the cuttlefish. Let it stand for 4–5 minutes, unrefrigerated.

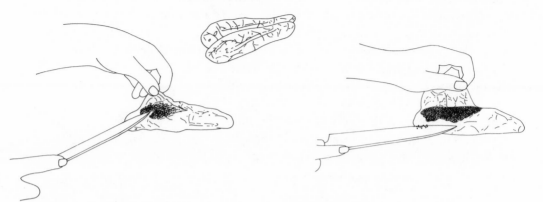

Slit open the cod roe and carefully scrape out the pink eggs, discarding the sac. Transfer the eggs to a small dry bowl and pour the remaining rice wine over them. Stir to distribute evenly.

Pat dry the cuttlefish and slice it in half or thirds lengthwise, then across into ribbons ⅛ inch wide. Toss the ribbons in the pink dressing and cover and refrigerate if not serving immediately.

小鯛の刺身   F R E S H   P O R G Y *(Kodai No Sashimi)*

Tender, translucent slices of impeccably fresh porgy look particularly inviting as they lie mounded on top of dark, aromatic *shiso* leaves, with a background of crisp, curly radish strips. Fiery horseradish and soy sauce served on the side provide just the right flavor accent to this elegant appetizer. *Serves 4–6.*

1 fresh whole porgy (weighing about
    1½ pounds)
Scant ¼ teaspoon salt
4–6 *shiso* leaves (green aromatic leaves
    of the beefsteak plant)
2-inch piece of *daikon* (Japanese white
    radish)

1–1½ teaspoons *wasabi* (fiery green
    horseradish) paste or reconstituted
    powder
4–6 tablespoons soy sauce

Fillet the fish (see pages 28–30) and lightly salt it. Let the fillets stand for 5–10 minutes (the salt will cause the fish to "sweat" a bit) then gently pat away any accumulated moisture. Slice the fish very thin and slightly on the diagonal. Chill until serving time.

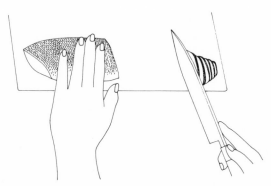

Rinse the *shiso* leaves under cold water, and one at a time pat them dry. Then lay a single leaf on the palm of your open hand and slap it with your other open hand. This will release the leaf's unique aroma. Place a single leaf on each of 4–6 small plates. Peel the radish, then cut it *kaminari* style (page 24). Arrange some curly radish strips in a mound behind each *shiso* leaf.

Arrange the fish slices to make a small mountain in the center of each leaf. To the side of each "mountain" place a dab of horseradish (if you can coax it into a "hill" shape, all the better). In separate individual small plates with flanges put 1 tablespoon of soy sauce for each person. At the table, each person dissolves some of the horseradish in the soy sauce, then dips the fish lightly in it before eating.

NOTE: Red snapper, tile fish, grouper, flounder, sole and halibut also make delicious *sashimi* (raw fish). Just be sure that the fillets you buy are fresh enough for such a use. (Ideally, the fish should be no more than 8 hours out of water and refrigerated but not frozen in the interim. Filleting should be done as close to serving time as possible.)

白 和 え JAPANESE VEGETABLES WITH THICK WHITE DRESSING *(Shira Aé)*

Tōfu, a smooth custard-like cake often referred to as "bean curd," is a common ingredient in many Japanese dishes. Here it is used to make a rather bland dressing for cooked vegetables. In a Japanese meal, this nicely balances the more intense flavors of braised or pickled foods. The thick white dressing resembles fine-curd cottage cheese in appearance, though its taste is unique. This dressing can be nicely adapted to a Western meal by using it to stuff tomatoes. Thick white dressing will keep for 1–2 days covered in the refrigerator. *Yields about ⅔ cup, to serve 3–4.*

White dressing:

½ cake *tōfu* (soybean curd), about 6 ounces
1¼ tablespoons superfine sugar
Pinch of salt

Drop of soy sauce (preferably *usu kuchi shōyu*; soy sauce)
½ teaspoon *saké* (rice wine)

5–6 *kikuragé* ("woodtree ears," mushrooms)
⅓ cake *konnyaku* (a pearly-toned gelatinous cake made from a tuber vegetable)

⅓ cup *dashi* (Basic Soup Stock, page 55)
2 tablespoons sugar
2 tablespoons soy sauce
¼ cup carrot, cut in fine julienne strips

Boil the soybean curd in water to cover for 2–3 minutes and then drain it in a cloth-lined colander. Gathering up the edges of the cloth to make a bag, twist and squeeze, to wring out all excess moisture. Mash the soybean curd before seasoning it with the sugar, salt, soy sauce and rice wine listed in the dressing ingredients.

Soak the dried mushrooms in warm water for 15–20 minutes. They will soften and expand to many times their original size. Rinse the softened but slippery mushrooms and pat them dry before slicing into extra fine julienne strips.

Cut the *konnyaku* into julienne strips and blanch it in boiling water for 1–2 minutes. Drain, and let it cool to room temperature naturally.

Combine the soup stock, sugar and soy sauce in a small saucepan. Over low heat, simmer the carrot, *konnyaku* and mushrooms in this liquid for about 15 minutes. Drain the vegetables and let them cool before tossing in thick white dressing. Serve at room temperature, or slightly chilled.

SPINACH WITH SESAME SEED DRESSING
(Hōrensō No Goma Aé)

ほうれん草のごま和え

This is a standard dish served in almost every home and restaurant throughout Japan. As soon as you taste it, you'll understand the reason for its wide popularity. Variations on this theme are possible with cooked-but-still-crisp green beans or cooked-until-tender Brussels sprouts. *Serves 3–4.*

¾ pound fresh spinach
3 tablespoons white sesame seeds

1 tablespoon superfine sugar
2½ tablespoons soy sauce

Remove the stems before washing and patting dry the spinach leaves. Bring a large pot of salted water to a rolling boil and cook the spinach until it barely wilts. Drain and refresh the spinach under running cold water. Squeeze out excess moisture before chopping the spinach coarsely.

Dry roast the sesame seeds (see page 16) over medium-high heat and transfer them to a *suribachi* (page 17) while still warm. Crush the sesame seeds well before adding the sugar. Continue to grind the sesame and sugar until the mixture is quite pasty, then add the soy sauce and blend well. If using a blender or food processor, you may need to double or triple quantities in order to have enough volume to engage the blades of your machine; store excess in a tightly sealed jar and refrigerate.

Toss the chopped spinach in the sesame seed dressing and serve chilled or at room temperature.

くるみ和え WALNUT PASTE *(Kurumi Aé)*

In some northern areas of Japan, walnuts are used instead of sesame seeds to make a thick, rich paste for dressing cooked vegetables. Traditionally, carrots and *konnyaku* (a pearly-toned gelatinous cake made from a tuber vegetable) are sliced in extra fine julienne strips, blanched for a minute or so, and drained before being tossed in the dark walnut paste. Try this paste too as a dip for raw celery and cucumber sticks. *Yields ¼ cup.*

⅓ cup coarsely chopped, unsalted   scant tablespoon soy sauce
    walnut meats
½ tablespoon ungranulated or
    superfine sugar

Dry roast the walnut meats for 30–40 seconds over high heat (page 16). Crush the walnuts and grind them fine in a *suribachi* (page 17) or blender. Add the sugar and continue to grind and crush until the mixture resembles a fine powder. Add the soy sauce and continue to blend to a very thick, rather sticky paste. It will keep well for several days if covered and refrigerated.

茄
子
の
ご
ま
酢
じ
ょ
う
油
和
え

EGGPLANT SALAD WITH TART SESAME DRESSING
(Nasu No Goma Su-jōyu Aé)

This makes a wonderful summer salad when chilled and served on a bed of crisp lettuce. The same dressing, by the way, could transform the most mundane tomato and cucumber slices into an interesting Oriental salad. *Serves 2–3.*

1 eggplant, weighing about ¾ pound
1 tablespoon white sesame seeds
½ teaspoon superfine sugar
1 tablespoon soy sauce

1 tablespoon rice vinegar
Pinch of salt
½ tablespoon water OR *dashi* (Basic Soup Stock, page 55)

Peel the eggplant and slice it into ¼-inch-thick diagonal slices. Cut these slices into ¼-inch-thick strips and soak them in cold water for 5–6 minutes to avoid bitterness and discoloration. Drain the eggplant, then blanch it in boiling salted water for 2–3 minutes. Drain the cooked eggplant strips and pat them dry to remove excess moisture.

Dry roast the sesame seeds (page 16 for details) and crush them, while still warm, in a *suribachi* (page 17). Add the remaining ingredients, one at a time, stir-grinding after each new addition. If you are using a blender or other food processor to crush the seeds, you may have to triple all ingredients to provide enough volume to engage the blades. Store excess in a tightly sealed jar and refrigerate.

Just before serving, toss the eggplant strips in the tart sesame dressing. Serve at room temperature or chilled.

い
ん
げ
ん
の
ご
ま
味
噌
和
え

STRING BEANS IN THICK BEAN AND SESAME SAUCE (Ingen No Goma Miso Aé)

This aromatic bean and sesame sauce transforms ordinary string beans into an unusual side dish or salad. The sauce is delicious with fresh-cooked asparagus, broccoli or cauliflower, too. *Serves 3–4.*

½ pound fresh string beans
2 tablespoons *Saikyo miso* (light bean paste)

2 teaspoons sugar
1 tablespoon *saké* (rice wine)
2 tablespoons white sesame seeds

Wash and trim the string beans. Bring salted water to a rapid boil and cook the beans in it for 3–4 minutes. They should be bright green and crisp. Drain them and let them cool naturally before cutting them into 1-inch lengths.

Mix the bean paste, sugar and rice wine together in a small saucepan. Heat this mixture, stirring constantly with a wooden spoon, until the sugar has melted and the sauce is satiny. Remove from the heat and let the sauce cool while preparing the sesame seeds.

In a heavy skillet, dry roast the sesame seeds over medium heat (see page 16 for details). Transfer the seeds while still warm to a *suribachi* (mortar and pestle; page 17 for details) and grind them to a smooth paste. If using a blender or food processor to grind the sesame seeds, you may have to double or triple the amount of seeds to have sufficient volume to engage the blades of your machine. (Store excess in a tightly sealed jar and refrigerate.) Add the bean paste sauce to the sesame paste and blend thoroughly to make a thick, smooth, aromatic sauce.

Toss the string beans in the sauce lightly just before serving. Serve at room temperature or slightly chilled.

CLAMS IN MUSTARD AND BEAN SAUCE
(Asari No Karashi Miso Aé)

あさりのからし味噌和え

A lovely hors d'oeuvre, this dish combines a variety of interesting flavors and textures. Both the sauce and clams can be prepared separately many hours ahead and chilled, making this a particularly good party dish. *Serves 4–6.*

½ pound cherrystone clams, shelled	3 tablespoons sugar
4–5 scallions	2 tablespoons rice vinegar
3 tablespoons *Sendai miso* (dark bean paste)	½ teaspoon prepared mild mustard

Rinse the shelled clams in salt water to remove all traces of sand. Blanch them for 30–40 seconds, then drain, and let them cool to room temperature naturally. Refrigerate the clams if not to be used within 30 minutes.

Trim the scallions and blanch them in boiling salted water for 30 seconds. Drain and refresh under cold water. Pat the scallions dry with paper towels, and cut them into 1-inch lengths.

Combine the bean paste, sugar and vinegar in a small saucepan. Stirring frequently with a wooden spoon, heat the mixture for a minute over medium heat until smooth and glossy. Let the sauce cool to room temperature before blending in the mustard. Chill the sauce if it is to accompany cold clams.

Toss the clams and scallions in the sauce just before serving. This dish may be enjoyed either chilled or at room temperature.

茄子のあんかけ

FRIED EGGPLANT WITH CHICKEN
AND BEAN SAUCE *(Nasu No An Kaké)*

The Japanese do many things with their eggplants—they pickle, roast, sauté, blanch, braise, steam and fry them, to be exact. Here, fried eggplant is napped with a sweet and pungent sauce. In a Japanese meal this might be the main or featured dish, accompanied by white rice, a clear soup and tart salt-pickled greens. A more Western approach might be to serve the eggplant with a fluffy omelet and a crisp green salad. *Serves 4.*

2 tablespoons *Sendai miso* (dark bean
   paste)
2½ tablespoons sugar
3 tablespoons *saké* (rice wine)
½ chicken breast, approximately ¼
   pound

2 eggplants, each weighing
   approximately ½ pound
Vegetable oil for deep frying
Sansho (Japanese fragrant pepper)
4 small sprigs of parsley

Combine the bean paste, sugar and rice wine in a small saucepan and stir until smooth. Cook the sauce, stirring frequently, for 2–3 minutes over medium heat.

Remove skin and bone from the chicken breast and trim off the fat; chop the meat to a fine dice. Add the chopped chicken to the bean paste sauce and cook, stirring often, for 2–3 minutes over medium heat. The sauce will thicken and the chicken will turn white. (This sauce can be made several hours in advance and reheated just before serving.)

Wash and pat dry the eggplants before slicing them in halves lengthwise. Slice off just enough of the rounded bottom of each piece to allow the eggplant to lie flat. Save a few of these slivers for testing the readiness of the oil for frying. Score the cut surface, shallowly around the rim and more deeply toward the center of each half.

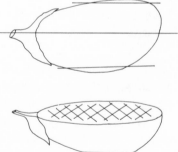

Heat the oil to approximately 325 degrees F. Test-fry one of the eggplant slivers. Small bubbles should appear within a few seconds and the eggplant should float on the surface of the oil. Deep fry each of the eggplant pieces, skin side down, for 1–2 minutes. Flip the pieces over and continue to fry for 3–4 more minutes. The cut surface of the eggplant should be golden brown and the flesh beneath it tender. (You can test this by inserting a wooden toothpick.) Drain the fried eggplant well.

Serve each eggplant half napped with some of the warm chicken and bean sauce. Sprinkle a pinch of Japanese pepper over the sauced eggplant and garnish with a sprig of parsley.

か
ぼ
ち
ゃ
の
鳥
あ
ん
か
け

SIMMERED SQUASH WITH CHICKEN SAUCE
(Kabocha No Tori An Kaké)

From late summer through the fall, several kinds of squash and pumpkin are on the market. The following recipe should make a flavorful addition to your bake-with-butter or pumpkin-pie repertory.

The basic recipe is for acorn squash, though butternut squash and pumpkin are delicious, too. Since butternut is often sweeter and softer than acorn squash, for it you may wish to reduce both the amount of sugar and the cooking time. Pumpkin, on the other hand, will require longer cooking (at least 10 minutes more unless cut into very small pieces). You will need to increase the amounts of stock, sugar and rice wine by a teaspoon or two. *Serves 4–6 as a side dish.*

1–1½ pounds winter squash (or pumpkin)	2 tablespoons soy sauce
1½ cups *dashi* (Basic Soup Stock, page 55)	1 tablespoon *saké* (rice wine)
	¼ pound ground raw chicken meat
Scant ¼ cup sugar	2 teaspoons cornstarch
	1½ tablespoons cold water

Cut the squash into 4–6 wedges and remove the seeds from each piece. Wash the skin and pat the pieces dry.

Combine the stock, sugar, soy sauce and rice wine in a saucepan just large enough to hold the squash in one layer. Heat the seasoned stock and stir it until the sugar has dissolved. Add the wedges of squash, skin side down, and simmer them until tender but firm (about 15 minutes). For best results in simmering the squash, use a dropped lid *(otoshi-buta)*. If cooking without one, be sure to ladle the seasoned stock over the squash frequently.

When the squash is tender, remove it from the saucepan and add the chicken meat to the remaining liquid. Simmer, stirring constantly to separate the pieces of ground meat, for about 3 minutes, or until the meat has turned white and is thoroughly cooked.

Mix the cornstarch and cold water together before adding it to the meat and liquid. Stir over high heat while the sauce thickens. Pour the sauce over the cooked squash. Serve warm or at room temperature.

RED TUNA WITH CREAMY POTATO SAUCE
(Maguro No Yama Kaké)

まぐろの山かけ

Smooth, bright blocks of tender raw tuna are topped with a thick potato sauce and garnished with a dusting of green laver. A classic in its native land, this dish has an unusual taste and texture surprise for you. *Serves 4–6.*

½ pound fillet raw tuna
2 tablespoons soy sauce
3–4 inches (about 6–8 ounces) *yama imo*
   (glutinous yam)
1 teaspoon *ao nori* (green laver flakes)

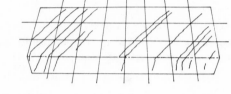

Cut the fillet into ¾-inch cubes. Toss and marinate the tuna cubes in the soy sauce for 5 minutes. Meanwhile, peel and grate the sticky potato. (Once peeled, this tuber vegetable can be irritating to sensitive skin. Wearing plain white cotton gloves will protect your hands. If they should begin to itch, dip them in vinegar and wash with plain soap and water. The irritation is temporary and does not affect the eating of this extraordinary potato.) The grated potato will be thick, glossy and slightly sticky.

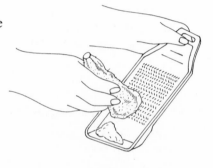

Lift the pieces of tuna from their marinade and make a small pyramid of blocks on each person's plate. Pour several spoonfuls of grated potato over the top of each pyramid. Sprinkle a bit of green laver over the very top of each portion, and serve immediately.

NOTE: Impeccably fresh raw tuna is available at an increasing number of fish markets. It often comes frozen, though, and if that is the case where you live, allow the fillet to defrost naturally, with several layers of paper toweling under it to absorb the excess liquid. You can cut the fillet into blocks while it is still partially frozen (in fact you may find it easier then) but never refreeze the fish. Fresh or defrosted raw tuna can be held in the refrigerator for 8 hours.

Pickles

(TSUKÉ MONO)

Though pickles are found in nearly every cuisine throughout the world, the Japanese take particular pride in their own vast assortment. Pickling was begun as a practical approach to food preservation, but developed into a highly refined art as early as the fourteenth century. Referred to as "the fragrant things" by Masters of the Tea Ceremony, aromatic pickles run the gamut from pungent to mild. The Japanese use a variety of pickling agents, though rice bran *(nuka)* and coarse salt *(shio)* are the most commonly found in home kitchens. Vegetables predominate, but fish and occasionally fruits are pickled, too.

❖

ぬか漬 Rice Bran Pickles *(Nuka-Zuké)*

These pickles are traditionally a homemade delicacy, pungent in aroma yet mellow in flavor. Highly nutritious, they harbor a wealth of minerals and vitamins found in rice bran. They are particularly good when served as a side dish to grilled or fried foods. Unlike some pickled products, vegetables prepared in this manner keep for only a short period of time—usually less than a week. *Nuka-zuké* pickles are not at all difficult to make. Once you've got a good pickling medium going, it is simple to maintain and it will provide you with months, even years, of delicious crisp pickled vegetables.

Preparing the Pickling Medium

You will need a wide-mouthed glazed ceramic pot or glass jar that has a tight-fitting lid. Plastic or metal containers are unacceptable since unpleasant chemical reactions occur. Wooden bowls should be avoided, since they absorb too much moisture from the pickling paste. Your pickling pot should have at least a 2-quart capacity.

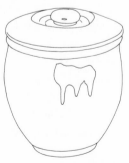

Purchase a package of *iri nuka* (roasted rice bran) or dry roast plain *nuka* (rice bran) yourself. Either method should yield 5½–6 cups of dry-roasted rice bran. With your hands, thoroughly mix the rice bran with 1¾–2 cups of cold water to make a thick paste. Check with the clerk when purchasing your rice bran to see if salt has already been added (some brands have salt and other enzymes mixed in). If not, sprinkle 1 tablespoon of salt over your paste and mix again. The salt aids development of a mature pickling paste. Some brands of *iri nuka* are packaged with a small piece of *konbu* (dried kelp), while others are not. If it is not in your package, add a 2–3-inch strip of dried kelp to your paste. This helps to maintain the proper balance of moisture and it lends a slightly sweet sea aroma to the finished pickles. Dried hot red peppers *(tōgarashi)* should also be added to the pickling paste. One or 2 whole peppers should be enough to add the right sharpness of flavor (the *tōgarashi* also discourages bugs from entering the mixture). In addition, 1–2 cloves of garlic (peeled but not cut) and/or a small knob of fresh ginger (peeled) added to the *nuka* paste provide a piquancy much favored by the Japanese.

It will take several days before your pickling paste begins to ripen. This process can be assisted by adding already matured *nuka* paste from a friend's pot. If you have some vegetable scraps (peels from unwaxed cucumbers, carrots, eggplant, wilted cabbage leaves) these can also be put in the basic paste. These scraps should be removed and discarded the following day. A ripe pickling paste has a rather heady aroma and is the consistency of damp sand. If you are unsure as to the ripeness of your paste, try pickling a piece of unwaxed cucumber or zucchini for 8 hours. Rinse the sample piece under cold water and pat dry. The vegetable should still be bright green but limp, pleasantly salty, slightly tangy, and crunchy though no longer as crisp as when raw. There should be a mellow, almost earthy aftertaste that lingers for several moments.

If your pickling paste is in constant use, you may wish to replenish it by adding 1–2 cups of dry-roasted rice bran every month or so. Sprinkle the additional rice bran over the existing mixture and combine well with your hands. If the mixture should be very dry, you may need to add a few tablespoons of water, too. The dried red peppers, kelp, garlic and ginger do not need to be changed more than once or twice a year. Should your pickles seem too salty, 2–3 crushed raw eggshells can be tossed into the paste. These will have a mellowing effect and you need not worry about removing them as they will gradually decompose over a period of several months. If your pickling paste becomes too watery, stand a small ceramic or glass cup in the center. The pickling mixture should completely surround the cup without spilling over into it. Excess moisture will drain into the cup, which should be removed in a few days.

If a whitish mold should appear on the surface of your pickling paste there is no cause for alarm. Merely scrape it off with a wooden spoon. This mold is harmless and, if removed promptly, will not alter the flavor or quality of your pickles.

Your pickling medium should be kept at room temperature, tightly covered. It should be aerated at least 3 times a week, by mixing and folding bottom over top. Your bare hand is the best implement, though you can use a wooden spoon. If properly cared for, your pickling paste will last for several years.

冬のぬか漬

WINTER RICE BRAN PICKLES *(Fuyu No Nuka-Zuké)*

Serves 5–6 people

3 small white turnips (preferably with
    leaves attached)
Pot of ripe *nuka* pickling paste

2 small stalks broccoli
½ teaspoon soy sauce

Slice off the leaves from the turnips and discard any wilted ones. Rinse and shake dry, then tie them together with string. Rinse the turnips but do not peel them. Slash each, making a deep X in the stem end and bury the turnips deep in the *nuka* paste. Press the bundle of leaves into the paste, leaving the string exposed for easy removal.

Wash the broccoli well and trim off any tough stems. Break into 1-inch flowerets before burying deep in the pickling paste. Make sure that all the vegetables are entirely covered with paste, put the lid on your pot and wait 1–1½ days for the leaves and 1½–2 days for the turnips and broccoli to mature. They will be limp and have a salty tang. Refrigerate any pickles that are not to be eaten immediately (they can be held for 2–3 days). Just before serving, rinse off any pickling paste that may be clinging to the vegetables and pat the pickles dry.

Cut the turnips into half moons ½ inch thick; chop the leaves and broccoli into bite-size pieces. Serve at room temperature with a drop or two of soy sauce.

夏のぬか漬

SUMMER RICE BRAN PICKLES *(Natsu No Nuka-Zuké)*

Serves 5–6 people

2 small eggplants
1 zucchini

Pot of ripe *nuka* pickling paste
½ teaspoon soy sauce

Wash and pat dry the eggplants, and slash them lengthwise not quite in half. Wash and pat dry the zucchini, slice it in half lengthwise and if too long for your pot, cut in half crosswise. Bury the eggplant and zucchini pieces deep in your pot of pickling paste. Put on the lid and wait 6–10 hours for the pickles to mature. They will be limp, but still bright-colored.

Remove the pickles and refrigerate any that are not to be eaten immediately (pickles may be held for 2–3 days in the refrigerator). Just before serving, rinse off any paste that may be clinging to the pickles, pat them dry, trim off the end pieces and slice the vegetables into half moons ¼ inch thick. Serve at room temperature with a few drops of soy sauce.

一年中ぬか漬 ## YEAR-ROUND RICE BRAN PICKLES
(Ichinen Ju Nuka-Zuké)

Serves 5–6 people

1 carrot OR 2 half-inch-thick wedges
   acorn squash
2 unwaxed cucumbers

Pot of ripe *nuka* pickling paste
½ teaspoon soy sauce

Scrape the carrot and cut it in half, lengthwise, if more than 1½ inches thick. If using squash, peel, rinse and pat it dry, removing any seeds. Cut the cucumber in half, crosswise, if too long for your pot. Bury the vegetables deep in the pickling paste, cover and wait 6–8 hours for cucumbers and 10 hours to 1½ days for the carrot or squash to mature. They will mature more rapidly in hot weather. The cucumbers should be limp but still bright-colored, the carrots or squash firm but mellow.

Remove the pickles as they mature and refrigerate any that are not eaten immediately (they can be held for up to 4 days). Just before serving, rinse off any paste that clings to the pickles and slice into ¼-inch-thick half moons or other bite-size pieces. Serve at room temperature with a few drops of soy sauce.

塩漬 ## Salt Pickles *(Shio-Zuké)*

Good salt pickles are bright-colored, crisp and with a bit of lingering sharpness to the taste. Most are less perishable than the rice bran pickles if hermetically sealed at maturation. Salt pickles go particularly well with hot white rice and faintly sweet braised dishes.

Basic Instructions

The principle involved in making these pickles is really quite simple. Pressure is brought to bear upon salted food, causing it to release a certain amount of liquid. This liquid, in turn, becomes the brine in which that food is pickled. In other words, the salt acts as a catalyst, seasoning and preservative. Salted "pressure" pickles are the oldest known form of preserved food in Japan. Although commercially prepared salt pickles are increasingly available, this kind of pickling is basically a home endeavor.

Traditionally, pressure for salt pickling was provided by large flat stones of various weights. Wooden or ceramic tubs were filled with fresh, though slightly sun-dried, produce. Coarse salt was sprinkled liberally over each layer of food and a wooden lid was placed on top. Heavy weights were then placed on the lid until a fair amount of brine was formed. The weight was then lessened a bit as the pickles matured in the brine.

Of course salt pickling can still be done in this traditional manner. If you have no access to stones, then bricks, books or even a sack of potatoes can act as an appropriate weight. Wrap your weights in a plastic bag since they sink into the brine as the pickles mature.

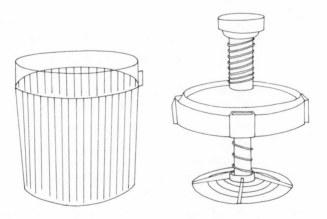

The modern Japanese have come up with a compact plastic jar fitted with a screw-type device called a *shokutaku tsuké mono ki* that simplifies matters greatly and which I highly recommend to any serious salt pickle eaters. Do not, however, use this jar for vinegared pickles or rice bran pickles. Also, it should be washed and dried by hand. When applying pressure, screw until the inner lid fits quite snugly against the top layer of food. Then screw twice more for good measure.

Whether using weights or a screw-type device, be sure your foods are laid flat, in several layers, and seasoned evenly.

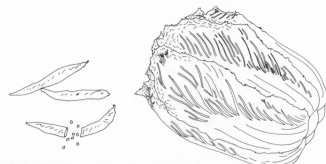

冬
の
塩
漬
WINTER SALT PICKLES *(Fuyu No Shio-Zuké)*

Serves 8–10 people

1 small *hakusai* (Chinese cabbage),
    about 1¼ pounds
1–2 teaspoons coarse salt
1 *tōgarashi* (dried hot red pepper)
Peel from ¼ lemon sliced in julienne
    strips, optional

Pickling tub and 8–10 pounds of
    pressure OR a *shokutaku tsuké mono
    ki* (screw-type device)
½ teaspoon soy sauce

Remove any outer leaves of cabbage that may be wilted or damaged and save them to use as a cover if you are going to weight your pickles. Rinse the cabbage, pat dry and cut lengthwise into 1½-inch wedges. Lay them out to dry in a sunny spot for 3–4 hours.

Rub the cabbage wedges with half the salt. Lay some of the cabbage on the bottom of your pickling tub and sprinkle a bit more salt over it. Break open the hot red pepper and sprinkle some of the seeds over the cabbage. Break the pod into 4 or 5 pieces and lay a few of them over this first layer. For a lighter, fruitier pickle, add some slivers of lemon peel. Continue to make 2 or 3 more layers of cabbage and seasonings until all the ingredients have been used up.

If using weights, make a cover from wilted leaves to protect the pickles. Lay a flat lid or plate over the cover and add 8–10 pounds of pressure, distributed as evenly as possible over the surface. As soon as enough brine has been formed to cover part of your weights (this may take as long as 8 hours), reduce the pressure to 3–5 pounds and let the pickles mature in their own brine for another 12–18 hours.

If using a screw-type device, secure it snugly (some brine may cover the screw from the start) and keep it tight for 5–6 hours. Then loosen the screw by a turn or two and let the pickles mature in their own brine for 12–18 hours. Refrigerate in their brine any pickles that are not to be eaten immediately. They will keep for about a week. Just before serving, rinse the pickled cabbage under cold water and squeeze it dry. Chop coarsely or cut into 1-inch lengths. Serve at room temperature with a few drops of soy sauce.

NOTE: If you want to keep your pickles longer, transfer them, in their brine, when they have reached maturity to Mason-type jars and seal according to the manufacturer's instructions. Keep refrigerated for up to 2 months.

夏 の 塩 漬　SUMMER SALT PICKLES *(Natsu No Shio-Zuké)*

Serves 5–6 people

1 small eggplant	Pickling tub and 8–10 pounds of
Scant teaspoon salt	pressure OR a *shokutaku tsuké mono*
1 unwaxed cucumber	*ki* (screw-type device)
OR zucchini	½ teaspoon soy sauce

Wash and pat dry the eggplant. Cut it in half lengthwise and rub some salt into the cut surfaces. Lay the eggplant flat against the bottom of your pickling tub.

Wash the cucumber or zucchini and pat it dry. Using the tines of a fork, scrape the cucumber or zucchini along its length. Rub salt over the entire surface and slice the vegetable in halves lengthwise or quarters, if necessary, to fit your pickling tub. Lay the cucumber or zucchini over the eggplant as evenly as possible. If using weights, lay a flat lid or plate over the vegetables, then apply 8–10 pounds of pressure as evenly as possible. It may take as long as 8 hours for the brine to rise an inch or so above the weights. When it does, reduce the pressure to 3–5 pounds, and let the pickles mature in their brine for another or another 3–4 hours.

If using a screw-type device, secure it very snugly for 4–5 hours, then loosen it by a turn or two. Let the pickles sit in their brine for 4–5 hours. If you are concerned about discoloration, add a pinch of alum or a rusty nail to the brine after reducing the pressure. Refrigerate the pickles in their brine until ready to eat (they will keep for about one week). Just before serving, rinse the pickles under cold water, squeeze them dry and cut into bite-size pieces. Serve at room temperature with a few drops of soy sauce.

NOTE: If you want to keep your pickles longer, transfer them in their brine to Mason-type jars. Seal the jars according to the manufacturer's instructions. Refrigerate up to 2 months.

一年中の塩漬

YEAR-ROUND SALT PICKLES *(Ichinen Ju No Shio Zuké)*

Serves 7–8 people

2–3-inch piece of *daikon* (Japanese
    white radish), about 1½–2 ounces
Some green *daikon* tops if you have
    them
1 unwaxed cucumber OR zucchini
Peel from ¼ lemon

½ small carrot
1 teaspoon salt
Small pickling tub and 8–10 pounds
    pressure OR a *shokutaku tsuké mono
    ki* (screw-type device)
½ teaspoon soy sauce

Peel the radish and slice it into julienne strips. Rinse, pat dry and chop fine any green
stems and leaves from the radish. Wash and pat dry the cucumber or zucchini and
slice it on the diagonal, then into julienne strips. Scrape the carrot, and cut it into fine
julienne strips. Slice the lemon peel into thin slivers. You should have about 2½–3
cups vegetable and fruit peel strips. Put the vegetables and lemon peel into a large
bowl and sprinkle the salt over all.

Let stand for a minute before lightly squeezing to release liquid. Transfer the
wilted vegetables and brine to a small pickling tub, lay a flat lid or plate over them
and apply 8–10 pounds of pressure distributed as evenly as possible over the surface.
It may take up to 5 hours for the brine to rise above the lid. Once the brine partially
covers the weights, let the vegetables pickle for 4–5 hours. Reduce the pressure by
half, and let the pickles mature for another hour or two.

Or use a screw-type device and secure the lid very snugly. As the vegetables wilt
and brine is formed (about 3–4 hours) tighten the screw snugly again. Let the
vegetables pickle for 3–4 hours, then loosen the screw slightly. Let the pickles mature
in their brine for another hour or two.

Either way, refrigerate in the brine for up to three days any pickles not to be eaten
that day. Just before serving, lightly rinse the pickles under cold water and squeeze
dry. Serve with a few drops of soy sauce.

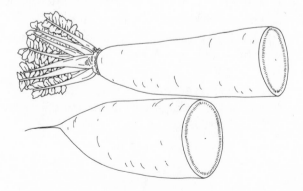

Commercially Prepared Pickles

Some pickling processes are rather complicated or require considerable time and effort. And some Japanese pickles are regional delicacies with their "secrets" carefully guarded.

奈良漬 *Nara-zuké* ("pickle of Nara," a culture center near Kyoto) is a fine example: they take several years to reach maturity after being placed in a pungent malty yeast paste that is difficult to make. Traditionally, *shiro uri* (a zucchini-like vegetable native to the area) and small, round eggplants are pickled in this manner. In Japan, *Nara-zuké* are sold in wooden tubs, though in the West you will most likely see them packaged in vacuum-sealed plastic bags. After breaking the seal, refrigerate any pickles that are not eaten that day. They will keep for several weeks. A plastic container with a tight-fitting lid is good for storage. Just before eating *Nara-zuké* pickles, rinse off any excess pickling paste and towel dry the vegetables. Cut in thin slices or chop to a coarse dice. Since these pickles are very aromatic, they are best enjoyed with bland foods such as steamed fish and hot white rice.

たく庵 *Takuan* (yellow pickled radish) are distinctive pickles to be found in many parts of Japan. Ranging in color from pale gold to bright yellow, *takuan* are crisp and pungent. They make a colorful highlight to an otherwise earthy-toned meal, and they contrast well with fried foods. Packaged in vacuum-sealed plastic bags, the radish should be refrigerated once the seal has been broken. It will stay fresh for about 1 week. Just before eating, rinse the *takuan* in cold water and pat it dry. Slice in half lengthwise and then into half moons ¼ inch thick.

桜漬 *Sakura-zuké* ("cherry-blossom" pickles) are made from thin slices of *daikon,* or Japanese white radish. Salted and pickled, then tinted a pale pink with *aka-jiso* (a leaf and berry) and seasoned with sweet syrupy wine, *sakura-zuké* are crisp, colorful and mild. Packaging and storage are the same as for *takuan,* above.

柴漬 *Shiba-zuké* are a bright purple assortment of pickled cucumber, eggplant, ginger and *myōga* (a root vegetable native to Japan). Kyoto is famous for making these piquant pickles. Even in Japan they are most likely to be packaged in vacuum-sealed plastic bags. Storage suggestions are the same as for the other pickles described above; *shiba-zuké* will keep for several weeks. Just before eating, rinse off the vegetables and discard the wrinkled dark leaves (these are *aka-jiso,* which provide the unique color and flavor to these pickles). Chop *shiba-zuké* to a fairly fine dice. They are very good with *sushi* and other seasoned rice dishes.

広島菜漬 *Hiroshimana-zuké* are made from a deep-green leafy vegetable similar in flavor to collard greens. They are pickled in a salty brine in much the same way homemade salt pickles are. The *Hiroshimana-zuké,* found in most Oriental groceries in the United States, are made on the premises from local produce (either greens resembling the original are substituted or the "real thing" is grown from imported seeds). Most that I've sampled have been excellent, with a truly authentic flavor. *Hiroshimana-zuké* make a delicious contrast to braised foods. They will keep for 4–5 days if refrigerated in their original brine. Rinse off the leaves just before eating and chop fine, or cut into ½-inch lengths and align them to form a bundle. You may wish to pour a few drops of soy sauce over the pickles.

紅しょうが *Béni shōga* (red pickled ginger) is readily available in the West. Packaged in chunks, slices and julienne slivers, *béni shōga* will last for months if refrigerated in its original brine after opening. The color is the result of a natural food dye, called *shoku béni,* not the feared A-2 red dye. Drain off excess brine just before serving. Red pickled ginger goes well with seasoned rice and noodle dishes.

甘酢しょうが *Amazu shōga* (pink pickled ginger) is also available at most Oriental groceries. Thin slices are packaged in vacuum-sealed bags and, like red pickled ginger, it will last for months if refrigerated in its own brine after opening. The color is completely natural— caused by a chemical reaction when marinating blanched yellow ginger in a sweet and sour brine. Drain the slices of excess brine before serving. *Amazu shōga* is the traditional accompaniment to *sushi* (vinegared rice dishes) and also provides a mouth-refreshing touch with grilled fish or poultry.

Sweet Things and Beverages

(KANMI/NOMI MONO)

Fresh fruit in season is good at the end of a Japanese meal, though certainly not essential. The Japanese do not eat dessert in the Western sense of the word, and their sweets are more likely to be served as mid-afternoon snacks. Here is a small selection of the sweet things I find the most appealing. Serve them, if you like, at the end of an otherwise Western meal or for tea, or for your own version of a Japanese meal.

Traditional Japanese tea cakes filled with bean paste are time-consuming and difficult to make, and since they quite frankly remain unappreciated by most Westerners I have decided not to include them. Such cakes are best enjoyed as part of the Tea Ceremony, since the bitter, frothy, vividly green tea is a perfect complement to them.

❖

かりんとう

SWEET STICKS (Karintō)

The Japanese eat these sweet sticks as a light snack with numerous cups of hot green tea, though black or cinnamon-and-clove-spiced tea would be nice, too. Served with ice cream or fruit sherbet, these sweet sticks make an interesting dessert for a Western or Oriental meal. *Makes about 100 sticks.*

1 tablespoon honey
¼ teaspoon salt
4 tablespoons warm water
1 egg, well beaten
1⅔ cups all-purpose flour (plus up to
   ¼ cup for board)

2 teaspoons baking powder
Oil for deep frying
1 cup firmly packed brown sugar
⅓ cup water

Put the honey, salt and warm water into a bowl and stir until well blended. Add the egg and continue to stir until the mixture is well combined.

Combine flour and baking powder and sift it into the egg mixture, a little at a time. Stir to blend well after each addition. When all the flour has been added, form the soft dough into a ball and turn it out on a floured board. Knead the dough until it is satiny and smooth. Roll it out evenly to ¼-inch thickness. Cut the dough into sticks 1½ inches long and ⅛ inch wide.

Fry these in 4–5 batches in deep oil, using medium-low temperature (325–350 degrees F.) for best results. The sticks should puff but not color at first, and the oil will be quite foamy. Fry for 2–3 minutes, or until golden brown and cooked through. Test a stick by cutting it in half; the inside should be dry. Drain the sticks well on paper towels before spreading them out on a cookie sheet.

Combine the brown sugar and ⅓ cup water in a small saucepan and heat it. Stir constantly as the syrup bubbles and thickens. Check the temperature with a candy thermometer; the syrup should be about 245 degrees F. Or use a simple cold-water test: Drop a little syrup into a bowl of cold water. It should form a firm but pliable ball. Let the hot syrup cool for a few seconds before pouring it over the fried sticks. Toss and stir constantly until each stick has been coated with syrup. Continue to toss and stir to separate the sugar-frosted sticks. Store in an airtight canister.

For a tasty variation, knead 1 teaspoon ground black sesame seeds into the dough before rolling it out. Use refined white sugar instead of brown for the syrup.

大学いも CANDIED SWEET POTATOES *(Daigaku Imo)*

Known as a sweet and enjoyed throughout the Orient, candied sweet potatoes are a surprising combination of cool, sweet, chewy syrup and pieces of warm, soft potato, with black sesame seeds as a crunchy and colorful accent. *Makes about 35–40 pieces.*

¾ pound sweet potatoes
Oil for deep frying
4 tablespoons sugar
2 tablespoons water
1 tablespoon soy sauce
1 tablespoon whole black sesame seeds

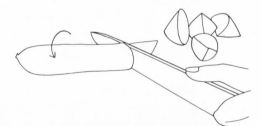

Wash and peel the potatoes, or scrub the skins very well and leave the potatoes unpeeled, then cut them in half lengthwise. Cut the long pieces into oblique shapes about 1½ inches long. Soak them in a bowl of cold water for 10 minutes, then carefully pat dry.

Fry the potatoes in deep oil at a medium temperature (approximately 350 degrees F.) until tender and lightly colored. Test a piece or two by piercing with a toothpick—there should be no resistance. Drain the potatoes well.

In a small saucepan, combine the sugar, water and soy sauce and heat the mixture, stirring constantly. Cook the bubbly syrup a few minutes or until it is about 245 degrees F. Check the temperature with a candy thermometer or make a simple cold-water test (when a little syrup is dropped into a bowl of cold water it should form a firm but pliable ball). Dry roast the sesame seeds (see page 16) and add them to the syrup.

Arrange your work space so that the fried potatoes, hot syrup, chopsticks or tongs, bowl of ice water, slotted spoon and a lightly oiled serving platter are all ready and within easy reach. From here on swift action is required. Add the potatoes, a few at a time, to the hot syrup and coat them quickly and thoroughly. With chopsticks or tongs, immediately lift the pieces out of the syrup, one at a time, and plunge them into the bowl of ice water. With a slotted spoon, quickly remove them from the water and transfer the candied potatoes to your serving platter. For fullest enjoyment, eat them within 15–20 minutes.

あんず寒 JELLIED APRICOT LOAF *(Anzu Kan)*

The Japanese enjoy gelatin as much as anyone and this loaf makes a refreshing snack or dessert in the heat of the summer. One of the nicest things about Japanese gelatin is its firmness. It won't "weep" or lose its shape at room temperature as Western gelatin often does. Many variations are possible, perhaps the simplest being to use prepared orange or apple juice and add well-drained slices of canned *mikan* (tangerine-like fruit). *Serves 5–6.*

1 strip white *kanten* (agar-agar, Japanese gelatin)	2 cups water
	1 tablespoon sugar
½ cup dried apricots	2 teaspoons lemon juice

Break the strip of agar-agar into 3 or 4 pieces and soak them in cold water to cover for 15 minutes. Squeeze out the water and shred the softened agar-agar into a bowl.

Combine the apricots and water in a saucepan and simmer them until the apricots are soft and the liquid a deep amber color (about 20 minutes). Strain the liquid into a measuring cup, reserving the cooked apricots. Add cold water if necessary to make 1¼ cups. Season this liquid with the sugar and lemon juice.

Purée the reserved apricots. The Japanese use an *uragoshi* (page 33), and this results in a velvety, thick purée. You can use a blender or food processor if you like, and add the seasoned apricot liquid to obtain the proper consistency for your machine. Strain the purée to remove any skins or fibers.

In a saucepan, combine the purée, shredded agar-agar and reserved apricot liquid if it has not already been added when puréing. Stir over low heat until the agar-agar has melted and all ingredients are well mixed. Pour into a mold (traditionally a rectangular one, called a *nagashi-bako,* page 39) and let it set. It will jell at room temperature but chilling speeds the process a bit. Because this particular loaf is a purée, it takes quite some time to jell firmly—about 1½ hours at room temperature or a little under 1 hour if refrigerated.

Unmold as you would any gelatin preparation, or if using a *nagashi-bako* lift out the loaf and slice it once lengthwise, then crosswise 5 times, yielding 10 rectangular blocks. A single serving is traditionally 2 pieces.

三色だんご THREE-COLORED TAFFY BALLS *(Sanshoku Dango)*

Most traditional Japanese cakes or pastries are made from steamed rice flour. They are soft and chewy, often filled with thick sweet bean paste. Not many Westerners like them—I think it is as much a question of texture as it is of taste. On the other hand, taffy balls with a variety of garnishes are more likely to find Occidental fans. An interesting variation can be had by roasting ungarnished taffy balls as you would marshmallows at a campfire. Drizzle the roasted taffy balls with honey and sprinkle with black sesame seeds. *Makes 1 dozen balls.*

Taffy balls:

⅔ cup *jōshinko* (fine rice flour)	Pinch of salt
1 tablespoon sugar	¼ cup warm water

Garnishes:

1 tablespoon *kinako* (soy flour)	½ tablespoon black sesame seeds
½ tablespoon brown sugar	½ tablespoon sugar
Pinch of powdered cinnamon	

Combine the rice flour, 1 tablespoon sugar and salt in a bowl. Add the warm water, a little at a time, and mix well. Gather the dough into a smooth, though sticky, ball. Pinch into 6 or 7 smaller balls and place them on a damp cloth lining the rack of your steamer. Steam the balls for 25 minutes.

Remove the steamed balls on their damp cloth and transfer them to a board. Dampen another cloth and wrap it around your hand. Punch and knead the hot taffy balls until they form one smooth, satiny mass (about 5 minutes). If your hands are as sensitive to heat as mine are, you'll want to wet your hand cloth in cold water several times (being careful to wring out all excess water) during the kneading. Divide the kneaded taffy into 12 small perfectly round balls.

Mix well the soy flour, brown sugar and cinnamon in a small bowl.

In a heavy skillet, dry roast the black sesame seeds (page 16 for details). Mix with the ½ tablespoon sugar in another small bowl.

While they are still warm, roll 4 of the taffy balls in the soy and brown sugar mixture and 4 of them in the black sesame mixture.

On each of 4 short bamboo skewers, place 1 black, 1 white and 1 brown ball. Serve them at room temperature within 24 hours. It is not a good idea to refrigerate the taffy because it gets crusty and hard. However, that's all right if you plan to roast them later (in which case don't add the final garnishes).

きんかんの甘露煮 KUMQUATS IN SYRUP *(Kinkan No Kanro Ni)*

Fresh kumquats are in season in the cold months and I always make *kinkan no kanro ni* whenever I see this luscious orange fruit. In Japan kumquats in syrup are a New Year's delicacy, but there's no reason why they can't be enjoyed as a garnish or dessert at any Western meal. *Makes 25–30.*

25–30 firm fresh kumquats	1½ cups sugar
1½ teaspoons *saké* (rice wine)	¾ cup water

Remove any leaves from the kumquats, wash the fruit well, and pat it dry. Make 3–4 small, vertical, shallow slits in each kumquat, being careful not to cut completely through. The Japanese remove the seeds, since it is considered poor etiquette to leave them on your plate while eating. This is a time-consuming task with the heavily seeded American variety of the fruit, but if you wish to be authentic here is how to do it. Hold each kumquat between thumb and forefinger, and squeeze lightly so that the slits part to expose flesh and seeds. Insert a toothpick, and carefully poke and pick out seeds.

Put the kumquats in a saucepan with cold water to cover and add the *saké*. Bring this to a boil rapidly, then reduce the heat to maintain a steady simmer for 10–15 minutes. Drain the soft, tender fruit.

In a saucepan combine the sugar and ¾ cup water, and cook it, stirring constantly, for 2–3 minutes or until syrupy. Add the drained cooked kumquats and simmer the fruit in the syrup for 8–10 minutes. Let them cool in the saucepan, and just before serving, drain them of any excess syrup. Refrigerate any leftovers, covered in syrup, for up to 4 days. If you wish to store for a longer period of time, transfer the hot fruit and syrup to sterile Mason-type jars, and seal them according to the manufacturer's instructions.

栗
き
ん
と
ん
CHESTNUTS IN YAM PASTE *(Kuri Kinton)*

Golden, glossy chestnuts in a swirl of sweet, bright-colored yam paste are also a Japanese New Year's tradition. They are wonderful as a decorative accompaniment to a Western-style roast turkey or baked ham. Try decorating your platter next time with whole chestnuts, piping out the sweet yam paste in circlets around them. *Makes about 2½ cups.*

2 seven-ounce bottles of yellow chestnuts in syrup (sold as *kuri no kanro ni* in Oriental groceries)	1–1¼ pounds yams ½ cup sugar 2 tablespoons *mirin* (syrupy rice wine)

Drain the chestnuts, reserving ¼ cup of the syrup. Cut very large chestnuts in half.

Peel the yams and cut them into 1-inch-thick slices before cooking them in water to cover for 15 minutes. They should be very tender when tested with a fork or chopstick. Drain the yams and mash them, preferably using an *uragoshi*. Or force your mashed yams through a strainer to eliminate any stringy vegetable fibers. Either way, you should have about 1¾–2 cups velvety mashed yams.

Place the warm yam paste in a small saucepan with the sugar and stir to mix well. Add the reserved chestnut syrup and simmer, stirring occasionally, for 3–4 minutes. Stir in the *mirin* and the drained chestnuts. Remove the saucepan from the heat and let it cool, uncovered, for 5 minutes. Spread the paste onto a cookie sheet and let it cool thoroughly. Serve the chestnuts swirled in yam paste either chilled or at room temperature. They may be stored for up to 2 months by covering the cooled paste with plastic wrap (make sure there are no air pockets), and refrigerating it.

A Word about Tea
and Other Beverages

The Japanese are forever drinking tea—to quench the slightest thirst, to formalize a business or social occasion, to provide an excuse for gossip—in fact, nearly every interpersonal relationship in Japan seems to indicate tea drinking. For most such occasions, roasted green tea leaves *(ocha)* are placed in small ceramic pots and allowed to steep for 2–3 minutes in very hot water—boiling water would be too much of a shock to the delicate tea leaves—before being poured into individual cups.

There are many grades of *ocha,* but price is usually a good indication of quality. Unless you are particularly attuned to the finer nuances of flavor and aroma, a middle price range should suit you. Figure on about 1 heaping tablespoon of *ocha* tea leaves for every 2–2½ cups of scalding hot water. These same leaves can be used again within 10–15 minutes, if you like. Most Japanese teapots do not have very fine filters so that leaves do come through. They usually settle to the bottom of individual cups, but stems which remain standing vertically are considered a lucky sign. By the way, Japanese etiquette indicates that tea cups should be filled only two-thirds full.

Occasionally tea leaves are mixed with roasted rice kernels, and this combination is called *génmai cha.* It has a distinctive smoky flavor, and since it is cheaper than regular tea, it is considered less elegant. It is prepared in the same manner as *ocha.*

Mugi cha is made from roasted barley and is served chilled. It is wonderfully refreshing during the hot, humid summer months, though it may take a few glassfuls to win you over. Fill a large kettle with 1½–2 quarts of cold water. Add ¾–1 cup *mugi cha* and bring it to a rapid boil. Reduce to a simmer and cook for 3–4 minutes. Strain the tea through a cloth-lined colander into a large bowl filled with 20–30 ice cubes. Chill the dark amber tea and serve it plain or over ice.

Another summertime drink is *Calpis.* Made from a sweet, chalky, fermented milk-based syrup of the same name, it is diluted to taste with cold water (three times as much water as syrup) and served over ice. Occasionally *Calpis* will come in orange and grape flavors, too.

Plum wine is an adult hot-weather refresher. Many families make their own in June during the rainy season. The green fruit is at its peak then; it is sweetened with rock sugar and fermented with rice wine. The ingredients necessary for home brews are not to be found in the West, but the bottled finished product is. Serve it chilled and on the rocks.

Beer is drunk year round in Japan with meals and on social occasions though it is particularly favored in the hot weather. Sapporo, Kirin, Asahi and Suntory are the best-known brands and are increasingly available in American liquor stores.

Nihon shu (literally "Japanese wine") is the official name for drinking *saké* (rice wine). Distilled from rice, it is a clear, colorless liquid that is consumed in large quantities at parties and other special gatherings. It is usually served warm and brought to the table in small serving containers with matching small cups. Proper etiquette requires your host or another guest to fill your cup, then you return the courtesy.

IN THE JAPANESE KITCHEN: FOODSTUFFS

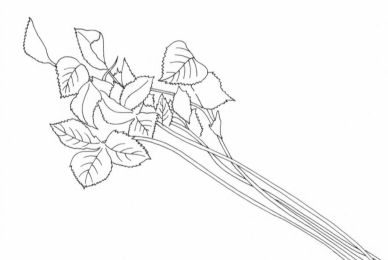

I am not sure at just what age an American child realizes that milk must be kept in the refrigerator and that green peas and carrots are "good for you," but it's an early bit of learning, I'm sure. Ask almost any three-year-old raised in a Japanese household if *sushi* gets refrigerated and you'll be told authoritatively, "Never!" Japanese children learn very soon that *hijiki* (a kind of sea vegetation) and *tōfu* (bean curd) are "good" for them, too. It's a matter of personal experience, of course. If you are not very familiar with the ingredients used in Japanese cooking, it can seem overwhelming and frustrating at times. It needn't be. Here is a list—in alphabetical order—of foodstuffs with information on their purchasing, storage and nutritional value.

For those of you just starting to cook Japanese food, I've underlined the basic things you'll need for most recipes in this book. You probably have some of them already; others are easily available at most Oriental groceries.

❖

油
あ
げ   ABURA AGÉ *(fried bean curd)*, available in the refrigerated or frozen-food compartments of Oriental groceries, is highly perishable and should be eaten within three days of purchase if not kept frozen. Do not refreeze. Canned *abura agé* is also available, though inferior in flavor and texture to the fresh or frozen product. Some canned products are already seasoned (usually called *Inari-zushi no Moto*) and not appropriate for the recipes in this book. One slice is approximately 70 calories.

甘酢しょうが

AMAZU SHŌGA *(pink pickled ginger)* is most commonly available in thin slices in vacuum-sealed cellophane packs; large chunks are often bottled. After opening, keep pickles and brine in a covered container and refrigerate. *Amazu shōga* will stay fresh for many months.

青のり

AO NORI *(flakes of green laver, a type of sea vegetation)* is sold in small glass bottles or tins, usually with a sprinkling spout on the top of the container. Store in a dark, dry spot at room temperature. Used primarily as a garnish for rice and noodle dishes, *ao nori* is rich in calcium and vitamin A. Caloric value for this and other types of sea vegetation is not available but thought to be very low.

浅草のり

ASAKUSA NORI is most commonly referred to as "seaweed" though this is a misnomer. It is laver, a type of sea vegetation, which is rinsed, chopped and then laid upon a rectangular frame to be dried. Thin, crisp sheets of very dark laver result. Packaged in tins or cellophane, the sheets are a standard 6 by 10 inches though these may be folded in half. After opening, store any leftovers in an airtight canister along with the anti-moisture pellets that come with the original package. Although dried laver does not spoil easily it does lose its aroma quickly. Keeping it in the freezer, though, helps to preserve the original quality. Laver defrosts almost instantaneously but should be dry roasted (page 16) before use. Return to the freezer any sheets not to be used that day. Laver may be frozen for up to 3 months.

As with all sea vegetation, *Asakusa nori* is highly nutritious; caloric value is not available, but it is suspected to be very low.

bamboo shoots—see TAKÉNOKO.

bean curd—see TŌFU.

bean paste—see MISO.

bean sprouts—see MOYASHI.

紅しょうが

BÉNI SHŌGA *(red pickled ginger)* is most commonly available bottled in chunks with pickling brine. It is also available in smaller vacuum-sealed cellophane packs. After opening, pickles and brine should be stored in a covered container and refrigerated. *Béni shōga* will stay fresh for many months.

bonito flakes—see KATSUO BUSHI.

burdock root—see GOBŌ.

カ
ル
ピ
ス

CALPIS is a brand name of a popular sweet, chalky syrup from which a soft drink is made. It comes in bottles and is diluted to taste, chilled and served over ice. The bottle should be refrigerated after opening, but will stay fresh for several months. Occasionally orange and grape flavors are available in addition to the basic white syrup. There are about 150 calories in a 6-ounce glass.

Chinese cabbage—see HAKUSAI.

chrysanthemum leaves—see SHUNGIKU.

中
華
そ
ば

CHŪKA SOBA *(thin yellow noodles for soups and salads)* is one Japanese version of Chinese soup noodles. Sold in cellophane bags in fresh and "instant" dried forms, these noodles may be used interchangeably with *ramen.* Fresh noodles are highly perishable and should be eaten within 2 days of purchase. Never refreeze any fresh noodle product.

大
根

DAIKON *(Japanese white radish or Japanese radish)* is a nutritious, versatile vegetable in season most of the year which can be found in most well-stocked Oriental groceries. Its shape and size may vary from quite large, fat and bulbous to a tapered, slender root slightly larger than a carrot. Good *daikon* is firm and white with a luminous cast. It has a tuft of stiff pale-green stems with short dark-green ruffled leaves. The entire vegetable is edible. The root, a good source of vitamin C, is sweet with a slightly sharp aftertaste. The stems and leaves are rich in calcium and vitamin A and are reminiscent of cabbage.

Only the fresh vegetable is used unless a recipe specifically calls for dried *daikon. Daikon* cannot be frozen for storage. It will keep for 4–5 days in the refrigerator, wilting and shriveling a bit toward the end. Recipes requiring thin, crisp slices of raw *daikon* (such as Red and White Salad, page 173) should be made within a day or two of purchase. Grated *daikon,* used as a condiment for fried foods (such as *tempura,* page 157), can be made successfully within three days of purchase. *Daikon* for use in soups or casseroles (such as *nabé mono,* page 116) need not be so crisp. Pickle the stems and roots (page 196) or blanch them quickly in salted water and slice thin. Add these slices to a salad instead of cabbage or celery. For the calorie conscious, ¼ cup shredded or grated *daikon* is about 25 calories.

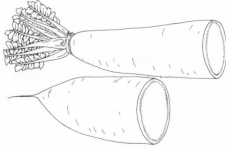

大豆 DAIZU *(dried soybeans)* are rich in protein, minerals and the B vitamins. Sold in small cellophane bags, the dried beans should be stored in a dry, dark place. With care, shelf life is six months. The beans are soaked, simmered and eaten as a vegetable. They are also the raw material for many other soybean products: *nattō* (fermented beans), *miso* (fermented bean paste), *shōyu* (soy sauce), *tōfu* (bean curd), *yuba* (thin, brittle sheets of dried soy milk "skin"), *okara* (a by-product of *tōfu* making), and *kinako* (soy flour). One tablespoon of cooked beans is approximately 50 calories.

出し DASHI *(basic soup stock)* is made from *konbu* (kelp) and *katsuo bushi* (bonito shavings) and is a clear, subtly flavored broth that will keep well if refrigerated, but not frozen, for 3–4 days.

There are several powdered *dashi* mixes and *dashi* "tea bags" on the market. Although convenient at times, they cannot compare to fresh stock made with care from fine materials.

枝豆 ÉDA MAMÉ *(fresh soybeans)* are delicious and nutritious. From late spring through the summer months, clusters of bright green pods on stiff stems can be seen in any Japanese market. The beans, cooked and served in their pods and shelled as they are eaten, are most often enjoyed as a snack with cold beer or iced barley tea. To remove the fuzz on the outside of the pods and season them, too, toss ¼ pound of them into a *suribachi* (serrated mortar) and sprinkle a teaspoon of coarse salt over all. Rub the salt into the pods by stirring them around. Cook in a quart or more boiling water for 3 minutes and drain immediately. Fan the cooked beans to cool them quickly (brighter color) and to avoid condensation (better flavor). Cooked beans will keep for 2–3 days if refrigerated. About 200 calories for 1½ cups cooked beans (about ¼ pound with pod).

えのきだけ ÉNOKIDAKÉ *(slender white mushrooms)* are found fresh in the fall and early winter months in most well-stocked Oriental groceries selling fresh produce. They come packaged in cellophane bags, with only the tops visible. The bottoms of these clusters of mushrooms are always orange-brown and a bit moldy looking—this is not a sign of spoilage. Really fresh *énokidaké* are never limp or slippery, though (until cooked, that is). Canned *énokidaké* are more readily available, but I think they taste awful; the delicate, almost perfume-like aroma just doesn't stand up to canning. It is difficult to calculate caloric units for all mushrooms, but *énokidaké* are rich in trace minerals.

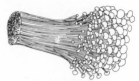

fried bean curd—see ABURA AGÉ.

玄
米
茶 GÉNMAI CHA *(combination of green tea leaves and roasted rice kernels).* Tea prepared from it has a smoky aroma and flavor. It is often sold in cellophane packages, but should be transferred to an airtight container after opening. Store in a dark, dry spot at room temperature.

ginger—see SHŌGA.

glutinous rice—see MOCHI-GOMÉ.

glutinous rice cakes—see OMOCHI.

ご
ぼ
う GOBŌ *(burdock root)* should be purchased fresh whenever possible; canned burdock root has lost the woodsy flavor and crunch of the fresh vegetable. Look for skinny roots (slightly thicker than your thumb) about 1–1½ feet long with brown earth still clinging to them. Fresh burdock root is never limp. It should be scrubbed just before it is cooked. Wrap it in newspaper and store in the vegetable bin of your refrigerator, washing and scraping or peeling as you need it. It has maximum flavor and texture for the first 3 days, but won't spoil for a week to 10 days. Cut surfaces often turn reddish or grayish-brown; this is no cause for alarm. *Gobō* has approximately 100 calories in 3 ounces; it is a good source of vitamin B$_1$ and trace minerals.

ご
ま GOMA *(sesame seeds)* are used extensively in Japanese cooking for seasoning and garnishing. White unhulled seeds are called *shiro goma;* white hulled seeds are *muki goma;* black seeds are *kuro goma;* and a mixture of black seeds and coarse salt is called *goma shio.* Unless otherwise indicated, use white (either hulled or unhulled) seeds in

all recipes calling for sesame seeds. Store all sesame seeds in dry containers with tight-fitting lids at room temperature away from direct sunshine. With care, shelf life is several years. Dry roasting sesame seeds brings out their marvelous aroma and should be done as close to mealtime as possible. They are a fine source of calcium, magnesium, protein and carbohydrates; 12 calories per tablespoon for white seeds, 68 per tablespoon for black.

green onion—see SCALLIONS.

はじかみ酢漬 HAJIKAMI SU-ZUKÉ *(whole young ginger, pickled)* is used as a garnish for grilled fish and many *sushi* (vinegared rice) dishes. The name *hajikami* refers to the "youthful blushing" pink color of these pickles—another bit of Japanese culinary poetry. Sold in glass jars, *hajikami su-zuké* will stay fresh for 3–4 months if refrigerated after opening.

白菜 HAKUSAI *(Chinese cabbage)* is available fresh during the fall and winter months in most Oriental markets selling fresh produce. Look for compact heads with snowy white stems and pale green ruffled leaves. A few black speckles on the outer leaves are quite common. Store wrapped in damp paper toweling and an unsealed plastic bag in your vegetable bin. It has superior flavor and texture for the first three days, wilting soon thereafter (best to pickle at this stage) but not spoiling for a week to 10 days. *Hakusai* is a good source of vitamin C if not overcooked, and is low in calories (about 5 per ounce).

HASU *(lotus root)*—see RENKON.

ひじき HIJIKI *(a type of sea vegetation)* is a mass of black kinky and brittle strands when purchased dried. But soak it, then braise it in a sweetened soy broth and it becomes a tender, lustrous vegetable with a licorice-like flavor. Store *hijiki* in its original cellophane bag in a dark, dry spot at room temperature until opened, then transfer any *hijiki* not prepared the same day to an airtight container. Caloric value of all sea vegetation is difficult to determine, though it is thought of as "not particularly

fattening" by the Japanese. *Hijiki* is an excellent source of calcium (one reason why the Japanese can balance their diet without dairy products) and minerals.

horseradish—see WASABI.

上
し
ん
粉   JŌSHINKO *(fine, white rice flour)* is used in making taffy-like sweets. Many similar products, such as *shiratamako* ("white jewel" flour) and *mochiko* (rice cake flour) are available, but for best results, use *jōshinko*. Check the label with the clerk to make sure you are getting what you want. Store as you would any other flour.

か
ま
ぼ
こ   KAMABOKO *(a steamed sausage prepared from different varieties of white fish)* is often decoratively trimmed in pink. Available at most large Oriental groceries, it is sold in a loaf 6–7 inches long. It must be kept refrigerated but should not be frozen and should be eaten within 3–4 days of purchase.

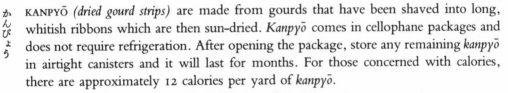

か
ん
ぴ
ょ
う   KANPYŌ *(dried gourd strips)* are made from gourds that have been shaved into long, whitish ribbons which are then sun-dried. *Kanpyō* comes in cellophane packages and does not require refrigeration. After opening the package, store any remaining *kanpyō* in airtight canisters and it will last for months. For those concerned with calories, there are approximately 12 calories per yard of *kanpyō*.

寒
天   KANTEN *(agar-agar)* is a type of gelatin processed from the algae fancifully named "heavenly grass" *(tengusa)*. The chemical composition of *kanten* is quite different from that of ordinary gelatin. It will jell without refrigeration, though chilling will quicken the process somewhat. And all fruits, including fresh pineapple, will set in it.

    Kanten (gelatin) is sold dried, in thick brittle sticks or occasionally in powdered form. The recipes in this book call for white (shimmering, translucent, no-color) sticks. Stored in a cool, dry spot, *kanten* will last for years.

片栗粉 **KATAKURIKO** *(Japanese thickening powder)* is a fine white powder, similar to cornstarch and to arrowroot. Dissolved in water, it is used to thicken sauces. Used alone or in combination with all-purpose flour, foods dredged in *katakuriko* before frying are extra crispy. Sold in cellophane bags, it should be transferred to a moisture-proof container after opening. Either cornstarch or arrowroot could be used as a substitute.

鰹節 <u>**KATSUO BUSHI**</u> *(flakes of dried bonito)* are used in stock making and occasionally as a garnish for vegetable dishes. Most often sold in cellophane packages, some are called "fresh packs" and contain many single portions of 5 grams each; more common are large bags of 100–150 grams with enough flakes for several gallons of stock. Freshness is essential to fine flavor. Check the import label for the date—anything older than 6–8 months will have lost its delicacy; anything older than one year isn't worth buying. By the way, although the dating system in Japan theoretically follows the Gregorian calendar, you will in fact encounter a different system of dating used for most things—including labels on food packages. Each emperor of Japan has a name assigned to his reign. *Showa* is the name of the present Emperor Hirohito's reign. The years are counted from one for the first year of the reign until the emperor's death. 1980 is Showa 55. So if a package is labeled 55-2-6, it means February 6, 1980.

In Japan, many people make their own shavings from dried fillets of fish. The fillet looks much like a polished piece of mahogany and the shavings a bit like sawdust. Store *katsuo bushi* in an airtight, moisture-proof container at room temperature, out of direct sunlight. Rich in many trace minerals, ¼ cup of flakes has only 25 calories.

きくらげ **KIKURAGÉ** *(thin, dark mushrooms)* grow at the foot of certain trees and resemble the human ear in size and configuration. In Japanese (and Chinese, too) the name is written with the characters for "wood" or "tree" and "ear." The English name most commonly found on the cellophane bags sold in the U.S. is "woodtree ears." In their dried state they are black and brittle. When soaked in warm water they expand and soften to thin, very dark brown, slightly slippery discs. *Kikuragé* do not have the strong, deep flavor of most other fungi. They are cultivated and enjoyed more for their unusual chewy, almost crunchy texture. Dried *kikuragé* should be stored in a

canister or other container with a tight-fitting lid. Avoid exposing them to moisture and heat, and they should keep for many years.

黄な粉 KINAKO *(soy flour)* is a fine pale-beige flour made from soybeans. It is highly nutritious but spoils rather easily. The package should be refrigerated after opening and its contents used within a few weeks.

木の芽 KI NO MÉ *(aromatic leaf of the prickly ash tree)* is difficult to obtain in the U.S., but if you should see these delicate leaves in the springtime, by all means buy them. Chopped and tossed in a salad or floated whole in a bowl of clear soup, their unique aroma and sharp flavor will surely captivate you. Store wrapped in damp paper towels and plastic wrap in the vegetable bin of your refrigerator. Just before eating, rinse the leaves lightly, then gently pat them dry. Open your hand, lay several leaves on your open palm, and slap down on them with your other hand. This will release the unique aroma of the leaf. It is rich in vitamin A with just a few calories.

切り干し大根 KIRI-BOSHI DAIKON *(shredded dried Japanese white radish)* looks much like a pile of straw in its cellophane or clear plastic bags. Softened and braised, it becomes a tasty vegetable to serve with meat, poultry and fish. Store in the vegetable bin of your refrigerator in its original or other plastic bag. Soften only the amount you wish to cook at a particular time; in its dried state it will keep for 3–4 weeks. Do not freeze either the dried or softened vegetable. Low in calories (1 cup, cooked in sweetened soy broth, is less than 50) and rich in minerals.

昆布 KONBU *(kelp)* looks like so many dusty strips of dark leather in its dried state. Used primarily for stock making, it imparts an elusive sweetness to the water in which it is cooked. You can keep the kelp you've used for making stock, covered in plastic wrap, in the refrigerator 3–4 days, then use to make fish rolls or beans and assorted vegetables. Store dry kelp in its original cellophane bag at room temperature until opening, then transfer remaining pieces to an airtight, dry container. Kelp is rich in calcium and other minerals; caloric count is not available but thought to be low. *Hidaka konbu* or *hidaka dashi konbu* from Hokkaidō (the northernmost island of the Japanese archipelago) is considered the best.

こんにゃく KONNYAKU *(pearly-toned gelatinous cake made from a tuber vegetable with the exotic name of devil's tongue)* is often labeled on cans or packages as "yam cakes" or "alimentary paste." There are light, dark, and speckled varieties of *konnyaku*. For the recipes in this book, any of these are acceptable. *Konnyaku* has no distinctive taste of its own, but is very porous and quickly absorbs the flavor of cooking liquids. Upon first opening the package, it has a slightly rancid offensive odor, which disappears with a quick blanching and is not an indication of spoilage. Refrigerate any leftover *konnyaku* in fresh cold water to cover. Change the water each day and it will stay fresh for 4–5 days. *Konnyaku* should not be frozen. It is thought to cleanse one's digestive tract of irritating and poisonous substances, and in Japan it is recommended to those with ulcers, upset stomachs and other digestive disorders. *Konnyaku* has no calories.

栗の甘露煮 KURI NO KANRO NI *(cooked chestnuts in sweet syrup)* are large, bright-yellow bottled chestnuts. Sold at most Oriental groceries in 7- or 12-ounce sizes, they are far less expensive than French *marrons glacés* or chestnut purée. In this book, there are one rice dish and one sweet calling for *kuri no kanro ni,* but they are perfectly gorgeous used in many Western recipes.

LEEKS *(called négi or naganégi in Japanese)* are favored by the Japanese in most dishes requiring an onion-like flavor. Select firm, white, thick leeks with dark-green tops, preferably with earth still clinging to the roots. Leeks should be stored in the vegetable bin of your refrigerator and washed and trimmed just before using.

lotus root—see RENKON.

み
か
ん MIKAN *(Japanese orange)* is a tangerine-like fruit in season throughout the winter in Japan. They are nearly impossible to obtain fresh in the United States, though cans of peeled *mikan* sections in light syrup are readily available in most Oriental groceries. Approximately 70 calories for ½ cup; a fairly good source of vitamins A and C.

味
醂 MIRIN *(sweet, syrupy rice wine)* is used to glaze foods as well as to flavor them. If for some reason you cannot find *mirin,* a reasonable substitute can be made by using equal parts of sugar and *saké.* Heat through until the sugar dissolves, stirring constantly. Continue to cook, stirring, until the liquid is reduced by nearly half.

    Mirin, once opened, has a shelf life of several months if kept tightly capped and away from direct heat and light. Refrigeration is not required. Be sure to wipe the rim of the bottle clean after each use before replacing the cap, otherwise the bottle cap can become "glued" on, as with honey or other syrups.

味
噌 MISO *(bean paste or soybean paste)* is a fermented soybean mash used to thicken and season soups, sauces and marinades. It comes in a wide variety of flavors, colors and textures, though they fall into three basic classifications: *aka* ("red," really dark brown) is pungent, *chū* ("medium," usually golden toned) is mild, and *shiro* ("white," actually pale tan) is mellow with a touch of sweetness. The recipes in this book call for *Sendai miso* (a brand and regional name) for dishes requiring "red" *aka* miso. *Shinshu Ichi miso* (again a brand and regional name) is used when "medium" *chū* miso is required. *Saikyo miso* (brand and regional name) is used in recipes that need pale *shiro miso.* Other brand names are available for each of these types and may prove more to your individual liking. The important thing to remember in substituting one *miso* for another is to use an alternate brand of the same classification. For example, you may prefer to use *Marukomé miso* instead of *Shinshu Ichi miso* but since both are of the same *chū* or "medium" type this presents no problem. If in doubt about substitutes ask the clerk when making your purchase.

    For best home storage, transfer the *miso* to a plastic, glass or ceramic container with a tight-fitting lid. Although *miso* will not spoil if kept in a cool spot, refrigeration is preferable. Freezing, though, ruins the texture and aroma. *Miso* will stay fresh for several months, but superior flavor is limited to the first few weeks.

    All *miso* has a very high sodium content, and those on special diets should be aware of this. It is also rich in protein, trace minerals and calcium. Calories run about 50 per tablespoon.

三つ葉 MITSUBA *(trefoil)* is a delicate-looking plant with a slender stalk and three flat leaves. It is sold fresh in bunches at most well-stocked Oriental groceries that sell fresh produce and should be available fairly regularly throughout the year. It is similar in appearance to coriander and flat-leafed parsley, though more delicate in flavor. Wrap in damp paper toweling and store in the vegetable bin of your refrigerator. *Mitsuba* will wilt after a few days, but will not spoil for a week. *Mitsuba* has only a few calories, and is very rich in vitamins A and C.

もち米 MOCHI-GOMÉ *(glutinous rice)* is steamed rather than boiled and is used primarily for making rice cakes. Available at all Oriental groceries in small bags, it should be stored in a dark, dry spot at room temperature. There are about 200 calories in a small bowl of cooked rice.

もやし MOYASHI *(bean sprouts)* are used less in Japanese cooking than in many other Oriental cuisines, but they do find their way into several dishes. Fresh bean sprouts are increasingly available even at neighborhood markets; canned sprouts should be avoided—they are limp, tasteless and nearly devoid of nutrition. Fresh sprouts are rich in vitamin C and only 15 calories per cup, but are highly perishable. Eat within 2 days of purchase.

麦茶 MUGI CHA *(roasted barley tea)* makes a nutritious and refreshing beverage. *Mugi cha* is sold in cellophane packages, but should be stored in airtight moisture-proof canisters after opening and used within 3 months.

mushrooms—see SHIITAKÉ (black Oriental), ÉNOKIDAKÉ (slender white), NAMÉKO (slippery orange), KIKURAGÉ (thin, dark).

なめこ NAMÉKO are firm, round, orange or gold mushrooms naturally coated in a slippery, almost slimy, substance. They have a rich, earthy, full-bodied flavor. Canned *naméko* are available in most Oriental groceries and have a shelf life of several years. Once opened, though, they should be used immediately or refrigerated in a closed plastic container or glass jar. Stored in this manner, they will stay fresh for 3–4 days.

煮干し NIBOSHI *(dried sardines for stock making)* are sold in cellophane bags at most Oriental groceries. After opening, store in a moisture-proof container. The dried fish may be dipped in soy sauce and eaten as a snack. They are extremely rich in calcium, magnesium and protein, and the stock made from *niboshi* is also.

NIHON SHU—see SAKÉ.

noodles—see CHŪKA SOBA (thin yellow), RAMEN (Chinese style), SOBA (buckwheat), SŌMEN (thin white), UDON (thick white).

ぬか NUKA *(rice bran)* is the by-product of hulling white rice and is used by the Japanese primarily as a pickling agent. It is extremely rich in the B vitamins and trace minerals, and vegetables pickled in a damp *nuka* paste are nutritious, with a tangy crispness quite different from most Western vinegared pickles and relishes. *Nuka* is sold in cellophane bags (sometimes in boxes) and the date on the label should be checked for freshness. In anything older than 2 months the nutritional value is cut in half; older than 6 months, the flavor will suffer greatly. *see* KATSUO BUSHI for how to decipher the Japanese dating of labels.

Rice bran for pickling is sold as plain *nuka, iri nuka* (dry-roasted rice bran; slightly less perishable than raw bran), and *nuka-zuké no moto* ("the essence of pickling," or an already "seasoned" mixture needing only water or water and salt). If the store where you shop has packaged its own rice bran (as a by-product of hulling freshly harvested rice), by all means buy it and dry roast it yourself. Spread it on a cookie sheet and place in a very slow oven for 20 minutes, or heat it in a dry skillet over medium heat (shaking and rotating the pan constantly) for 5 minutes. Allow the rice bran to cool to room temperature, then store it in an airtight container at room temperature. Prepackaged rice bran should be stored at room temperature in its original package until opened, then transferred to an airtight container.

お茶 OCHA *(green tea)* is enjoyed throughout the day by everyone in Japan. There are many grades, but price is usually a good indication of quality. And, unless you are a connoisseur of this drink, a medium range should suit you. *Ocha* is sold in canister-like tins or boxes containing vacuum-sealed aluminum packs. Since the delicate, musky aroma of green tea suffers with exposure to air, store it in an airtight, moisture-proof canister. Room temperature is fine. Or store in the freezer for up to 3 months.

おぼ
米 OKOMÉ *(raw rice, hulled)* is the mainstay of the Japanese diet and is prized for its simplicity and purity of flavor. The Japanese favor a short-grained rice best known throughout the U.S. as California Rose or Blue Rose rice. It is available at any well-stocked Oriental grocery in 2-, 5- and 10-pound bags. Store in an airtight container at room temperature away from direct sunlight. Freshness is important; really fine rice is never more than 6 months old. Traditional harvesting time is late summer through early fall. *Shin mai* or new rice just harvested is particularly prized by the Japanese, but may require a teaspoon or so more water per cup for cooking. Plain cooked rice is approximately 90 calories for a single ½ cup serving. For those of you who are concerned with the nutrients lost in hulling, a product called *vita-raisu* is available at most Oriental groceries. Yellow in color but shaped just like rice, these vitamin kernels can be mixed into hulled rice (approximately ½ teaspoon for every cup of raw rice) before cooking. There is a slight vitamin odor when you first remove the lid after cooking, but this quickly disappears. As the *vita-raisu* cooks with the rice, it pales considerably, so that the final dish looks and tastes very similar to plain rice. Do not use *vita-raisu* for rice that is to be seasoned with vinegar later.

おも
ち OMOCHI *(glutinous rice cakes)* are made by pounding cooked glutinous rice and kneading and pulling it much as we do taffy; though no sugar or salt is added. Really fresh *omochi* is divine—soft, stretchy and chewy. Wintertime, and particularly the New Year, is the season for grilling and boiling these cakes and putting them in soups, or winding them up in sheets of crisp laver. At most family-run Oriental groceries, they will make *omochi* fresh if there are enough customers who request it. Find out what day they plan to make it, and if they do it by traditional pounding (rather than by kneading in a machine similar to a pasta machine) go watch the fun. The cakes are usually round if hand-formed and square if rolled into a sheet and cut with a sharp knife. Traditionally, squares are grilled and rounds are boiled, but truthfully the shape makes no difference in flavor. Store fresh cakes in clear wrap in the refrigerator for a week; or wrap it and freeze for up to 3 months. In either case, bring the cakes back to room temperature before boiling or grilling them. *Omochi* is yummy, but fattening: about 250 calories per 3–4-inch piece. (Vacuum sealed, commercially prepared *omochi* is awful—especially if you've ever sampled freshly made rice cakes.)

pickled ginger, pink—see AMAZU SHŌGA.

pickled ginger, red—see BÉNI SHŌGA.

pickles—see TSUKÉ MONO and the section on home and commercial pickling, page 189.

radish—see DAIKON.

ラーメン RAMEN *(Chinese-style noodles)* are sold as fresh, fresh-dried and instant noodles at almost every Oriental grocery in the U.S. Some of the precooked instant packages come with packets of soup mix and aren't bad for a quick snack. But really to enjoy the Japanese version of Chinese soup noodles, buy fresh or fresh-dried noodles and try the recipes on pages 104, 105, and 108. Fresh noodles should never be refrozen; eat within a day or two of purchase. Fresh-dried noodles have a long shelf life if stored in a dry, dark spot at room temperature. Instant noodles have all sorts of preservatives added, so that spoilage is rarely a problem. *Ramen* may also be labeled as *larmen* (originally a misspelling, which has persisted) and the weird "English" name of "alimentary paste."

れんこん RENKON *(lotus root)* is also called *hasu* in some parts of Japan. When prepared, it is a pretty vegetable, though the root itself is not particularly attractive. Unless cut through to expose the many hollow canals within the vegetable, lotus root is a string of several grayish speckled or streaked oblongs. It may be sold in small pieces of a few ounces each, or as a chain of several roots. It should be firm, unscarred and with clean canals. Fresh lotus root may be stored, unpeeled, in a plastic bag in the refrigerator for up to 5 days. Any peeled or cut surface will change from pure white to purple, gray or brown. After peeling and cutting, slices should be soaked in acidulated water to preserve their color. Lotus root is low in calories (approximately 70 calories in ¼ pound) and rich in vitamin C.

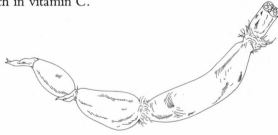

rice—see OKOMÉ.

rice cakes—see OMOCHI.

SAIKYŌ MISO—see MISO (bean paste).

酒 SAKÉ *(rice wine)* is often referred to as *nihon shu* or "Japanese wine" by the Japanese themselves. It is a light white wine used extensively in cooking. *Saké* is also served, slightly warm, as a beverage at parties or large dinners. Several grades exist, but price should be a good indication of quality. Most Oriental groceries do not have the required license to sell alcoholic beverages, and so *saké* must be purchased throughout most of the U.S. at liquor stores. It is becoming easier, though, to find *saké* at local liquor stores outside Oriental neighborhoods. *Saké* has about 200 calories per cup.

さんしょう SANSHO *(Japanese fragrant pepper)* is the green berry of the prickly ash, which is crushed to a fine powder to make a delightfully aromatic spice. Try using it, too, instead of white pepper in Western soups and sauces. *Sansho* is sold in small bottles and is occasionally referred to as *kona-zansho* or *kona sansho* meaning "powdered" pepper.

ささげ豆 SASAGÉ MAMÉ *(small dried red beans)* can be cooked with rice, or made into sweet bean jam for stuffing rice-flour cakes, are sold in small cellophane bags. Store in an airtight container at room temperature up to 3 months. Rich in protein, carbohydrates, magnesium, and vitamin B_1, a half cup has about 300 calories.

里いも SATO IMO *(Japanese country potatoes)* are often sold as taro potatoes. Dark brown and hairy outside, they are smooth and pale gray inside. Occasionally irritating to sensitive skin, the "potatoes" are tastiest and least likely to cause irritation if peeled in a basin of cold water. When cooked, these "potatoes" have an unusually mellow flavor and soft, almost slippery texture. Store in the vegetable bin of your refrigerator if not to be used within a day or two of purchase.

さつまいも SATSUMA IMO *(Japanese sweet potatoes)* have lovely reddish skins and golden yellow flesh. Not nearly as sweet as American yams, Japanese sweet potatoes are delicious baked in their jackets with no seasonings at all! They are occasionally available at Oriental markets selling fresh produce; store as you would Irish potatoes. One-quarter pound has approximately 140 calories.

さやえんどう SAYA ÉNDŌ *(snow peas)* are crisp, young pea pods available fresh in the spring and frozen year round. You may need to "string" fresh pods. Snap off the stem and pull back the string for the entire length of the pod. If you're going to use frozen pods, stir-fry or blanch them without defrosting first.

scallions are known as *wakégi* in Japanese. The tender green stalks and white bulbs are usually chopped and used as a garnish in soups or noodle dishes. Buy small bunches with firm stalks, wrap them in slightly damp paper toweling and store in the vegetable bin of your refrigerator up to 5 days.

seaweed—see ASAKUSA NORI (black sheets of laver), AO NORI (flakes of green laver), HIJIKI (black, licorice-like), KONBU (kelp for stock making), WAKAMÉ (lobe-leaf).

SENDAI MISO—see MISO (bean paste).

sesame seeds—see GOMA.

七味唐がらし SHICHIMI TŌGARASHI *(7-spice hot pepper)* is sold in tins at all Oriental groceries. It is a combination of dried hot peppers, rape, sesame seeds, mustard, and sea vegetation. Store in a cool, dry spot out of direct sunlight. It has a shelf life of at least a year.

椎茸 SHIITAKÉ *(black Oriental mushrooms)* are on the market fresh in Japan from the fall to the spring. Dried, they are used year round in a variety of dishes. Unfortunately fresh *shiitaké* are hard to find even in well-stocked Oriental groceries in the U.S. If you're lucky enough to see some buy them and use the fresh black mushrooms in soups or one-pot casseroles. Or skewer and grill them, serving with lemon wedges and soy sauce on the side. For braising and simmering, though, dried *shiitaké* are preferred. Though expensive, the small, thick black-with-beige-striped mushrooms are magnificent. Treat yourself to a few ounces of these for special occasions. Save the stems (dried) for stock making, and buy a package of the less-expensive broken pieces for ordinary use. Store in an airtight container at room temperature in a dark spot. All fungi are rich in vitamins and minerals, though caloric value is not available.

SHINSHŪ ICHI MISO—see MISO (bean paste).

白板昆布 **SHIRATA KONBU** *(translucent kelp)* is used here primarily to decorate a mackerel and rice loaf known as *saba-zushi*. To make *shirata konbu*, a thick, pale-green sea plant is dried, then shaved and scraped (these shavings are marketed as *tororo konbu*, by the way, a melt-in-your-mouth gauzy-looking strip of sea vegetation used as a garnish in some rice dishes and soups). The core that remains is the *shirata konbu*; it is quite pliable— a pale golden-toned green ribbon. When this ribbon is simmered in sweet and sour sauce it becomes translucent and delicious. It is difficult to find *shirata konbu* in the U.S., but if you are able to order it, do so. In addition to being used in the mackerel and rice recipe, after simmering it can be chopped and tossed into any mixed *sushi* dish. Once the original cellophane or vacuum-sealed bag has been opened, store in a plastic bag in the refrigerator. It will stay fresh for a month or more. Calories are difficult to determine for all sea vegetation, but thought to be very low. *Shirata konbu* is rich in minerals, particularly calcium.

しらたき **SHIRATAKI** *("white waterfall")* are thin transparent gelatin-like noodles made from a tuber vegetable (devil's tongue root). Sold in sealed plastic bags or suspended in liquid in cans, they have a slightly unpleasant odor when opened. If they are drained and quickly blanched, this odor disappears. Store cans as you would any other canned product; bags should be kept refrigerated (up to one week unopened, for two days after opening). Never freeze *shirataki*. It has no calories and no other real nutrients either, but the Japanese feel that this and *konnyaku*, both made from the same tuber vegetable, cleanse the intestinal tract.

しそ **SHISO** *(an aromatic dark green leaf of the beefsteak plant)* grows easily in moderate climates. Available fresh during the summer months (at some stores you may have to special-order it; better yet, try to order the seeds and grow some yourself!), *shiso* is rich in vitamins A and E. To store, wrap the leaves in a sheet of damp paper toweling, then clear plastic wrap, and keep in the vegetable bin of your refrigerator. It will have maximum aroma for the first three days, but the leaves can be chopped and added to salads for up to a week.

しょうが SHŌGA *(fresh ginger)*, also called *né shōga,* is used extensively in Japanese cooking. Use only fresh or pickled ginger, *never* the dried and powdered form. Store, unpeeled and unwrapped, in the vegetable bin of your refrigerator. It will dry out a bit around the edges after several days, but will not spoil for weeks. (If you wrap it in damp paper toweling, it will stay moist for about 4 days, but mold and spoil quickly thereafter.) For most recipes, the root is peeled and grated to extract fresh juice. A small knob the size of your thumb has only 7 calories.

しょう油 SHŌYU *(soy sauce)* is a dark, slightly salty liquid seasoning used extensively in Japanese cooking. Regular or dark soy sauce *(koi kuchi shōyu)* should be used unless light soy sauce *(usu kuchi shōyu)* is specifically indicated in any recipe. *Usu kuchi shōyu* is lighter in color, though saltier, than regular soy sauce. Check the labels with the sales clerk when purchasing. Do not use Chinese soy sauce—it is too strong. *Kikkoman* is the best-known Japanese brand, and both bottles and cans of various sizes are readily available everywhere. Soy sauce may be stored in the original container, but avoid exposure to light or heat. Soy sauce has a shelf life of several years, though a sediment may form at the bottom of your container after several months. Do not stir it up, just use the remaining liquid. Soy sauce has approximately 10 calories per tablespoon.

春菊 SHUNGIKU *(chrysanthemum leaves or dandelion greens)* are at their best in the fall. They are increasingly available at even the smaller Oriental groceries. Don't pass them up when you see them. If sold with the roots still attached, all the better—they should last 2–3 days longer that way. Wrap the stems in a sheet of damp paper toweling, then place the entire bunch in a loose-fitting plastic bag. Keep in the vegetable bin of your refrigerator until needed, trimming off the roots and stems and discarding any flowering buds only just before cooking. Chrysanthemum leaves will stay really fresh for 3 days, but won't spoil for a week. A 2–3 ounce bunch has only 20 calories but 2000 units of vitamin A.

snow peas—see SAYA ÉNDO.

そば SOBA is the name both of a thin beige-colored noodle and of the grain (similar to buckwheat) from which the noodle is made. Available at all Oriental groceries, usually fresh-dried, but occasionally homemade. The dried noodles have a shelf life of about 6 months if kept dry.

素麺 SŌMEN *(thin white noodles)* are available in fresh-dried form only, and have a shelf life of several years. In fact many Japanese think they mellow with a year of storage. *Sōmen* are packaged in small bundles (each about 2–3 ounces) in cellophane packages or occasionally in wooden crates.

soybeans—see ÉDA MAMÉ (fresh soybeans) and DAIZU (dried soybeans).

soy sauce—see SHŌYU.

stock—see DASHI.

酢 SU *(rice vinegar)* is a mild, mellow vinegar made from rice. It should be used in all recipes calling for vinegar. Ordinary vinegar is too harsh. *Mitsukan* is the most popular brand name of Japanese rice vinegar and it is widely available in bottles. You'll find the more delicate Japanese rice vinegar so much to your liking you'll be wanting to use it regularly in your American kitchen. One tablespoon has about 2 calories.

sugar—The Japanese use a great deal of refined, non-granulated white sugar in their cooking. In fact most people are shocked to discover just how much sugar they use. But it is necessary to complement the salty soy sauce or tangy vinegar, with which it is so often combined. I've cut traditional quantities whenever I felt the flavor would not suffer, but most braised foods require large amounts of sugar for taste and gloss.

In most recipes you can use regular granulated sugar. But in a few dishes where the texture is important I've called for superfine sugar (because granulated sugar would be unpleasantly gritty). You could, of course, use the kind of ungranulated sugar common in Japanese kitchens, but it would have to be purchased at a Japanese-owned Oriental grocery—and that seems an unnecessary nuisance.

寿
し
酢 SUSHI SU *(seasoned vinegar)* is used in making *sushi*. *Mitsukan* is the best-known brand, and bottles are available in most Oriental groceries—no special storage instructions. *Sushi su* has a shelf life of several years.

筍 TAKÉNOKO *(bamboo shoots)* are sold fresh in the springtime and shouldn't be missed—they have a delightful crunch and delicacy of flavor that just cannot stand up to canning. But, for year-round practicality, canned bamboo shoots (whole, pieces, and skinny "green" shoots) are available at every Oriental grocery. After opening, refrigerate in fresh cold water to cover. Change the water every day for up to one week. If the water should become cloudy before then, it's a sign of early spoilage and I would drain and blanch the remaining shoots and use immediately. About 120 calories for an 8-ounce shoot.

tea—see GÉNMAI CHA (roasted rice tea), MUGI CHA (barley tea), OCHA (green tea).

天
ぷ
ら
粉 TEMPURA KO *(low-gluten wheat flour)* is used specifically for making *tempura* batter. It is available in small paper bags. The most common brand name is *Nisshin*. All-purpose flour may be used instead.

天
つ
ゆ TENTSUYU is a dipping sauce for *tempura (batter-fried shrimp and vegetables)*. Canned concentrate (to be diluted with water) is convenient, though freshly made is superior in flavor. Store cans as you would any can of soup; fresh sauce can be kept refrigerated for several days.

照
り
焼
ソ
ー
ス TERI YAKI SŌSU *(a sweetened soy-based glaze)* is sold bottled or in powdered form everywhere. I prefer to make my own (with no MSG added). The recipe is on page 143. For finest flavor, *teri yaki* sauce should be used in the final half of grilling or broiling, not from the start.

手
打
ち
専
用
小
麦
粉 TÉ UCHI SENYŌ KOMUGIKO *(flour for making handmade thick white noodles)* is a brand name of flour put out by the Nisshin Seibun company. Not as readily available as it should be (little consumer demand from Americans up until now), try to order some if you can. Making your own noodles is fun and very rewarding. Store in an airtight container at room temperature for up to one month; refrigerate if longer storage is necessary.

豆腐 TŌFU *(bean curd)* is a pure white, custardlike loaf made from the curds of soybean milk. *Tōfu* provides an inexpensive, filling, protein-packed element to the Japanese diet. One loaf has approximately 180 calories. Store *tōfu* covered in fresh cold water, refrigerated. Change the water every day and it will stay fresh for 4–5 days. Do not freeze *tōfu* as this changes the texture entirely.

A fairly recent addition to the market is a powder to make your own *tōfu*. Although its flavor and texture are not quite as good as *tōfu* made from whole soybeans, the powdered mix will make *tōfu* available to many more people.

唐がらし TŌGARASHI *(dried hot red peppers)* are sold in small cellophane packets and should be stored in a cool, dry spot. Dried red peppers are used in a variety of ways in the Japanese kitchen—as a fiery seasoning to mild grated radish or salt-pickled cabbage, as a bug-deterrent in rice bran pickling, and as a hot and colorful garnish when sliced into thin rounds.

とんかつソース TONKATSU SŌSU *(dark, spicy sauce)* sold in plastic and glass bottles. Meant specifically for fried pork cutlets *(tonkatsu)*, it is also nice for other fried breaded foods. *Bull Dog* and *Kagomé* are the best-known brand names. Store at room temperature, with the cap tightly screwed on. It has a shelf life of several years, though the aroma and flavor are best within the first month or two.

漬物 TSUKÉ MONO *(pickles)* is the name commonly given to fresh or sun-dried vegetables pickled in a variety of ways. The two most frequently encountered types of pickles are *shio-zuké*, salt-pressure pickles, and *nuka-zuké*, rice-bran-paste pickles. Details on making and/or purchasing can be found on page 189, where an entire chapter has been devoted to the subject. Pickles are also known as *oshinko*, the "fragrant things."

うどん UDON *(thick white noodles)*. Handmade are far superior to commercially prepared, but precooked fresh and fresh-dried are available at most Oriental groceries. Fresh noodles are highly perishable and should be eaten within a day or two of purchase. Often they have been frozen for transport; do not refreeze such noodles. *Udon* are packaged in plastic bags in individual portions of about 4 ounces each. Fresh-dried noodles have a shelf life of several years; they are packaged in cellophane. Some noodles are as broad as ⅜ inch, most about half that. One pack yields approximately 4–5 servings.

梅干し UMÉ-BOSHI *(pickled plums)*. The dusty-pink-tinted ones have been pickled with a leaf called *aka-jiso* and are favored by most Japanese (the bright red or heliotrope ones are artificially colored and should be avoided). Packaged in plastic, cellophane or glass, they should be stored in a cool, dry spot. Peak flavor is within a half year of pickling, though they will keep for several years. Many Japanese think *umé-boshi* have medicinal properties, particularly for intestinal upsets. Only a few calories for each plum.

梅酒 UMÉ SHU *(plum wine)* is often a homemade affair in Japan. A rather sweet, slightly syrupy liquor, it is best chilled and served on the rocks. It is increasingly available at even small liquor stores throughout the U.S.

USU KUCHI SHŌYU—see SHŌYU (soy sauce).

vinegar—see SU (rice vinegar), SUSHI SU (seasoned rice vinegar).

若布 WAKAMÉ *(lobe-leaf, a type of sea vegetation)* is sold in its dried state and looks like a tangle of dusty, dark and stiff ribbons. Soaked and softened, it returns to its natural vibrant green color. *Wakamé* is slippery and sweet. Coarsely chopped it is used in soups and salads. It is rich in calcium and vitamin A; its exact caloric value is unknown but suspected to be low. Store in an airtight container after opening, in a dark spot at room temperature.

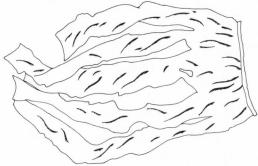

わ
さ   WASABI *(fiery green horseradish root)* is nearly impossible to obtain fresh in the United
び   States and very expensive when it is. Tins of powder (to be mixed with water) and
tubes of paste, though, are readily available at Oriental groceries. Store the powder
or paste in a cool dry spot and it will last for years.

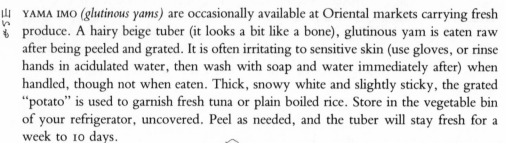

山   YAMA IMO *(glutinous yams)* are occasionally available at Oriental markets carrying fresh
い   produce. A hairy beige tuber (it looks a bit like a bone), glutinous yam is eaten raw
も   after being peeled and grated. It is often irritating to sensitive skin (use gloves, or rinse
hands in acidulated water, then wash with soap and water immediately after) when
handled, though not when eaten. Thick, snowy white and slightly sticky, the grated
"potato" is used to garnish fresh tuna or plain boiled rice. Store in the vegetable bin
of your refrigerator, uncovered. Peel as needed, and the tuber will stay fresh for a
week to 10 days.

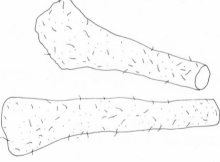

Suggestions for Ordering
Japanese Foodstuffs

Oriental foodstuffs have become increasingly popular and available throughout the United States. Should you have trouble, however, in obtaining certain items, I suggest you write to the Japan Food Corporation. It is the major supplier of Oriental foodstuffs in the continental United States, and the people there will be glad to inform you of stores in your area that handle mail orders. They have sales offices throughout the United States, but it's best to write to their head offices for information:

The Japan Food Corporation
445 Kauffman Court
South San Francisco, California 94080

If you live in a large metropolitan area, consult the yellow pages of your phone directory for local Oriental groceries.

In addition, here is a small list of stores that responded to my questionnaire about the availability of ingredients I mention in this book:

Rafu Bussan Company
344 East First Street
Los Angeles, California 90012

Star Market
3349 N. Clark St.
Chicago, Illinois 60657

K. Sakai Company
1656 Post Street
San Francisco, California 94115

Yoshinoya
36 Prospect Street
Cambridge, Massachusetts 02139

Asian Trading Company
2581 Piedmont N.E.
Atlanta, Georgia 30324

Kim's Korner
19517 West 7 Mile Road
Detroit, Michigan 48219

The Orient
P.O. Box 24
Portage, Michigan 49081

Maruyama, Inc.
100 N. 18th Street
St. Louis, Missouri 63103

Katagiri Company
224 East 59th Street
New York, New York 10022

Tanaka and Company
326 Amsterdam Ave.
New York, New York 10023

Mikado
4709 Wisconsin Avenue N.W.
Washington, D.C. 20016

A Glossary
of Japanese Terms

abura: oil

abura agé: fried bean curd

aé: mix, toss

aé mono: salads

agé: fry

agé mono: fried foods

aji: flavor

aka: red

aka-jiso: red leaf and berry

aka miso: dark bean paste

amai: sweet

amazu: Sweet and Sour Sauce

amazu shōga: pink pickled ginger

an: sauce; bean jam

an kaké: sauced food

anzu: apricot

ao nori: green flakes of seaweed

Asakusa nori: thin sheets of dark dried seaweed

asari: a kind of clam

atsu: thick

béni shōga: red pickled ginger

bō: stick

buta (niku): pork (lit. "pig meat")

Calpis: brand name of a syrupy drink

chirashi: scatter

chūka soba: Chinese egg noodles

chū miso: medium bean paste

daikon: Japanese white radish

daizu: dried soybeans

dango: ball

dashi: basic soup stock

déba-bōchō: cleaver

——*domburi;* ——*don:* bowl of rice with ——(a topping)

do nabé: earthenware pot

ebi: shrimp (prawn, lobster)

éda mamé: fresh soybeans

éndō mamé: snow peas

énokidaké: slender-stalked white mushrooms

fuki: vegetable similar to rhubarb

furai: fry

futo maki: fat rolls

génmai cha: roasted barley tea

——*giri:* ——cut

gobō: burdock root

gochisō sama deshita: "I've been royally feasted" (said after eating)

gohan: rice; meal

goma: sesame seeds

goma abura: sesame oil

gomai oroshi: 5-piece filleting (of flat fishes)

235

goma shio: sesame and salt combination, a garnish
gomoku: assorted
gyū (niku): beef (lit. "cow meat")

hajikami su-zuké: pickled whole young ginger
hakusai: Chinese cabbage
hamaguri: a kind of clam
hana-gata: "flower-shaped," a decorative cut
handai: wooden tub for mixing rice with seasonings
han gétsu-giri: "half-moon shaped," a decorative cut
hashi: chopsticks (also referred to as *ohashi*)
hasu: lotus root (also called *renkon*)
hibachi: lit. "fire-box," an open grill
hidaka dashi konbu: fine grade kelp for stock making
hijiki: black sea vegetable
hitashi: vegetables with clear broth sauce
hiyashi: chilled, cold
Hokkaidō: name of northern-most island in Japan
honé nuki: de-boning tweezers

ika: squid, cuttlefish
inari: often refers to food made with fried bean curd
ingen (mamé): string beans
iri: include, put in; dry roast; pan roast
iri nuka: dry-roasted rice bran
itadakimasu: "I receive" (said before eating)
itamé ni: sauté

jidō denshi hōn-gama: automatic rice cooker
jiru: soup
jōshinko: fine rice flour (for making Japanese pastries)
——jū: box filled with rice and topped with——
jū-bako: box used for serving food

kabayaki: grilled eel
kabocha: squash, pumpkin
kaiseki ryōri: elegant, formal dinner
kaki: persimmon; oyster
kamaboko: fish sausage
kaminari: "lightning," a fancy curlicue cut
kani: crab
kanpyō: dried gourd strips
kanro: sweet syrup
kanten: agar-agar, Japanese sea gelatin
kappa maki: *sushi* filled with cucumber and rolled in seaweed
kappogi: apron with sleeves
kara agé: deep crispy fry
karai: spicy, salty
karashi: mustard
katakuriko: cornstarch, arrowroot
katei ryōri: home-style cooking
katsuo bushi: bonito (fish) flakes for stock making and garnish
katsura muki: "wide-peel," a decorative cut
kayaku: assorted food mixed into rice or noodles
katsu: cutlet
Kikkoman: brand name of soy sauce
kikuragé: woodtree-ear mushrooms
kimono: Japanese traditional clothing
kinako: soy flour
ki no mé: aromatic leaf of the prickly ash tree
kiri: cut
kiri-boshi daikon: shredded sun-dried Japanese white radish
kirimi: slice (of fish, meat, etc.)
ko: flour; child
kodéba-bōchō: small, dagger-like knife
kōhaku: red and white, colors of felicity
kona sansho; kona-zansho: powdered Japanese pepper
konbu: kelp (for stock making and other dishes)
konnyaku: pearly-toned gelatinous cake made from a tuber vegetable
kōri: ice
kotatsu: under-the-table heating unit
kuchi: mouth, taste
kuri: chestnut

kuri no kanro ni: cooked chestnuts in sweet syrup

kuro goma: black sesame

kurumi: walnuts

kushi: skewer, stick; comb

kushi-gata: "comb-cut," a decorative cut

kyūri: cucumber

larmen: misspelling of *ramen* that has persisted

maki: roll, rolled

mamé: bean

maru: whole, round

Marukomé miso: brand name of medium fermented bean paste

matsuba: "pine needle," a decorative cut

Matsuri: festival, holiday

mikan: Japanese orange

mirin: syrupy rice wine

miso: fermented bean paste

miso shiru: soup thickened with fermented bean paste

mitsu: syrup

mitsuba: trefoil (slender-stalked 3-leaf vegetable)

Mitsukan: brand name of vinegar

mizu: water

mochi-gomé: glutinous rice

mochiko: flour made from glutinous rice

momiji oroshi: "autumn maple leaves" (grated radish with hot red pepper condiment)

mono: thing (food)

moritsuké: arrangement, presentation

moyashi: bean sprouts

mugi cha: barley tea

muki: peel, hull

muki goma: hulled sesame seeds

mushi: steamed

mushi mono: steamed foods

nabé: pot

nabé mono: one-pot cooking

nagashi-bako: rectangular metal mold

na-giri-bōchō: broad-bladed vegetable knife

naméko: slippery mushrooms

nasu: eggplant

nattō: fermented sticky soy beans

négi: leek, scallion, onion

né shōga: ginger

niboshi: dried sardines (for stock making)

nigiri: compress, compact (as in rice into a ball or oval)

Nihon shu: generic name of Japanese wine, *saké*

ni: braise, simmer

niku: meat

ni mono: braised or simmered food

ninjin: carrot

Nisshin: brand name of flour

noren: parted curtains to frame kitchen or restaurant entrance

nori: sheets of seaweed

nori maki: sushi filled with gourd and rolled in seaweed

nuka: rice bran powder

nuka-zuké: rice bran pickles

nuka-zuké no moto: seasoning for making rice bran pickles

"o" is an honorific prefix added to many words

ocha: green tea

ohitashi, see "H," *hitashi*

okara: by-product of fresh tōfu-making

okayu: porridge

okomé: raw rice

omochi: glutinous rice cakes

oroshi-gané: grater

oshinko: pickles ("fresh fragrance")

osushi: vinegared rice dishes

otoshi-buta: "dropped" lid

oya: parent

oyako nabé: chicken and egg dish

ōya-san: landlord; landlady

ramen: Chinese noodles served in soup

ran-giri: oblique cut

renkon: also *hasu,* lotus root

robata yaki: open-hearth cooking
ryōri: food, cooking

saba: mackerel
Saikyō miso: light bean paste, a brand and regional name
sakana: fish
saké: rice wine
sanmai oroshi: 3-piece filleting
sansho: Japanese fragrant pepper
Sapporo: name of large city in Hokkaidō
sarashi: cotton cloth
sasagaki: whittle cut
sasagé mamé: small dried red beans
sashimi: "fresh slice," usually uncooked fish
sashimi-bōchō: long, sharp knife for slicing meat and fish
sashimizu: "adding water" technique for cooking dried noodles
sato imo: country potato
satsuma imo: sweet potato, yam
saya éndō: snow peas
Sendai miso: dark bean paste, a brand and regional name
sen-giri: julienne slicing
shaké cha-zuké: salmon and rice dish
shamoji: wooden, paddle-like spoon
shichimi tōgarashi: 7-spice hot pepper
shiitaké: black Oriental mushrooms
shimofuri: blanch
shin mai: new rice
Shinshū Ichi miso: medium bean paste, a brand and regional name
shio: salt
shirataki: "white waterfall," shredded *konnyaku;* gelatin-like noodles
shirata konbu: pale-green broad kelp
shiratamako: flour for making Japanese pastries
shiro: white
shiro goma: white sesame seeds
shiromi: white meat (fish)
shiro miso: white (or light) bean paste
shiro uri: vegetable native to Japan, similar to zucchini
shiru: soup

shiso: dark aromatic leaf of beefsteak plant
shōga: fresh ginger
shoku béni: red food coloring
shokutaku tsuké mono ki: screw-type pickling jar
shōyu: soy sauce
shungiku: chrysanthemum leaves
soba: buckwheat noodles
soboro: "fine-crumb" texture to food
su: rice vinegar
subasu: sweet and sour lotus root
sudaré: slatted mat for rolling foods
suéhiro: fan cut
sugata: whole; in the shape of ——
sui mono: soup
su-jōyu: vinegar and soy sauce
sukiyaki: beef and vegetable sauté
sukiyaki nabé: wrought-iron skillet for cooking *sukiyaki*
su no mono: vinegared foods
suribachi: mortar (bowl)
surikogi: pestle (stick)
sushi: vinegared rice
sushi oké: wooden tub used in seasoning rice for *sushi*
sushi su: seasoned vinegar for *sushi* making

také no kawa: bamboo bark
takénoko: bamboo shoots
takuan: yellow pickled radish
tamago: egg
tamago yaki nabé: rectangular omelet pan
tazuna: "braid," a decorative cut
tekka: raw tuna
tekkyū: stand for supporting skewers
tempura: deep-fried, batter-coated food
tempura ko: flour for making batter
tempura nabé: pan for cooking *tempura*
tengusa: "heavenly grass"; a sea gelatin
tentsuyu: dipping sauce for *tempura*
teppan: griddle
teri: glaze
teri yaki: glaze-grilling
té uchi: hand made
té uchi senyō komugiko: flour made especially for making thick white noodles

tōfu: bean curd
tōgarashi: dried hot red peppers
tonkatsu: pork cutlet, fried
tonkatsu sōsu: dark, spicy sauce for *tonkatsu*
tori (niku): chicken (meat)
tori cha-zuké: chicken and rice in tea soup
tororo konbu: kind of melt-in-your-mouth sea
    vegetation
tsuké mono: pickled foods
tsuya: gloss, shine
tsuyu: seasoned liquid, clear sauce

uchiwa: flat fan
udon: thick white noodles
umé-boshi: pickled plums
umé shu: plum wine
una; unagi: eel
uragoshi: sieve
uroko tori: scaler (for cleaning fish)
usu: thin
usu kuchi shōyu: thin or light soy sauce

vita raisu: vitamin-injected rice kernels

wakamé: lobe leaf, a type of sea vegetation
wakégi: scallion
wan: bowl (of soup)
wari-bashi: disposable wooden chop sticks
wasabi: fiery green horseradish

yaki: grill, broil
yaki mono: grilled or broiled foods
yama-gata: "mountain-shaped," a decorative cut
yama imo: glutinous yams
yori udo: curlicue peels of vegetable
yuba: thin brittle sheets of soy milk (by-product
    of *tōfu*-making)

zaru: woven tray; strainer, colander
zenmai: bracken, mountain vegetable

Index

A Note About the Author

Elizabeth Andoh was raised in New York and graduated from the University of Michigan. In 1966 she went to Japan to study Japanese, and later attended the Yanagihara School of Classical Japanese Cooking for six years. It was there that she became inspired to offer classes to other Westerners living in Japan, and she wrote a series of articles on Japanese cooking for *Gourmet* magazine. Elizabeth Andoh married into a traditional Japanese family, and after more than thirteen years of living in Japan, she returned in 1980 with her husband and young daughter to America. She now teaches Japanese cooking frequently in this country and has contributed to several magazines.

A Note About the Type

The text of this book has been film set in a type face named Bembo. The roman is a copy of a letter cut for the celebrated Venetian printer Aldus Manutius by Francesco Griffo, and first used in Cardinal Bembo's *De Aetna* of 1495—hence the name of the revival. Griffo's type is now generally recognized, thanks to the researches of Mr. Stanley Morison, to be the first of the old face group of types. The companion italic is an adaption of the chancery script type designed by the Roman calligrapher and printer Lodovico degli Arrighi, called Vincentino, and used by him during the 1520's.

This book was composed by Monotype Composition Company, Inc., Baltimore, Maryland, and printed and bound by the Murray Printing Company, Forge Village, Massachusetts. The Japanese characters were set by Dai Nippon Printing Company, Ltd., Tokyo, Japan. Typography and binding design by Elissa Ichiyasu. Illustrations by Michikó Fujiwara.